Spanish Grammar
FOR
DUMMIES®

by Cecie Kraynak, MA

WILEY

John Wiley & Sons, Inc.

Spanish Grammar For Dummies®

Published by
John Wiley & Sons, Inc.
111 River St.
Hoboken, NJ 07030-5774
www.wiley.com

For general information on our other products and services, please contact our Customer Care Department within the U.S. at 877-762-2974, outside the U.S. at 317-572-3993, or fax 317-572-4002.

For technical support, please visit www.wiley.com/techsupport.

Wiley publishes in a variety of print and electronic formats and by print-on-demand. Some material included with standard print versions of this book may not be included in e-books or in print-on-demand. If this book refers to media such as a CD or DVD that is not included in the version you purchased, you may download this material at http://booksupport.wiley.com. For more information about Wiley products, visit www.wiley.com.

ISBN 978-1-118-02380-8 (pbk); ISBN 978-1-118-22201-0 (ebk); ISBN 978-1-118-23576-8 (ebk); ISBN 978-1-118-26065-4 (ebk)

Manufactured in the United States of America

10 9 8 7 6 5 4 3 2 1

WILEY

About the Author

Cecie (Mary) Kraynak is a Spanish teacher, ESL coordinator, and author/editor of numerous Spanish books, including *Spanish For Dummies* and *Spanish Verbs For Dummies* (both published by Wiley).

Cecie inherited her love of the Spanish language and culture from her mother, Jo Anne Howard, who cultivated Cecie's innate interest and encouraged her to travel and study abroad. From the heartland of Crawfordsville, Indiana, Cecie first set out to study at the University of the Americas in Cholula, Mexico, and later spent her junior year abroad at the Universidad Complutense in Madrid, Spain. She earned her bachelor's degree in Spanish and secondary education in 1980 and her master's degree in Spanish literature in 1983 from Purdue University. During her grad school years, Cecie taught Spanish to undergraduates and served as the graduate assistant for Purdue's summer study program in Mexico City.

Dedication

In memory of my father, Frank Howard, who never lost his sense of adventure.

Author's Acknowledgments

Thanks to my acquisitions editor, Michael Lewis, for choosing me to work on *Spanish Grammar For Dummies* and for working closely with me during the initial stages to formulate the vision for this book. Thanks also to my project editor, Georgette Beatty, for carefully shaping the manuscript and shepherding the text through production and to my copy editor, Amanda Langferman, for purging the manuscript of any typos and ugly grammatical errors. Thanks also to the technical reviewers, Diane de Avalle-Arce and Greg Harris, for their expertise and careful attention to detail. Last but not least, thanks to my husband, Joe, who assisted in preparing the manuscript.

Publisher's Acknowledgments

We're proud of this book; please send us your comments at http://dummies.custhelp.com. For other comments, please contact our Customer Care Department within the U.S. at 877-762-2974, outside the U.S. at 317-572-3993, or fax 317-572-4002.

Some of the people who helped bring this book to market include the following:

Acquisitions, Editorial, and Vertical Websites

Senior Project Editor: Georgette Beatty

Acquisitions Editor: Michael Lewis

Copy Editor: Amanda M. Langferman

Assistant Editor: David Lutton

Editorial Program Coordinator: Joe Niesen

Technical Editors: Diane de Avalle-Arce, Greg Harris

Editorial Manager: Michelle Hacker

Editorial Assistant: Alexa Koschier

Cover Photo: © iStockphoto.com/artvea

Cartoons: Rich Tennant (www.the5thwave.com)

Composition Services

Project Coordinator: Sheree Montgomery

Layout and Graphics: Carl Byers, Joyce Haughey, Christin Swinford

Proofreader: Tricia Liebig

Indexer: Valerie Haynes Perry

Special Help
Danielle Voirol

Publishing and Editorial for Consumer Dummies

    Kathleen Nebenhaus, Vice President and Executive Publisher

    Kristin Ferguson-Wagstaffe, Product Development Director

    Ensley Eikenburg, Associate Publisher, Travel

    Kelly Regan, Editorial Director, Travel

Publishing for Technology Dummies

    Andy Cummings, Vice President and Publisher

Composition Services

    Debbie Stailey, Director of Composition Services

Contents at a Glance

Table of Contents

Part II: Constructing Simple Sentences and Asking Questions 81

Introduction

When you're learning your first language, you don't need to know much about grammar to speak correctly. Assuming you grew up around people who spoke proper English, you instinctively acquired the ability to express yourself appropriately. When you're picking up a second language, like Spanish, however, grammar is essential, especially if you want to say something more than **¡Hola!** and **¡Muchas gracias!** After all, grammar is the structure on which you hang the words you want to say:

Grammar + Vocabulary = Ability to Communicate

If you know the grammatical rules and your vocabulary, you can say and understand just about anything, including both questions and statements. In addition, you can communicate more creatively, expressing exactly what you want to say rather than just reciting an expression you memorized.

Although grammar may sound boring, it's actually what makes Spanish fun and exciting. When you begin to think — and even dream — in Spanish, you'll see what I mean.

About This Book

Each chapter of *Spanish Grammar For Dummies* tackles a specific Spanish grammar topic, explaining it in detail, providing plenty of examples, and giving you plenty of practice exercises to help you put that particular topic to use. At the end of each chapter is an answer key that allows you to check your work.

The book starts you off with the basics — nouns and verbs — so you can figure out how to compose simple sentences in the present tense right away. Each chapter then explains how to embellish your simple sentences with additional details, including adverbs, prepositional phrases, and different verb conjugations.

You don't have to read this book from cover to cover (although I would love it if you did!); you can simply read the sections or chapters that interest you the most.

Conventions Used in This Book

I've used the following conventions to make navigating this book a little easier:

- Spanish words and sentences appear in **boldface** to make them stand out.

- English equivalents, set in *italics*, follow the Spanish words and sentences.

- When translating Spanish expressions, I usually present the English equivalent, which isn't always the literal translation. For example, you can translate the Spanish phrase

de nada literally as *of nothing*, but in English, the equivalent is *you're welcome* (as in *think nothing of it*). This book usually gives the *you're welcome* translation.

✔ At the end of every chapter is an answer key that provides the correct answers to all the questions in the practice exercises in that chapter.

To make verbs and their many uses stand out, I present verb conjugations in tables like this:

cantar (*to sing*)	
yo **canto**	nosotros/nosotras **cantamos**
tú **cantas**	vosotros/vosotras **cantáis**
él/ella/usted **canta**	ellos/ellas/ustedes **cantan**

Note that the Spanish verb and its English translation are at the top followed by six verb forms that vary according to who or what is performing the action: *I; you* (singular, informal); *he, she,* and *you* (singular, formal); *we; you* (plural, informal); and *they* and *you* (plural, formal).

One more note: With the exception of Chapter 2 (which is all about sounding out Spanish words), this book doesn't feature pronunciations after Spanish text. Instead, it focuses on grammar and written communication. Feel free to use a Spanish dictionary for any pronunciation questions you may have.

What You're Not to Read

Of course, I'd like to think you're going to read every word in this book, but that may not be the practical option or even the best approach in your case. If you're short on time or you have a few grammatical areas that you know you need more help with, feel free to skip around to the stuff that interests you most.

As you read, you can safely skip the exercise examples. If the exercise seems obvious to you, don't waste your time checking out the examples before you dive into the exercise questions themselves. Along the same lines, if I present several examples to illustrate a particular grammar rule and you understand the rule after reading the first example, don't bother with the rest of them.

Foolish Assumptions

When writing this book, I made the following assumptions about you:

✔ You already have a background in Spanish and may even be able to carry on a conversation, but you want to be able to communicate more creatively, especially in writing. (If you're a rank beginner, I suggest you start with *Spanish For Dummies,* 2nd Edition, written by yours truly and published by Wiley.)

✔ You want to practice everything you learn so you can be sure you've "got it" and will retain your newly acquired knowledge.

✔ You love Spanish (like I do!) and find grammar fascinating . . . okay, that may be pushing it just a little.

How This Book Is Organized

Spanish Grammar For Dummies is divided into six parts. The following sections introduce the parts and describe the contents of each one.

Part 1: Starting with the Basics

This part is for beginners or for those of you who need a brief refresher on the basics before you dive into any heavy-duty grammar. Here you find a brief overview of Spanish grammar; discover how to pronounce Spanish words so you can sound like you know what you're doing; find out how to deal with the whole number/gender thing with nouns, articles, and adjectives; practice counting and telling time; and brush up on dates, days of the week, and months of the year.

If you already know this stuff, feel free to use these chapters as confidence boosters to build the momentum you need to tackle the more challenging Spanish grammar topics I cover in the rest of this book.

Part II: Constructing Simple Sentences and Asking Questions

Grammar is all about stringing words together to form sentences that make sense. The most basic sentences consist of a subject and a verb in the present tense; for example, **Ella camina** (*She walks*). In this part, you find out how to put together a subject and a verb to express yourself with simple sentences and how to use pronouns in place of nouns. You also figure out how to use the present tense and the present progressive tense and how to ask questions so you can find out what else you need to know.

Part III: Beefing Up Your Sentences with More Description

In this part, I explain how to make sentences more descriptive by adding adverbs, prepositional phrases, and other parts of speech. You also discover how to use the reflexive to describe actions performed on oneself; employ the passive voice to stress the action instead of the doer of the action; make comparisons; and add negative words to completely change the meaning of a sentence.

Part IV: Talking about the Past or Future

Spanish has fourteen verb tenses broken down into seven simple and seven complex tenses. Fortunately for you, this book focuses on verb tenses you're likely to use on a daily basis: the present, preterit (past), imperfect (past but ongoing or repeated), and future. While Part II covers conjugating verbs in the present tense, this part covers the preterit, imperfect, and future.

As a bonus, I explain how to use the helping verb **haber** to transform the simple tenses into compound tenses — a trick that doubles the number of verb tenses you have at your disposal!

Part V: Expressing Conditions and Giving Commands

No grammar book is complete without coverage of the conditional and imperative, and this part gets you up to speed in a hurry. *Conditional* statements go something like this:

Yo iría contigo, pero tengo que estudiar. (*I would go with you, but I have to study.*)

In other words, my being able to go is conditional upon not having to study.

You use the *imperative* to issue commands like this one:

¡Por favor, pase el guacamole! (*Please pass the guacamole!*)

Part VI: The Part of Tens

Every *For Dummies* title has a Part of Tens, and this one's no different. Here you find a list of ten common Spanish grammar mistakes (and how to avoid them) and ten Spanish idioms that'll make you sound like a native Spanish speaker!

Icons Used in This Book

To make particular types of information easier for you to find, I use the following icons in this book:

This icon highlights information that you should remember long after you read this book. If you read anything in this book, it should be text marked with this icon!

This icon points out tips for understanding Spanish grammar more easily.

Beware the pitfalls of Spanish grammar that I mark with this icon!

Practice makes perfect when it comes to Spanish grammar; this icon denotes practice problems that you can use to sharpen your skills.

Where to Go from Here

Where you go from here really depends on where *here* is for you. If you're looking for a quickie on Spanish grammar, head to Chapter 1. Beginners and anyone else who's looking for a warm-up session would probably do best to start with Chapter 2 on sounding out Spanish words or Chapter 5 on numbers, dates, and times. Chapters 3 and 4 are essential for helping you make sure your nouns, articles, and adjectives all agree in gender (masculine or feminine) and number (one or more than one).

Otherwise, feel free to skip around and dive in wherever you like. Every chapter is a stand-alone module. The more modules you complete, the more fluent you'll become in Spanish grammar. **¡Buena suerte!** (*Good luck!*)

Part I
Starting with the Basics

In this part . . .

Consider this part the lighter side of Spanish grammar — strictly beginner stuff. Here, you get up to speed in a hurry with a brief overview of Spanish grammar; discover how to pronounce Spanish words so you can sound like you know what you're talking about; figure out how to deal with nouns, articles, and adjectives in terms of number and gender; master the art of counting and telling time; and practice working with dates, days of the week, and months of the year.

If you're ready to get your head in the game of Spanish grammar, you've come to the right place!

Chapter 1

Spanish Grammar in a Nutshell

∙∙∙

In This Chapter
▶ Getting to know your parts of speech
▶ Taking a quick look at conjugating verbs in different tenses
▶ Slapping together a simple sentence
▶ Asking questions, posing conditions, and giving orders

∙∙∙

Spanish grammar is fairly complex, so many people benefit from getting an overall picture of everything that's involved — the framework on which all the details ultimately find their place — before they jump into any one part. This chapter presents this framework, bringing you up to speed in a hurry on Spanish grammar basics and rooting that framework in what you already know — English.

Luckily for everyone, the Spanish language is very phonetic, which makes speaking it fairly simple. Even so, you need to be aware of the importance of pronunciation when you're learning Spanish to make sure that what you're saying not only conveys the meaning you intended but also sounds grammatically correct. Skip to Chapter 2 for everything you need to know about Spanish pronunciation.

Recognizing the Parts of Speech

Learning a second language is a whole lot easier if you know a little something about your own language, especially when the languages are as similar as Spanish and English. To grasp the fundamentals of either of these languages, you need to know your *parts of speech* — the various categories that describe what purpose different types of words serve and how those different types of words relate to one another.

Don't worry if you can't recall your parts of speech. The following sections provide a quick review.

Nouns and pronouns

A **nombre** or **sustantivo** (*noun*) is a person, place, or thing that can serve as a subject, direct object, or indirect object:

✔ **Subject:** Whoever or whatever performs the action

✔ **Direct object:** What or whom the action is performed on

✔ **Indirect object:** To or for whom or what the action is performed

For example, in **Paco le dijo a María una mentira** (*Paco told María a lie*), **Paco** is the subject because he's performing the action (telling), **una mentira** (*a lie*) is the direct object (what **Paco** is telling), and **María** is the indirect object (the one to whom the lie is told). Chapter 3 introduces Spanish nouns in more detail.

To mix things up, you can use different types of **pronombres** (*pronouns*) in place of nouns so you don't have to keep repeating the same noun:

✔ **Subject (personal) pronouns: Yo** (*I*), **tú** (*you* singular, informal), **él** (*he*), **ella** (*she*), **usted** (*you* singular, formal), **nosotros/nosotras** (*we*), **vosotros/vosotras** (*you* plural, informal), **ellos/ellas** (*they*), and **ustedes** (*you* plural, formal) are the subject pronouns. They take the place of the doer of the action.

✔ **Direct object pronouns: Me** (*me*), **te** (*you* singular, informal), **lo** (*him* or *you* masculine, singular, formal), **la** (*her* or *you* feminine, singular, formal), **nos** (*us*), **os** (*you* plural, informal), and **los/las** (*them* or *you* plural, formal) are the direct object pronouns. They take the place of the person, place, or thing the action is performed on.

✔ **Indirect object pronouns: Me** (*to/for me*), **te** (*to/for you* singular, informal), **le** (*to/for him, her, it,* or *you* singular, formal), **nos** (*to/for us*), **os** (*to/for you* plural, informal), and **les** (*to/for them* or *you* plural, formal) are the indirect object pronouns that take the place of the recipient of the action.

✔ **Reflexive pronouns: Me** (*myself*), **te** (*yourself*), **se** (*himself, herself,* or *yourself*), **nos** (*ourselves*), **os** (*yourselves*), and **se** (*themselves* or *yourselves*) are reflexive pronouns that take the place of the recipient of a reflexive action (an action that the subject of the sentence performs on itself).

✔ **Interrogative pronouns: ¿Quién(es)?** (*Who?*), **¿Cuál(es)?** (*What?* or *Which one[s]?*), **¿Qué?** (*What?*), **¿Cuánto(a)?** (*How much?*), and **¿Cuántos(as)?** (*How many?*) are the interrogative pronouns. They take the place of the nouns given in the answers to these questions.

Flip to Chapter 9 for the full scoop on Spanish pronouns.

Articles

Artículos (*articles*) are the tiny words commonly used to introduce nouns. They come in two flavors:

✔ **Definite articles: El, la, los,** and **las** (*the*)

✔ **Indefinite articles: Un** and **una** (*a, an*) and **unos** and **unas** (*some*)

An article must agree with the noun it modifies in gender (masculine or feminine) and number (singular or plural). That's why you have four articles in each category: **el** and **un** are masculine, singular, **la** and **una** are feminine, singular, **los** and **unos** are masculine, plural, and **las** and **unas** are feminine, plural. Chapter 3 covers this agreement issue in greater detail.

Verbs

Verbos (*verbs*) breathe life into expressions, so you really can't do anything without them. For example, in the simple sentence, **Selena canta** (*Selena sings*), **Selena** is the subject and **canta** is the verb.

In most languages, verbs are the most challenging part of speech because every verb has so many variations, depending on who's performing the action and when they're performing it — in the present, past, future, and so on. I touch on this issue later in this chapter in the section "Conjugating Verbs in the Present Tense."

Adjectives and adverbs

Adjetivos (*adjectives*) and **adverbios** (*adverbs*) are descriptive words that colorize otherwise drab expressions:

- ✔ *Adjectives* describe nouns.
- ✔ *Adverbs* describe verbs, adjectives, and other adverbs.

Here's an example of what you can do to a sentence simply by adding adjectives and adverbs:

> **Before: El edificio se derrumbó.** (*The building collapsed.*)

> **After: El edificio alto poco a poco se derrumbó.** (*The tall building slowly collapsed.*)

The second sentence is much more interesting, don't you think? That's the magic of adjectives and adverbs. Chapter 4 tells you all about Spanish adjectives; I cover Spanish adverbs in detail in Chapter 12.

You often use adjectives and adverbs to make comparisons, such as **Susanna es más alta que Ricardo** (*Susanna is taller than Ricardo*). If you're wondering how to compare two or more people or things (or actions), head to Chapter 16 for more about making comparisons.

Prepositions

A **preposición** (*preposition*) is a word that typically accompanies a noun or pronoun and describes its relationship usually in terms of time, space, or direction. Simple prepositions include **a** (*to* or *at*), **ante** (*before* or *in the presence of*), **contra** (*against*), **durante** (*during*), **hasta** (*until*), and **tras** (*after*). Here's an example of a simple preposition in action:

> **Ella va a la tienda.** (*She is going to the store.*)

In this example, the simple preposition **a** (*to*) joins with **la tienda** (*the store*) to form a prepositional phrase that describes where she's going. For more about prepositions and the rules for using them, check out Chapter 13.

Conjunctions

Conjunciones (*conjunctions*) connect words and phrases in a sentence. Common conjunctions include **y** and **e** (*and*), **ni** (*neither/nor*), **o** and **u** (*or/either*), **pero** (*but*), **porque** (*because*), and **que** (*that*). In Chapter 6, you find out how to use conjunctions to form compound sentences by joining two simple sentences.

Conjugating Verbs in the Present Tense

When you want to describe an action, you have a lot to consider besides which verb to use. You have to choose the right form of the verb that does all of the following:

- ✔ Matches the subject in person (first, second, or third) and number (singular or plural)
- ✔ Describes when the action is taking place (verb tense), which can be present, past, future, and so on
- ✔ Reflects the correct *mood* (the attitude of the speaker), which can be *indicative* (certain), *subjunctive* (uncertain or hopeful), *conditional* (what if), or *imperative* (commanding)
- ✔ Reflects the right voice (active or passive)

To conjugate a verb, you start with the infinitive form and add endings that represent the person, number, tense, mood, and voice. The following sections break down the process of conjugating verbs in the present tense.

Identifying infinitives

The *infinitive* form of a verb is pure action or being — when nobody's doing it or being it and time doesn't matter. In other words, the infinitive is the verb without a subject or tense. In English, you form the infinitive by adding *to* before the verb, as in *to run*, *to skip*, and *to jump*. In Spanish, the infinitive forms end in **-ar**, **-er**, or **-ir**. Here's an example of each type of verb: **hablar** (*to talk, to speak*), **correr** (*to run*), and **vivir** (*to live*).

When you conjugate a verb, you start with the infinitive form, drop the ending, and add the appropriate conjugated ending according to the subject of the sentence and the tense that you're using.

Establishing subject-verb agreement

To know which conjugated verb form to use, you need to know the subject of the verb — whatever or whoever is performing the action — because the verb must agree with the subject in both person (for example, *I*, *you*, or *he*) and number (for example, *I* is singular and *we* is plural). When conjugating verbs, use the subject pronouns that I list in the earlier section "Nouns and pronouns" to substitute for actual nouns.

Several different types of Spanish verbs exist; I outline their present tense conjugations in the following sections. You can turn to Chapter 6 for additional information on using the present tense.

Regular verbs

To conjugate most regular verbs in the present tense, you drop the infinitive's **-ar, -er,** or **-ir** ending to create the verb *stem* and then add the verb's present tense endings. The endings you add vary according to whether you're conjugating an **-ar, -er,** or **-ir** verb:

Verbs That End In	Use These Endings
-ar	**-o, -as, -a, -amos, -áis, -an**
-er	**-o, -es, -e, -emos, -éis, -en**
-ir	**-o, -es, -e, -imos, -ís, -en**

As you may have guessed, this gives you six forms of the verb. Here's an example, showing the verb **practicar** (*to practice*) conjugated in the present tense. Be sure to drop the **-ar** ending to form the stem (**practic-**) before adding the endings.

practicar (*to practice*)	
yo **practico**	nosotros/nosotras **practicamos**
tú **practicas**	vosotros/vosotras **practicáis**
él/ella/usted **practica**	ellos/ellas/ustedes **practican**

Unlike in English, you can usually tell who the subject of a Spanish sentence is just by looking at the verb ending. Thus, Spanish allows you to drop the subject out of your sentence when it's unnecessary. If I'm practicing something, for example, I don't have to say **yo practico.** I can simply say **practico.** Only two forms may be ambiguous — the third person singular and the third person plural. These two forms represent more than one possible subject; therefore, you have to establish who the subject is before you can drop it from the sentence.

Stem-changing, spelling-changing, and irregular verbs

Knowing how to conjugate regular verbs in the present tense is a great start, but unfortunately, Spanish has some stem-changing, spelling-changing, and irregular verbs that don't play by the rules:

✔ **Regular stem-changing verbs:** With regular stem-changing verbs, you don't just drop the verb ending to form the stem. In all conjugated forms except the **nosotros/nosotras** and the **vosotros/vosotras** forms, the stem changes from **e** to **i, o** to **ue,** or **e** to **ie,** as in the case of **empezar** (*to begin, to start*), whose stem changes from **empez-** to **empiez-.**

✔ **Regular spelling-changing verbs:** Certain verbs change spelling to help with pronunciation when the verb is conjugated into its different forms. For example, when conjugating **incluir** (*to include*), you drop the **-ir** ending and add **-y** in all forms except the **nosotros/nosotras** and the **vosotros/vosotras.**

✔ **Irregular verbs:** These verbs are just plain weird. Some change irregularly in the stem, while others change irregularly in the endings or only in certain forms, such as the **yo** form. For example, the **yo** form of **caber** (*to fit*) is **yo quepo**. The verb **estar** (*to be*) is irregular in all of its forms except the **nosotros/nosotras** and **vosotros/vosotras** forms. (*Note:* The verbs **estar** and **ser,** which both mean *to be,* are especially unusual; I discuss them in detail in Chapter 7.)

Composing a Simple Sentence

When you have some vocabulary under your belt and you know how to conjugate verbs, forming a simple sentence in Spanish is easy. All you do is start with a subject and then tack on a verb that agrees with the subject in person and number and reflects the desired tense, mood, and voice. One of the simplest sentences you can come up with is **Yo soy** (*I am*). In Spanish, you can simplify it even further — **Soy** (*I am*) — because the verb ending indicates the subject of the sentence.

After you have a simple sentence in place, you can start to embellish it with the other parts of speech that I describe earlier in this chapter — articles, adjectives, adverbs, pronouns, and prepositions — and use conjunctions to combine words, phrases, and even entire sentences! Head to Chapter 6 for an introduction to simple sentences in the present tense. In Chapter 8, you find out how to compose sentences in another simple tense — the present progressive.

Another very basic form of communication in any language is to express what you like and dislike. In Spanish, you do this with the verb **gustar** (*to be pleasing*). Turn to Chapter 10 for more details.

In Spanish (as in English), you sometimes need to express things in the negative, such as **Yo nunca quiero ver a ellos jamás** (*I never want to see them again*). Both languages use the word **no** for **no**, but they also have many other words that express the negative. For more on negative words and expressions, see Chapter 17.

Asking Questions

A good portion of daily communication revolves around asking and answering questions. One of the easiest ways to ask a **sí/no** (*yes/no*) question is to take a statement, like **Usted tiene un dolor de cabeza** (*You have a headache*) and bracket it with an upside-down and right-side-up question mark: **¿Usted tiene un dolor de cabeza?** (*Do you have a headache?*) (Literally: *You have a headache?*). Another option is to invert the subject and the verb, as in this example: **¿Tiene usted un dolor de cabeza?** Answering such questions, assuming you understand them, is easy. You just say **sí** or **no** or shake your head in agreement (or disagreement).

Asking an interrogative question to actually elicit some information is a little more difficult. First, you need to form your question by inverting the subject and verb. Then you have to add an interrogative word, such as **¿Quién(es) . . . ?** (*Who . . . ?*) or **¿Cuándo . . . ?** (*When . . . ?*), to the beginning of the sentence. Here's an example:

¿Cuándo quieren ellos ir al cine? (*When do they want to go to the movies?*)

Obviously, answering an interrogative question and understanding the answer to an interrogative question you asked are more challenging than dealing with a **sí/no** question, because you have to deal with additional information. If you've ever asked someone for directions in a Spanish-speaking country, you know what I mean.

To answer an interrogative question, you drop the interrogative word, invert the question to place the subject at the beginning, and then add the information being requested. Here's an example:

> **¿Cuándo quieren ellos ir al cine?** (*When do they want to go to the movies?*)
>
> **Ellos quieren ir al cine a las 7:00 de la noche.** (*They want to go to the movies at 7:00 p.m.*)

Do you have additional questions about Spanish questions? Chapter 11 gives you the info you're looking for.

Moving On to Other Verb Tenses

Spanish has fourteen verb "tenses" — seven simple and seven compound tenses. (I put "tenses" in quotes because some tenses are really a combination of tense and mood.) In this book, I focus on the four simple tenses you use most often: present, preterit (past), imperfect (ongoing past action), and future. I also explain how to combine a verb with a helping verb to transform simple tenses into compound tenses, which include the pluperfect (more past than the past tense) and future perfect (an action completed before another future action).

The following sections introduce you to the three main simple tenses (besides the present tense, which I cover earlier in this chapter) and the compound tenses.

Like English, in addition to different tenses, Spanish has different voices — active and passive. With the active voice, the subject performs the action, as in **El mecánico arregló el coche** (*The mechanic repaired the car*). With the passive voice, the subject of the sentence receives the action, as in **El coche fue arreglado por el mecánico** (*The car was repaired by the mechanic*). For more about the passive voice, see Chapter 15.

Preterit and imperfect

The *preterit* or *past tense,* which I explain in Chapter 18, describes action that's been completed or is clearly in the past. Use the preterit like the past tense in English. Here's an example:

> **Ustedes salieron a las nueve.** (*You* [plural] *left at nine.*)

The *imperfect tense* is vague and imprecise, the equivalent to *used to* or *always* in English, as in **Yo solía ir a las corridas de toros** (*I used to go to the bullfight*). The action occurred in the past, but you don't know exactly when it occurred. You may also use the imperfect to describe two or more ongoing past actions that occurred simultaneously, as in **Mientras mi mamá cocinaba mi padre leía el periódico** (*While my mom was cooking, my father was reading the newspaper*). Chapter 19 provides additional examples, along with more uses for the imperfect.

When choosing whether to use the preterit or the imperfect to describe a past action, keep in mind that the preterit describes an action or a series of actions completed in the past — they're done, over, stick a fork in it. The preterit also expresses an action, event, or state of mind that happened in the past and was completed at a specific moment or period. The imperfect describes an ongoing or continuous past action, without focusing on the beginning or end.

Future

The future tense describes what *will* or *might* happen. Use the future tense to

- Describe an action or a state of being that will occur in the future, as in the following example:

  Yo limpiaré la casa este fin de semana. (*I will clean the house this weekend.*)

- Express probability or conjecture in the present. In English, you'd do this with such terms as *I wonder, could it be, must be,* and *probably,* as in the following example:

  ¿Serán ya las diez? (*Could it already be ten?*)

You *will* find out more about the future tense in Chapter 20.

Whether you're describing present, past, or future events, you often need to add some specific words about when the action occurred, such as **el sábado a las diez** (*on Saturday at ten o'clock*). To find out about numbers, dates, and time, check out Chapter 5.

Compound

The *compound tenses* (also referred to as *complex tenses*) add the verb **haber** (*to have*) to the main verb so that a verb in the past tense can be more past, a conditional statement can be completed, and a future action can be finished. Spanish has seven compound tenses. The two most commonly used compound tenses are

- **Present perfect:** Describes actions that *have happened* — recently completed actions, as in **Yo he comido un sandwich** (*I have eaten a sandwich*), and past actions that continue to remain true, as in **Yo he comido aquí todos los sábados por cinco años** (*I have eaten here every Saturday for five years*).

- **Pluperfect:** The *pluperfect* describes actions that happened in the past before another past action. It's the same as saying that something *had happened* in English. For example, in the sentence **Ellos habían comido antes de llegar** (*They had eaten before arriving*), the eating happened before they arrived.

Compound tenses are made up of two elements:

- **Helping verb:** All compound tenses require the *helping verb* (or *auxiliary verb*) **haber** (*to have*).

✔ **Past participle of the action verb:** All compound tenses require the past participle, or the ed/en form, of the verb whose action has or had been done. In Spanish, you form the past participle of most verbs by adding **-ado** or **-ido** to the end of the verb's stem:

- For an **-ar** verb, drop the **-ar** and add **-ado**.
- For an **-er** verb, drop the **-er** and add **-ido**.
- For an **-ir** verb, drop the **-ir** and add **-ido**.

The great thing about the compound tenses is that you don't have to learn how to conjugate a bunch of different verbs. All you need to know is how to conjugate **haber** and how to form the past participle of the action verb. Find out all the details about compound tenses in Chapter 21.

Wondering "What If" with the Conditional Mood

The *conditional mood* describes what will or would happen if something else occurs. You can use the conditional to describe something you (or someone else) would like or would do, to conjecture about something that occurred in the past (what might have happened), or to express probability about a past action (what must have happened).

Forming the conditional with regular **-ar**, **-er**, and **-ir** verbs is pretty easy. You take the entire verb infinitive (don't drop anything) and then add the imperfect verb endings you use for **-er** and **-ir** verbs (see Chapter 19). Following are the three different types of verbs conjugated in the conditional.

preparar (*to prepare*)	
yo **prepararía**	nosotros/nosotras **prepararíamos**
tú **prepararías**	vosotros/vosotras **prepararíais**
él/ella/usted **prepararía**	ellos/ellas/ustedes **prepararían**

vender (*to sell*)	
yo **vendería**	nosotros/nosotras **venderíamos**
tú **venderías**	vosotros/vosotras **venderíais**
él/ella/usted **vendería**	ellos/ellas/ustedes **venderían**

escribir (*to write*)	
yo **escribiría**	nosotros/nosotras **escribiríamos**
tú **escribirías**	vosotros/vosotras **escribiríais**
él/ella/usted **escribiría**	ellos/ellas/ustedes **escribirían**

Here's an example of a very basic use of the conditional:

Me gustaría tomar un refresco. (*I would like to have a soft drink.*)

You can find out more about the conditional mood in Chapter 22.

Forming Simple Commands

Use the *imperative mood* to give commands — to tell someone what to do or what not to do. In most cases, you bark out commands in one of the *you* forms, **tú** (*you* singular, informal), **usted** (*you* singular, formal), **vosotros/vosotras** (*you* plural, informal), or **ustedes** (*you* plural, formal). But you can also use the **nosotros** (*we*) form of the imperative so that your command comes across as more of a "*Let's . . .*" suggestion than a direct command.

The imperative is called a *mood* rather than a tense because it deals with wants and desires and because the time is always *now*.

To form singular informal commands, drop the **-s** from the present tense **tú** form of the regular **-ar**, **-er**, and **-ir** verbs:

Hablas. (*You speak.*) becomes **¡Habla!** (*Speak!*)

Comes. (*You eat.*) becomes **¡Come!** (*Eat!*)

Escribes. (*You write.*) becomes **¡Escribe!** (*Write!*)

To form negative singular informal commands, add **No** (*No*) to the beginning of the sentence, remove the **-o** from the present tense **yo** form of the verb, and add **-es** for regular **-ar** verbs and **-as** for regular **-er** and **-ir** verbs, as in the following examples:

Hablo. (*I speak.*) becomes **¡No hables!** (*Don't speak!*)

Como. (*I eat.*) becomes **¡No comas!** (*Don't eat!*)

Escribo. (*I write.*) becomes **¡No escribas!** (*Don't write!*)

In Spanish, you can use an upside-down exclamation point at the beginning of your command and a right-side-up exclamation point at the end to show emphasis.

Singular informal commands should enable you to tell all the people within shouting distance what to do. However, you still need to know how to form commands in the informal plural and the formal singular and plural. For all that, skip to Chapter 23.

Chapter 2

Sounding Out Spanish Words

- -

In This Chapter

▶ Pronouncing vowels, consonants, and diphthongs

▶ Placing stress on the right *syl*-la-ble and adding accents to the right letters

▶ Adjusting your intonation for the desired effect

- -

When acquiring a second language, you're likely to read it first, then write it, listen to it, and understand it, and, last but definitely not least, speak it. Of course, the best way to learn to speak Spanish is to have a Spanish-speaking person model the spoken language for you and to listen to recordings. But seeing the pronunciation is also helpful, especially when you're learning a language as wonderfully phonetic as Spanish.

This chapter explains how to pronounce Spanish vowels, consonants, and diphthongs; how to tell which syllable to stress in any word; and how to adjust your *intonation* (the rise and fall of your voice) to convey meaning.

Vocalizing Vowels

Spanish has five vowels. (In case you're wondering, Spanish excludes the letter *y*.) The vowel sounds are easy to pick up because each vowel has only one possible sound:

✔ **a:** *ah,* as in *father*

✔ **e:** *eh,* as in *bet*

✔ **i:** *ee,* as in *seen*

✔ **o:** *oh,* as in *old*

✔ **u:** *ooh,* as in *moo*

Note: Spanish vowels are pronounced *staccato,* that is short and hard, versus the way English speakers (especially those from the South) round out their vowels. So when you say a Spanish vowel, cut off your airflow immediately after uttering it to get the desired effect.

Conversing with Consonants

Many Spanish consonants have the same sound as their English counterparts. These consonants are *d, f, k, l, m, n, p, s, t, w, x,* and *y.* (See, you already know a little Spanish!) The following consonants are exceptions:

- ✔ **b:** a cross between *b* and *v* (indicated as *bv*)

- ✔ **c:** *k* when in front of *a, o,* and *u; s* when in front of *e* and *i*

- ✔ **g:** *g* when in front of *a, o,* and *u; h* when in front of *e* and *i* (This *h* is more guttural than the English *h,* so it's indicated in pronunciations by a capital *H.*)

- ✔ **h:** silent

- ✔ **j:** *h* (This *h* is more guttural than the English *h,* so it's indicated in pronunciations by a capital *H.*)

- ✔ **ñ:** *ny,* like the sound *nio* in the word *onion*

- ✔ **qu:** *k*

- ✔ **r:** like the double *dd* in the word *ladder* (indicated as *r*)

- ✔ **v:** a cross between *b* and *v* (indicated as *bv*)

- ✔ **y:** *y* as in *yellow* or *ee* at the end of a word, such as **hoy** (*today*) or **hay** (*there is, there are*)

- ✔ **z:** *s*

In Spanish, the following double-letter combinations form unique sounds:

- ✔ **ch:** *ch,* just as in English

- ✔ **ll:** *y*

- ✔ **rr:** trilled *r*

    To pronounce the trilled *rr* sound, place your tongue up against the roof of your mouth and then blow air over it, causing your tongue to vibrate against the roof of your mouth.

Choose the correct pronunciation for the following words from the choices given. The stressed syllables appear in italics (you find out more about stressing syllables and adding accents later in this chapter). Here's an example:

Q. **hombre**

  a. *ohm*-bvreh

  b. hohm-*bvreh*

A. a. *ohm*-bvreh

1. **libro**

  a. *lee*-bvroh

  b. *leh*-bvroh

2. aquí

    a. ah-*gee*

    b. ah-*kee*

3. gato

    a. *gah*-too

    b. *gah*-toh

4. mano

    a. *mah*-noh

    b. *meh*-noh

5. muchacho

    a. mooh-*chee*-choh

    b. mooh-*chah*-choh

6. príncipe

    a. *preen*-see-peh

    b. *preen*-seh-peh

7. cereza

    a. seh-*ree*-sah

    b. seh-*reh*-sah

8. pera

    a. *peh*-rah

    b. *peh*-reh

9. manzana

    a. mahn-*zah*-nah

    b. mahn-*sah*-nah

10. árbol

    a. *ahr*-vohl

    b. *ahr*-bvohl

Doubling Up on Diphthongs

A *diphthong* is literally a double sound; it occurs in Spanish when the unstressed vowel *i* or *u* or the ending consonant *y* is combined with another vowel. Spanish considers *a, e,* and *o* to be the strong vowels and *i* and *u* to be the weak vowels.

Use the following rules to pronounce neighboring vowels:

- ✔ Two vowels almost always form a single syllable, such as in the word **bueno** (booh*eh*-noh) (*good*).

- ✔ If one vowel is strong and the other is weak and unaccented, the stronger vowel gets the stronger sound, as in the word **bien** (bee*ehn*) (*fine*).

- ✔ If both vowels are weak, you stress the second vowel, such as in the word **concluido** (kohn-klooh*ee*-doh) (*concluded*).

- ✔ If both vowels are strong, you pronounce the two vowels as separate syllables, such as in the word **feo** (*feh*-oh) (*ugly*), and they aren't considered a diphthong.

- ✔ If the weak vowel has an accent mark, you pronounce the two vowels as separate syllables, such as in the word **tío** (*tee*-oh) (*uncle*), and they aren't considered a diphthong.

A diphthong is also formed if a word ends in **-y.** Though *y* is a consonant in Spanish, it makes a vowel sound (like the English long *e*) when it's next to another vowel in the same syllable and when it's at the end of a word, such as in the following words: **muy** (mooh*ee*) (*very*), **hoy** (oh*ee*) (*today*), and **hay** (a*hee*) (*there is/are*).

Table 2-1 shows the possible vowel combinations that form diphthongs, along with their sounds and a word that contains the diphthong.

Table 2-1	Vowel Combinations That Form Diphthongs	
Diphthong	**Pronunciation**	**Example**
ai	a*hee*	**paisaje** (pa*hee*-*sah*-Heh) (*landscape*)
au	a*hooh*	**flauta** (fla*hooh*-tah) (*flute*)
ei	e*hee*	**peinado** (pe*hee*-*nah*-doh) (*hairstyle*)
eu	e*hooh*	**Europa** (e*hoo*-*roh*-pah) (*Europe*)
iu	ee*ooh*	**ciudad** (see*ooh*-*dahd*) (*city*)
oi	o*hee*	**moisés** (mo*hee*-*sehs*) (*wicker cradle*)
ua	ooh*ah*	**lengua** (*lehn*-gooh*ah*) (*language, tongue*)
ue	ooh*eh*	**bueno** (booh*eh*-noh) (*good*)
ui	*ooh*ee	**intuitivo** (een-tooh*ee*-*tee*-bvoh) (*intuitive*)
uo	ooh*oh*	**cuota** (kooh*oh*-tah) (*fee*)

Underline the diphthongs in the following words. Then rewrite the words phonetically in the space provided. Here's an example:

Q. **media** _____

A. **media** *meh*-deeah

11. **fui** _____

12. editorial _____

13. ruidoso _____

14. yegua _____

15. abuelo _____

16. fueron _____

17. aula _____

18. novio _____

19. nuero _____

20. italiano _____

Stressing the Right Syllables and Adding Accents

In Spanish, as in English, some syllables in a word get a stronger emphasis than others. In addition, you have to add an accent mark to some Spanish words to change their meaning or to clue the reader into the fact that you're asking a question (rather than making a statement) or using the reflexive in the present progressive. In the following sections, I reveal the rules that govern stress and accents.

Beginning with basic rules

Knowing which syllable to stress in Spanish is a pretty cut-and-dried affair. These three simple rules are all the guidance you need:

✔ If a word ends in a vowel or **-n** or **-s,** stress the next-to-last syllable, as in the words **casa** (*kah*-sah) (*house*), **mesa** (*meh*-sah) (*table*), and **pollo** (*poh*-yoh) (*chicken*).

✔ If a word ends in any consonant except **-n** or **-s,** stress the last syllable.

This rule applies to all verbs in the infinitive form, such as **bailar** (bahee-*lahr*) (*to dance*), **poder** (poh-*dehr*) (*to be able to*), and **suprimir** (sooh-pree-*meer*) (*to suppress*) (see Chapter 6 for details on infinitives), and other words that end in a consonant other than **-n** or **-s,** such as **feliz** (feh-*lees*) (*happy*), **hotel** (oh-*tehl*) (*hotel*), and **virtud** (beer-*toohd*) (*virtue*).

✔ If the word doesn't follow one of these two rules, stress the syllable that has the accent mark, as in the words **balcón** (bahl-*kohn*) (*balcony*), **carácter** (kah-*rahk*-tehr) (*character*), and **pájaro** (*pah*-Hah-roh) (*bird*).

Note: The accent mark doesn't affect how to pronounce the vowel. It affects only which syllable to stress.

When Spanish nouns end in **-n** and pluralize with **-es** at the end, the stressed syllable changes when the **-es** is added because it adds a syllable to the end of the word (see Chapter 3 for details on pluralizing nouns). Here are some examples:

- ✔ When a word ends in **-ión,** pluralize the word with **-es** and drop the accent mark, as in the following words:

  - **acción** (ahk-see-*ohn*) becomes **acciones** (ahk-see-*oh*-nehs) (*actions*)
  - **sección** (sehk-see-*ohn*) becomes **secciones** (sehk-see-*oh*-nes) (*sections*)
  - **conversación** (kohn-bvehr-sah-see-*ohn*) becomes **conversaciones** (kohn-bvehr-sah-see-*oh*-nehs) (*conversations*)
  - **televisión** (teh-leh-bvee-see-*ohn*) becomes **televisiones** (teh-leh-bvee-see-*oh*-nehs) (*televisions*)

- ✔ Some words, such as **examen** (ehk-*sah*-mehn) (*exam*), follow Spanish stress rules, so the stress is on the middle *a* naturally. Adding **-es** to pluralize this word throws off the stress, so you have to add an accent to the stressed syllable, making the plural form **exámenes** (ehk-*sah*-meh-nehs) (*exams*).

Adding an accent mark to change a word's meaning

Spanish uses accents for more than to show stress. Table 2-2 lists some single-syllable words that change meaning when you add an accent. Note that the accent doesn't affect the pronunciation of these words; it affects only their meaning.

Table 2-2	Single-Syllable Words That Change Meaning When Accented		
Unaccented Form	*Meaning*	*Accented Form*	*Meaning*
de	*of, from*	dé	*give* (the command form of the verb **dar**)
el	*the*	él	*he*
mas	*but*	más	*more*
mi	*my*	mí	*me*
se	*one's self*	sé	*I know* or *be* (the command form of the verb **ser**)
si	*if*	sí	*yes*
te	*you*	té	*tea*
tu	*your*	tú	*you*

Indicating interrogative words with accent marks

Every *interrogative word* (a word used to ask questions) in Spanish has an accent mark. Though this accent mark looks the same as the ones used in the preceding two sections, it doesn't change the meaning of the word being accented or show where stress is. It simply shows that you're dealing with question words. Without the accent mark, the same words you use to ask questions can be the words you use in statements or answers. Following are the most common interrogative words (see Chapter 11 for more details about them):

- **¿Dónde . . . ?** (*dohn*-deh) (*Where?*)
- **¿Adónde . . . ?** (ah-*dohn*-deh) (*To where?*)
- **¿De dónde . . . ?** (deh *dohn*-deh) (*From where?*)
- **¿Cómo . . . ?** (*koh*-moh) (*How?*)
- **¿Cuál(es) . . . ?** (kooh*ah*[lehs]) (*Which one[s]?*)
- **¿Cuándo . . . ?** (kooh*ahn*-doh) (*When?*)
- **¿Cuánto/Cuánta . . . ?** (kooh*ahn*-toh/kooh*ahn*-tah) (*How much?*)
- **¿Cuántos/Cuántas . . . ?** (kooh*ahn*-tohs/kooh*ahn*-tahs) (*How many?*)
- **¿Qué . . . ?** (keh) (*What?*)
- **¿Quién(es) . . . ?** (kee*ehn*[ehs]) (*Who?*)
- **¿Por qué . . . ?** (pohr keh) (*Why?*)

Accenting reflexive verbs in the present progressive

Another time you need to add accent marks is when you use reflexive verbs (see Chapter 14) with the present progressive (see Chapter 8). For example, to say *I am dressing . . . ,* you would say

> **Estoy vistiendo . . .** (ehs-*tohy* bees-tee*ehn*-doh).

To use the same verb reflexively and say *I am dressing myself,* you have to use a reflexive pronoun. The reflexive pronoun goes at the end of the *ing* word (in this case, **vistiendo**). Because you're adding a syllable to that word, you have to add a written accent mark, so the sentence *I am dressing myself* looks like this:

> **Estoy vistiéndome** (ehs-*tohy* bees-tee*ehn*-doh-meh).

The following Spanish words are italicized where the stress should be. Following the rules for stress and accents, rewrite the words that need a written accent mark, making sure to place the accent mark over the correct letter. If the word doesn't need a written accent mark, just mark it *okay as is*.

Q. pal*a*bra _____

A. palabra (okay as is)

21. le*er* _____

22. coordinaci*o*n _____

23. preg*u*nta _____

24. leccion _____

25. telefono _____

26. escucha _____

27. simpatico _____

28. contestar _____

29. millon _____

30. latin _____

Adjusting Your Intonation

Intonation refers to the way your voice rises and falls as you speak, such as when you ask a question. Intonation is important because it can change the meaning of what you're saying. As you speak in Spanish, follow these rules of intonation:

- ✔ End a statement in a falling pitch. For example, when you say **Me gusta tu suéter** (*I like your sweater*), the pitch of your voice should fall at the end of the word **suéter** (*sweater*).

- ✔ End a yes/no question in a rising pitch that conveys uncertainty. For example, when you ask **¿Vas al supermercado?** (*Are you going to the supermarket?*), the pitch of your voice should rise at the end of the word **supermercado** (*supermarket*).

- ✔ End interrogative questions (those that request more specific information than a yes/no question) in a falling pitch, as you do with a statement. Although this type of intonation sounds just like the intonation of a statement, the interrogative word at the beginning of the sentence signals that you're asking a question. For example, when you ask **¿Dónde está la biblioteca?** (*Where is the library?*), the pitch of your voice should fall at the end of the word **biblioteca** (*library*).

- ✔ For a question that offers a choice between two or more options, raise the pitch of your voice with each choice and then have it fall at the end of the final option. For example, when you ask **¿Cuál te gusta más, el color amarillo, rojo, o verde?** (*Which do you like the most, the color yellow, red, or green?*), the pitch of your voice should rise on **amarillo** (*yellow*) and **rojo** (*red*) and then fall at the end of the word **verde** (*green*).

Answer Key

1 a

2 b

3 b

4 a

5 b

6 a

7 b

8 a

9 b

10 b

11 **fui** *foo*hee

12 **editorial**
eh-dee-toh-ree*ahl*

13 **ruidoso**
roohee-*doh*-soh

14 **yegua** *yeh*-goohah

15 **abuelo**
ah-bvooh*eh*-loh

16 **fueron** fooh*eh*-rohn

17 **aula** *ah*ooh-lah

18 **novio** *noh*-bveeoh

19 **nuero** nooh*eh*-roh

20 **italiano**
ee-tah-lee*ah*-noh

21 **leer** (okay as is)

22 **coordinación**

23 **pregunta** (okay as is)

24 **lección**

25 **teléfono**

26 **escucha** (okay as is)

27 **simpático**

28 **contestar** (okay as is)

29 **millón**

30 **latín**

Chapter 3

Naming Things with Nouns and Articles

$\bullet$

In This Chapter

▶ Telling a girl noun from a boy noun

▶ Converting nouns to their plural forms

▶ Being more or less specific with definite and indefinite articles

$\bullet$

Spanish uses **nombres** (*nouns*) to talk about people, places, and things just as English does, except for one big difference: All Spanish nouns have a gender (masculine or feminine). This chapter explains how to tell whether a noun is masculine or feminine, how to pluralize nouns, and how to choose the right definite or indefinite article based on a noun's gender. (If you don't know what articles are or what they're used for, don't worry; this chapter explains that, too.)

Determining Whether a Noun Is Masculine or Feminine

Whenever you deal with nouns in Spanish, you have to deal with *gender* — whether the noun is masculine or feminine. Nouns that describe people, such as **tío** (*uncle*) and **tía** (*aunt*), are easy to figure out because masculine nouns describe males and feminine nouns describe females (makes sense, right?). But what happens when you're talking about non-person-related nouns, like **silla** (*chair*) or **banco** (*bank*)? Fortunately, you can use a few rules to determine the gender of the majority of Spanish nouns; I describe these rules in the following sections. Of course, these rules have exceptions, and I present those, as well. (In case you're wondering, **silla** is feminine and **banco** is masculine.)

Identifying masculine nouns

The majority of masculine nouns end in **-o.** Here are a few examples:

- ✔ **año** (*year*)
- ✔ **baño** (*bathroom*)
- ✔ **concierto** (*concert*)
- ✔ **durazno** (*peach*)
- ✔ **queso** (*cheese*)

- ✔ **tío** (*uncle*)
- ✔ **abuelo** (*grandfather*)
- ✔ **hijo** (*son*)

Nouns that end in **-aje** and **-ambre** are also masculine. Here are some examples:

- ✔ **alambre** (*wire*)
- ✔ **calambre** (*cramp*)
- ✔ **equipaje** (*luggage*)
- ✔ **lenguaje** (*language*)
- ✔ **personaje** (*character*)
- ✔ **salvaje** (*savage*)

Certain nouns that end in **-or** and **-án** are also masculine. Take a look at these examples:

- ✔ **amor** (*love*)
- ✔ **refrán** (*proverb*)
- ✔ **rencor** (*hate*)
- ✔ **azafrán** (*saffron*)
- ✔ **temblor** (*tremor*)
- ✔ **valor** (*courage, value*)

A group of nouns that end in **-a** are masculine; this group may be confusing because most nouns that end in **-a** are feminine (see the next section). The masculine nouns in this group end in either **-ama, -ema, -oma, -ma,** or **-ía.** Consider these examples:

- ✔ **clima** (*climate*)
- ✔ **crucigrama** (*crossword puzzle*)
- ✔ **día** (*day*)
- ✔ **dilema** (*dilemma*)
- ✔ **idioma** (*language*)
- ✔ **programa** (*program*)

Table 3-1 shows some additional noun groups that are masculine. (See Chapter 5 for full details on days of the week and months of the year.)

Table 3-1	Masculine Noun Groups
Noun Group	*Example(s)*
Days of the week	**El lunes es mi cumpleaños.** (*Monday is my birthday.*)
Months of the year	**Es un julio muy caluroso.** (*It is a very hot July.*)

Noun Group	Example(s)
Colors used as nouns	**El rojo es mi color favorito.** (*Red is my favorite color.*)
Names of languages (***Note:*** Names of languages aren't capitalized in Spanish.)	**Mi madre habla bien el francés.** (*My mother speaks French well.*)
Names of rivers, seas, and oceans	**El océano Pacífico está muy lejos de aquí.** (*The Pacific Ocean is very far from here.*)
Compound nouns (usually consisting of a noun-verb combination and usually ending in **-s** even when singular)	**abrelatas** (*can opener*) **lavaplatos** (*dishwasher*) **parabrisas** (*windshield*) **parachoques** (*bumper*) **paraguas** (*umbrella*) **portaaviones** (*aircraft carrier*) **sacacorchos** (*corkscrew*) **saltamontes** (*grasshopper*) **salvavidas** (*lifeguard*)

Identifying feminine nouns

The majority of feminine nouns end in **-a.** Here are some examples:

- **cabeza** (*head*)
- **columna** (*column*)
- **ensalada** (*salad*)
- **mesa** (*table*)
- **montaña** (*mountain*)
- **piscina** (*swimming pool*)

Fortunately (for your memory, at least), nouns that identify females also usually end in **-a.** For example:

- **abuela** (*grandmother*)
- **doctora** (*female doctor*)
- **enfermera** (*female nurse*)
- **hija** (*daughter*)
- **profesora** (*female professor*)
- **tía** (*aunt*)

A group of nouns that end in **-dad** and **-tad** are feminine. (In many cases, the English equivalent to these endings is **-ty.**) Here are some examples:

- **amistad** (*friendship*)
- **ciudad** (*city*)

- ✔ **dificultad** (*difficulty*)
- ✔ **dignidad** (*dignity*)
- ✔ **libertad** (*liberty*)
- ✔ **realidad** (*reality*)

A group of nouns that end in **-eza, -ie, -itis,** and **-sis** are feminine. Here are a few examples:

- ✔ **crisis** (*crisis*)
- ✔ **bronquitis** (*bronchitis*)
- ✔ **dosis** (*dose*)
- ✔ **especie** (*species*)
- ✔ **serie** (*series*)
- ✔ **tristeza** (*sadness*)

Nouns that end in **-ción, -sión, -tud,** and **-umbre** are feminine. See the following examples:

- ✔ **canción** (*song*)
- ✔ **costumbre** (*custom, habit, tradition*)
- ✔ **cumbre** (*summit*)
- ✔ **división** (*division*)
- ✔ **misión** (*mission*)
- ✔ **virtud** (*virtue*)

Based on the rules and exceptions governing noun gender, identify the following nouns as either masculine or feminine. Mark the masculine nouns with *M* and the feminine nouns with *F*. Here's an example:

0. lealtad ____

A. F

1. voluntad ____

2. tesis ____

3. zapato ____

4. fantasma ____

5. seguridad ____

6. tema ____

7. vapor ____

8. fraternidad ____

9. oficina _____

10. perro _____

Making a masculine noun feminine

Some nouns in Spanish describe professions for both males and females. To specify gender for these nouns, just change the article that precedes the noun, as I explain in the later section "Using articles to switch gender and meaning."

Other nouns require minor spelling changes to switch them from masculine to feminine; this change usually requires replacing the ending **-o** with **-a** or adding **-a** to the end of the word. Here's a list of some of those nouns in their masculine and feminine forms:

Masculine	*Feminine*
cartero (*male mail carrier*)	**cartera** (*female mail carrier*)
doctor (*male doctor*)	**doctora** (*female doctor*)
maestro (*male teacher*)	**maestra** (*female teacher*)
profesor (*male professor*)	**profesora** (*female professor*)

Some nouns change form when they describe males or females, as in the following examples (you just need to memorize these words):

Masculine	*Feminine*
actor (*actor*)	**actriz** (*actress*)
caballo (*horse*)	**yegua** (*mare*)
héroe (*hero*)	**heroína** (*heroine*)
hombre (*man*)	**mujer** (*woman*)
marido (*husband*)	**esposa** (*wife*)
padre (*father*)	**madre** (*mother*)
rey (*king*)	**reina** (*queen*)
varón (*male*)	**hembra** (*female*)
yerno (*son-in-law*)	**nuera** (*daughter-in-law*)

The following nouns can describe both males and females with a slight change to their spelling. This exercise provides the masculine form. Fill in the feminine form for each noun. Here's an example:

Q. **director** (*director*) _____

A. **directora**

11. **obrero** (*worker*) _____

12. **político** (*politician*) _____

13. **secretario** (*secretary*) _____

14. **abogado** (*lawyer*) _____

15. **niño** (*child*) _____

16. **panadero** (*baker*) _____

17. **conductor** (*conductor*) _____

18. **arquitecto** (*architect*) _____

19. **arqueólogo** (*archeologist*) _____

20. **biólogo** (*biologist*) _____

Recognizing some exceptions

Some nouns break-dance to the tune of a different drummer, or maybe they just like to be difficult. The only way to deal with these troublemakers is through practice and memorization.

The following nouns end in **-e** or a consonant and are masculine:

- **aceite** (*oil*)
- **antifaz** (*mask*)
- **arroz** (*rice*)
- **billete** (*ticket*)
- **cine** (*movie theater*)
- **cobre** (*copper*)
- **disfraz** (*costume, disguise*)
- **examen** (*exam*)
- **jarabe** (*syrup*)
- **lápiz** (*pencil*)
- **mes** (*month*)
- **papel** (*paper*)
- **plan** (*plan*)

These nouns end in **-e** or a consonant and are feminine:

- **base** (*base*)
- **clase** (*class*)
- **cruz** (*cross*)

- ✔ **gente** (*people*)
- ✔ **llave** (*key*)
- ✔ **luz** (*light*)
- ✔ **mente** (*mind*)
- ✔ **miel** (*honey*)
- ✔ **piel** (*skin*)
- ✔ **torre** (*tower*)
- ✔ **vez** (*time*)

To make things even more difficult, a few nouns break the mold and end in **-o** but are feminine. For example:

- ✔ The word **mano** (*hand*) ends in **-o,** but is feminine.
- ✔ The abbreviated form of **motocicleta** (*motorcycle*) is **moto** and the abbreviated form of **fotografía** (*photograph*) is **foto,** but they're both feminine (even though the abbreviated forms, which end in **-o,** are more commonly used).

Pluralizing Nouns

Often you need to describe more than one of something, so you have to be able to transform a noun from its singular form to its plural form. I provide some basic rules for pluralizing nouns, as well as a few exceptions to the rules, in the following sections.

The basic rules

The following three basic rules cover the pluralization of most Spanish nouns:

- ✔ If a noun ends in a vowel, add **-s,** as in the following examples:

artista (*artist*)	**artistas** (*artists*)
caballo (*horse*)	**caballos** (*horses*)
cine (*cinema*)	**cines** (*cinemas*)
menú (*menu*)	**menús** (*menus*)
coquí (*coqui*)	**coquís** (*coquis*)

- ✔ If a noun ends in a consonant, add **-es,** as shown here:

actor (*actor*)	**actores** (*actors*)
director (*director*)	**directores** (*directors*)
papel (*paper*)	**papeles** (*papers*)
profesor (*professor*)	**profesores** (*professors*)

✔ If a noun ends in **-z,** change the **-z** to **-c** and add **-es**; for example:

emperatriz (*empress*)	**emperatrices** (*empresses*)
luz (*light*)	**luces** (*lights*)
pez (*fish*)	**peces** (*fish*)

A few exceptions to the basic rules

Spanish has several nouns that don't conform to the three basic rules I list in the preceding section. Here are some additional rules for handling these exceptions:

✔ If the singular form of a noun has an accent mark on the last syllable, drop the written accent in the plural form, as demonstrated here:

autobús (*bus*)	**autobuses** (*buses*)
camión (*truck*)	**camiones** (*trucks*)
francés (*French*)	**franceses** (*French*)

✔ If a noun has an accent mark on the next-to-last syllable in its singular form, keep that accent in its plural form, as shown here:

azúcar (*sugar*)	**azúcares** (*sugars*)
lápiz (*pencil*)	**lápices** (*pencils*)

✔ If the singular form of a noun ends in an accented **-í** or **-ú,** form the plural by adding **-es** and keeping the accent mark, as in the following examples:

rubí (*ruby*)	**rubíes** (*rubies*)
tabú (*taboo*)	**tabúes** (*taboos*)

✔ If a word ends in **-n** and is stressed on the second-to-last syllable, add a written accent to that syllable when you add **-es,** as in the following examples:

examen (*exam*)	**exámenes** (*exams*)
joven (*young*)	**jóvenes** (*youths*)
origen (*origin*)	**orígenes** (*origins*)

✔ If a noun has more than one syllable and ends in an unstressed vowel and **-s,** don't change it for the plural form. See the following examples:

crisis (*crisis*)	**crisis** (*crises*)
tesis (*thesis*)	**tesis** (*theses*)

Note: This rule applies to all the days of the week except for Saturday (**sábado**) and Sunday (**domingo**). For the days Monday through Friday, use the singular form of the noun and change the article from **el** to **los** to form the plural, as in the following examples (see the next section for more about articles):

el lunes (*Monday*)	**los lunes** (*Mondays*)
el martes (*Tuesday*)	**los martes** (*Tuesdays*)
el miércoles (*Wednesday*)	**los miércoles** (*Wednesdays*)
el jueves (*Thursday*)	**los jueves** (*Thursdays*)
el viernes (*Friday*)	**los viernes** (*Fridays*)

✔ Just as you do in English, if the noun is always plural, use the same form for both singular and plural, as in the following examples:

> **afueras** (*outskirts*)
>
> **anteojos** (*eyeglasses*)
>
> **auriculares** (*earphones*)
>
> **gafas** (*eyeglasses*)
>
> **gemelos** (*binoculars*, *cuff links*, *twins*)
>
> **tijeras** (*scissors*)

Some Spanish nouns qualify as exceptions to the exceptions! That is, they don't even follow the rules for exceptions. For example, in some nouns, the accented syllable changes when you go from the noun's singular to plural form, as in these common examples:

✔ **carácter** (*character*)	**caracteres** (*characters*)
✔ **espécimen** (*specimen*)	**especímenes** (*specimens*)
✔ **régimen** (*diet*)	**regímenes** (*diets*)

Write the plural form of the following nouns, using the rules listed in the preceding sections. Here's an example:

0. restaurante _____

A. restaurantes

21. muchacha _____

22. mujer _____

23. abrigo _____

24. ciudad _____

25. hotel _____

26. relación _____

27. volumen _____

28. actriz _____

29. portal _____

30. músculo _____

Grasping Gender with Articles

English and Spanish both use definite and indefinite **artículos** (*articles*) to modify their nouns. English, for example, uses the definite article *the* and the indefinite articles *a, an,* and, in some cases, *some*. Spanish uses the definite articles **el**, **los**, **la**, and **las** for *the* and **un**, **una**, **unos**, and **unas** for *a, an,* and *some*. The reason Spanish has more definite and indefinite articles is that the article must agree with the noun both in number (singular or plural) and gender (masculine or feminine). The following sections go over articles and explain how to use them.

Getting specific with definite articles

Just as the name implies, *definite articles* refer to a specific or definite person, place, or thing. English has only one definite article that precedes the noun: *the*. In Spanish, the definite article also precedes the noun, but it has four forms: **el, la, los,** and **las**, as shown in Table 3-2.

Table 3-2	Definite Articles in Spanish
Article	*Example*
el (masculine, singular)	**el vestido** (*the dress*)
la (feminine, singular)	**la blusa** (*the blouse*)
los (masculine, plural)	**los vestidos** (*the dresses*)
las (feminine, plural)	**las blusas** (*the blouses*)

Spanish tends to use definite articles more than English does. So you may notice that in some translations, a definite article appears in Spanish but not in English. Spanish also differs from English in the various ways it uses definite articles. Here are the rules for using definite articles, along with a brief description and a few examples of each rule:

- ✔ Use the definite article before a noun to refer to a generalization about that noun. For example:

    La comida mexicana es la mejor del mundo. (*Mexican food is the best in the world.*)

    Los jugadores del fútbol son los más guapos. (*Soccer players are the most handsome.*)

    El azul es mi color favorito. (*Blue is my favorite color.*)

    Me gustan más las peras. (*I like pears the most.*)

- ✔ Omit the definite article after the verb **ser**, except when **ser** translates as *to happen, to take place,* as in the following examples (see Chapter 7 for details on the verb **ser**):

    Mañana es viernes. (*Tomorrow is Friday.*)

    La fiesta es el sábado. (*The party takes place on Saturday.*)

- ✔ Use the definite article with the days of the week and the seasons, but know that you may omit it when the day of the week is followed by the date or is in front of the season if the season is preceded by the preposition **en** and refers to a repeated occurrence. Here are some examples:

    La ópera es el viernes. (*The opera is on Friday.*)

    Hoy es viernes, el ocho de abril. (*Today is Friday, April 8th.*)

> **Me gusta el verano.** (*I like summer.*)
>
> **Vamos a Florida en invierno.** (*We go to Florida in winter.*)

✔ Use the definite article with the names of bays, mountains, oceans, regions, and rivers, as in the following examples:

> **El Mississippi está cerca de aquí.** (*The Mississippi is near here.*)
>
> **La Sierra Nevada es muy hermosa.** (*The Sierra Nevada is very beautiful.*)

✔ Use the definite article **el** in front of a verb infinitive when the infinitive is functioning as a noun, except when the infinitive is the subject of the sentence (in which case the definite article is sometimes omitted). Here are a couple of examples:

> **Viajar es el abrir de los ojos.** (*Traveling is the opening of one's eyes.*)
>
> **Mentir a sus amigos es peligroso.** (*Lying to your friends is dangerous.*)

✔ Use the definite article (rather than a possessive adjective) with body parts and clothing when the verb is in the reflexive form. (For more about reflexive verbs, see Chapter 14.) Here are some examples:

> **Me cepillo los dientes cada mañana.** (*I brush my teeth every morning.*)
>
> **Manuel se lava las manos.** (*Manuel is washing his hands.*)
>
> **Me pongo el vestido.** (*I'm putting on the [my] dress.*)

✔ Use the definite article as part of the names of some cities and countries, as in these examples:

> **El Cairo** (*Cairo*)
>
> **El Salvador** (*El Salvador*)
>
> **La Paz** (*La Paz*)
>
> **La República Dominicana** (*The Dominican Republic*)
>
> **Los Álamos** (*Los Alamos*)
>
> **Los Ángeles** (*Los Angeles*)
>
> **Las Vegas** (*Las Vegas*)

✔ Precede the names of some countries with the definite article, as in the following cases:

> **el Reino Unido** (*the United Kingdom*)
>
> **la India** (*India*)
>
> **los Países Bajos** (*the Netherlands*)

✔ Use definite articles in front of nouns of measurement, as in the following examples:

> **Cuesta un dólar el kilo.** (*It costs a dollar a kilo.*)
>
> **Las manzanas se venden a un dólar la libra.** (*Apples are sold at a dollar a pound.*)

✔ Use definite articles to tell time, as in these examples (see Chapter 5 for more about times):

> **Es la una.** (*It is one o'clock.*)
>
> **Son las tres.** (*It is three o'clock.*)

> ✔ Use the definite article **el** in front of the names of languages, except after the prepositions **de** and **en** or if the language is directly after the verb **hablar** (*to talk, to speak*). Spanish often omits the definite article directly following the verbs **aprender** (*to learn*), **enseñar** (*to teach*), **estudiar** (*to study*), **leer** (*to read*), **practicar** (*to practice*), and **saber** (*to know*).
>
> **Hablo inglés.** (*I speak English.*)
>
> **Él estudia francés.** (*He is studying French.*)
>
> **El español es muy fácil aprender.** (*Spanish is very easy to learn.*)

Fill in the blanks with the appropriate definite article (**el, la, los,** or **las**). (To figure out each noun's gender, follow the rules from the earlier section "Determining Whether a Noun Is Masculine or Feminine.") Here's an example:

0. _____ personaje

A. el personaje

31. _____ cruces

32. _____ billete

33. _____ papeles

34. _____ maestra

35. _____ llaves

36. _____ yerno

37. _____ torres

38. _____ paraguas

39. _____ misión

40. _____ hombres

Generalizing with indefinite articles

In both English and Spanish, when you're talking about people, places, or things that aren't specific, you use indefinite articles. English has three indefinite articles: *a* or *an* if the noun is singular and *some* if the noun is plural. Spanish has four indefinite articles to cover the masculine and feminine nouns in both their singular and plural forms: **un, una, unos,** and **unas.** Table 3-3 lists the four indefinite articles in Spanish, along with examples of their usage. Notice that, as in English, the indefinite article precedes the noun it modifies.

Table 3-3	Indefinite Articles in Spanish
Article	**Example**
un (masculine, singular)	**un vestido** (*a dress*)
una (feminine, singular)	**una blusa** (*a blouse*)
unos (masculine, plural)	**unos vestidos** (*some dresses*)
unas (feminine, plural)	**unas blusas** (*some blouses*)

Follow these rules for using indefinite articles in Spanish:

✔ If a noun in its singular form begins with a stressed **a-** or **ha-**, use either **el** or **un** before it, even if the word is feminine. But when these feminine nouns are in their plural form, use the feminine article **las** or **unas**. Here are a couple of examples:

el/un águila (*the/an eagle*)	**las/unas águilas** (*the/some eagles*)
el/un área (*the/an area*)	**las/unas áreas** (*the/some areas*)
el/un hábito (*the/a habit*)	**los/unos hábitos** (*the/some habits*)

Note: This rule doesn't apply if you're talking about the letter *a* (**la a**) or the letter *h* (**la hache**).

✔ Use the indefinite article with a noun that's part of a larger whole, as in the following examples:

Quisiera una ración de pizza. (*I would like a piece of pizza.*)

Se puede comprar y dedicar un ladrillo de la pared. (*You can buy and dedicate a brick from the wall.*)

✔ If a noun that refers to someone's gender, nationality, profession, religion, or social status is modified by an adjective or a phrase, precede it with an indefinite article. Check out these examples:

Juan es un buen electricista. (*Juan is a good electrician.*)

Javier es un hombre valiente. (*Javier is a brave man.*)

Don't use an indefinite article before a noun that refers to someone's gender, nationality, profession, religion, or social status when it follows a form of the verb **ser**, unless the noun is modified.

✔ Don't use the indefinite article in exclamatory phrases such as **¡Qué . . . !** (*What a . . . !*). For example:

¡Qué concierto! (*What a concert!*)

¡Qué chica! (*What a girl!*)

✔ Don't use the indefinite article in front of **cierto** (*a certain*), **medio** (*a half*), **otro** (*another*), or **ciento** (*a hundred*). Here are some examples:

Él tiene otro carro. (*He has another car.*)

Hay medio kilo de leche en la nevera. (*There is a half liter of milk in the refrigerator.*)

Rewrite the following words, using indefinite articles in place of the definite articles. Here's an example:

Q. la correa _____

A. una correa

41. la editorial _____

42. los refrescos _____

43. los cines _____

44. el deseo _____

45. las costumbres _____

46. el héroe _____

47. la limusina _____

48. la poeta _____

49. los exámenes _____

50. el caballo _____

Using articles to switch gender and meaning

Many nouns that identify professions and individuals end in **-a**, **-e**, **-ante**, or **-ista** and can be used to describe either a male or a female. In these cases, you have to specify gender through the article that precedes the noun, as shown in the following examples:

Masculine	*Feminine*
el atleta (*the male athlete*)	**la atleta** (*the female athlete*)
el cantante (*the male singer*)	**la cantante** (*the female singer*)
el dentista (*the male dentist*)	**la dentista** (*the female dentist*)
el electricista (*the male electrician*)	**la electricista** (*the female electrician*)
el intérprete (*the male interpreter*)	**la intérprete** (*the female interpreter*)
el pediatra (*the male pediatrician*)	**la pediatra** (*the female pediatrician*)
el poeta (*the male poet*)	**la poeta** (*the female poet*)
el turista (*the male tourist*)	**la turista** (*the female tourist*)

The meaning of some Spanish nouns changes based on whether you use a masculine or feminine article before them. Here are some common examples:

Masculine	Feminine
el capital (*capital, money*)	**la capital** (*capital city*)
el cometa (*comet*)	**la cometa** (*kite*)
el corte (*cut*)	**la corte** (*court*)
el cura (*priest*)	**la cura** (*cure*)
el editorial (*newspaper editorial*)	**la editorial** (*publishing house*)
el frente (*front*)	**la frente** (*forehead*)
el guía (*male guide*)	**la guía** (*female guide, guidebook,* or *telephone book*)
el orden (*order, sequence*)	**la orden** (*command, order*)
el Papa (*the Pope*)	**la papa** (*potato*)
el policía (*police officer*)	**la policía** (*the police force*)

Choose the masculine or feminine form of one of the nouns in the preceding lists to correctly answer the following statements. Here's an example:

0. *What do you use to make french fries?*

_____

A. **la papa**

51. *What do you fly when it's windy?*

_____

52. *What male leads you on a hike?*

_____

53. *What do you look for when you're sick?*

_____

54. *What do you write to express your opinion?*

_____

55. *Where do you find phone numbers?*

_____

56. *Where would you most likely find a judge?*

_____

57. *What does a sergeant give to his soldiers?*

_____

58. Who gives traffic tickets?

_____

59. What is the part of the body where parents check for a fever?

_____

60. Where does the president live?

_____

Answer Key

1	F	21	muchachas	41	una editorial
2	F	22	mujeres	42	unos refrescos
3	M	23	abrigos	43	unos cines
4	M	24	ciudades	44	un deseo
5	F	25	hoteles	45	unas costumbres
6	M	26	relaciones	46	un héroe
7	M	27	volúmenes	47	una limusina
8	F	28	actrices	48	una poeta
9	F	29	portales	49	unos exámenes
10	M	30	músculos	50	un caballo
11	obrera	31	las	51	la cometa
12	política	32	el	52	el guía
13	secretaria	33	los	53	la cura
14	abogada	34	la	54	el editorial
15	niña	35	las	55	la guía
16	panadera	36	el	56	la corte
17	conductora	37	las	57	la orden
18	arquitecta	38	el	58	el policía
19	arqueóloga	39	la	59	la frente
20	bióloga	40	los	60	la capital

Chapter 4

Describing Stuff with Adjectives

*I*f you want to add your personal opinion to a statement or more vividly describe something, **adjetivos** (*adjectives*) are the perfect tool for you. In English and Spanish, *adjectives* tell what color something is, how tall or short someone is, what country something or someone came from, how big or small something is . . . you get the idea.

In this chapter, I explain how to make an adjective agree with the noun or pronoun it describes and where to place the adjective in your sentence. I also highlight various ways that adjectives can make your sentences more colorful and descriptive.

Making Adjectives Agree with the Nouns They Modify

Just as articles have to agree with the nouns they precede in gender (masculine or feminine) and number (singular or plural), adjectives have to agree with the nouns they modify in both gender and number. The following sections explain the basic rules that govern adjective-noun agreement, as well as special circumstances in which Spanish tends to bend the rules. In doing so, these sections also present you with gobs of adjectives you'll find yourself using on a daily basis. (Flip to Chapter 3 for an introduction to nouns and articles.)

Brushing up on some basic rules

No matter what, an adjective must agree with the noun it modifies in both gender and number:

▶ **Gender:** If the noun is feminine, like **la muchacha** (*the girl*), the adjective must be feminine, too. For example, if you want to say the tall girl, you'd say **la muchacha alta** (*the tall girl*). If the girl has a brother who is also tall, you'd say **el muchacho alto** (*the tall* *boy*). (Refer to Chapter 3 to find out how to determine whether the noun you're using is masculine or feminine.)

✔ **Number:** If the noun is plural, the adjective must also be plural. For example, if you want to describe a group of tall girls, you'd say **las muchachas altas**. To describe a group of tall boys, you'd say **los muchachos altos**. Similarly, if the noun is singular, the adjective must be singular, too (see the preceding bullet for examples).

Here are a few more examples of adjectives that agree with the nouns they modify in both gender and number:

un examen difícil (*a difficult exam*)

un hombre español (*a Spanish man*)

un hotel bueno (*a good hotel*)

unas casas grandes (*some large houses*)

una chica inteligente (*a smart girl*)

una mujer hermosa (*a beautiful woman*)

unos crucigramas difíciles (*some difficult crossword puzzles*)

unos peces caros (*some expensive fish*)

unas reglas importantes (*some important rules*)

unos policías estrictos (*some strict policemen*)

unos programas interesantes (*some interesting programs*)

The following sections provide specifics on the gender and number rules for different types of adjectives.

Adjectives that follow the usual gender and number rules

Like nouns, most adjectives follow the general rule that masculine adjectives end in **-o** and pluralize with **-s** and feminine adjectives end in **-a** and pluralize with **-s** (see Chapter 3 for details on nouns and gender). Table 4-1 features some very useful adjectives that comply with this rule.

Table 4-1	Adjectives That Follow the Usual Gender and Number Rules			
Masculine Singular	**Feminine Singular**	**Masculine Plural**	**Feminine Plural**	**English Translation**
aburrido	aburrida	aburridos	aburridas	*bored, boring*
alto	alta	altos	altas	*tall*
antipático	antipática	antipáticos	antipáticas	*unpleasant*
bajo	baja	bajos	bajas	*short (height)*
barato	barata	baratos	baratas	*cheap*

Masculine Singular	Feminine Singular	Masculine Plural	Feminine Plural	English Translation
bonito	bonita	bonitos	bonitas	handsome, pretty
bueno	buena	buenos	buenas	good
cansado	cansada	cansados	cansadas	tired
cariñoso	cariñosa	cariñosos	cariñosas	affectionate
caro	cara	caros	caras	expensive
corto	corta	cortos	cortas	short (length)
delgado	delgada	delgados	delgadas	thin
delicioso	deliciosa	deliciosos	deliciosas	delicious
divertido	divertida	divertidos	divertidas	amusing, fun
enfermo	enferma	enfermos	enfermas	sick
famoso	famosa	famosos	famosas	famous
generoso	generosa	generosos	generosas	generous
gracioso	graciosa	graciosos	graciosas	witty
hermoso	hermosa	hermosos	hermosas	beautiful
honesto	honesta	honestos	honestas	honest
largo	larga	largos	largas	long
limpio	limpia	limpios	limpias	clean
listo	lista	listos	listas	clever
malo	mala	malos	malas	bad
necesario	necesaria	necesarios	necesarias	necessary
nervioso	nerviosa	nerviosos	nerviosas	nervous
nuevo	nueva	nuevos	nuevas	new
ocupado	ocupada	ocupados	ocupadas	busy
peligroso	peligrosa	peligrosos	peligrosas	dangerous
pequeño	pequeña	pequeños	pequeñas	little, small
perfecto	perfecta	perfectos	perfectas	perfect
preocupado	preocupada	preocupados	preocupadas	worried
rápido	rápida	rápidos	rápidas	fast
rico	rica	ricos	ricas	rich, delicious
serio	seria	serios	serias	serious
simpático	simpática	simpáticos	simpáticas	nice
sincero	sincera	sinceros	sinceras	sincere
sucio	sucia	sucios	sucias	dirty
viejo	vieja	viejos	viejas	old

Adjectives without gender

Adjectives that end in a consonant,-**e**, or -**ista** usually don't have masculine and feminine forms, but they do have singular and plural forms. To make an adjective that ends in -**e** or -**ista** plural, simply add -**s**. To make an adjective that ends in a consonant plural, add -**es**. Table 4-2 presents some very useful Spanish adjectives that follow this rule.

Table 4-2	Adjectives without Masculine and Feminine Forms	
Singular	*Plural*	*English Translation*
agradable	agradables	*agreeable, pleasant*
alegre	alegres	*happy*
arrogante	arrogantes	*arrogant*
brillante	brillantes	*brilliant (color)*
difícil	difíciles	*difficult*
excelente	excelentes	*excellent*
fácil	fáciles	*easy*
fuerte	fuertes	*strong*
grande	grandes	*big, large, great*
importante	importantes	*important*
inteligente	inteligentes	*intelligent*
interesante	interesantes	*interesting*
optimista	optimistas	*optimistic*
profesional	profesionales	*professional*
radiante	radiantes	*bright, intense (light, smile, sun)*
realista	realistas	*realistic*
responsable	responsables	*responsible*
terrible	terribles	*terrible*
triste	tristes	*sad*

Adjectives that end in -dor, -ón, and -án

With some adjectives that end in -**dor**, -**ón**, and -**án**, you add -**a** to form the feminine, -**es** to form the masculine plural, and -**as** to form the feminine plural. These adjectives, some of which are listed in Table 4-3, have four forms like the adjectives that end in -**o** that I describe in the earlier section "Adjectives that follow the usual gender and number rules."

Table 4-3		Adjectives That End in -dor, -ón, and -án		
Masculine Singular	*Feminine Singular*	*Masculine Plural*	*Feminine Plural*	*English Translation*
charlatán	charlatana	charlatanes	charlatanas	*talkative*
glotón	glotona	glotones	glotonas	*gluttonous*

Masculine Singular	Feminine Singular	Masculine Plural	Feminine Plural	English Translation
hablador	habladora	habladores	habladoras	talkative
peleador	peleadora	peleadores	peleadoras	combative, feisty
preguntón	preguntona	preguntones	preguntonas	inquisitive
trabajador	trabajadora	trabajadores	trabajadoras	hardworking

When a word that's accented on the last syllable pluralizes with **-es,** drop the accent. This follows the rule that any word ending in **-n, -s,** or a vowel has a natural stress on the second-to-last syllable. See Chapter 2 for more on accents and stress.

Adjectives that describe colors

The Spanish words for colors are a mixture of words that don't have a masculine or feminine form and words that follow the "masculine ends in **-o**" and the "feminine ends in **-a**" rule (I explain all these types of adjectives earlier in this chapter). Table 4-4 gives the masculine singular and plural, as well as the feminine singular and plural forms (when applicable), of the colorful adjectives. Note that some adjectives may drop or add an accent mark when they're pluralized (see Chapter 2 for more on accents).

Table 4-4		Common Colors		
Masculine Singular	Feminine Singular	Masculine Plural	Feminine Plural	English Translation
amarillo	amarilla	amarillos	amarillas	yellow
anaranjado	anaranjada	anaranjados	anaranjadas	orange
azul		azules		blue
blanco	blanca	blancos	blancas	white
gris		grises		grey
marrón		marrones		brown
morado	morada	morados	moradas	purple
negro	negra	negros	negras	black
rojo	roja	rojos	rojas	red
rosado	rosada	rosados	rosadas	pink
verde		verdes		green

Fill in the blank with the correct Spanish adjective, as shown in the following example. Make sure the adjective agrees in both gender and number with the noun it modifies.

Q. las flores _____ (*pink*)

A. las flores rosadas

1. **el biólogo** _____ (*intelligent*)

2. **el arroz** _____ (*brown*)

3. **los atletas** _____ (*strong*)

4. **la gente** _____ (*optimistic*)

5. **los exámenes** _____ (*easy*)

6. **el crucigrama** _____ (*difficult*)

7. **las luces** _____ (*bright*)

8. **la poeta** _____ (*interesting*)

9. **el color** _____ (*brilliant*)

10. **las actrices** _____ (*important*)

Modifying two or more nouns with one adjective

An adjective may modify more than one noun in a sentence. If the adjective modifies two nouns of the same gender, either singular or plural, you need to make the adjective agree with the nouns in number and gender, as in the following examples:

el perro y el gato peligrosos (*the dangerous dog and cat*)

el chico y el hombre graciosos (*the witty boy and man*)

la doctora y la enfermera simpáticas (*the nice doctor and nurse*)

los quesos y los duraznos deliciosos (*the delicious cheeses and peaches*)

los días y los años largos (*the long days and years*)

las chicas y las mujeres hermosas (*the beautiful girls and women*)

las obreras y las políticas sinceras (*the sincere workers and politicians*)

If the two nouns have different genders, whether they're both singular or plural, you use the masculine form of the adjective. Consider the following examples:

la cantante y el atleta famosos (*the famous singer and athlete*)

la miel y el queso deliciosos (*the delicious honey and cheese*)

las pediatras y los biólogos serios (*the serious pediatricians and biologists*)

los caballos y las yeguas hermosos (*the beautiful horses and mares*)

If one noun is singular and one is plural, you use the plural form of the adjective to modify them. If the nouns are both feminine, you use the feminine form of the adjective, but if one of the nouns is masculine and one is feminine, you use the masculine form of the adjective, as in the following examples:

> **el gato y las perras preciosos** (*the precious cat and dogs*)

> **los libros y la carpeta caros** (*the expensive books and folder*)

Give the appropriate form of the adjective shown in parentheses to complete the sentence. Make sure that the adjectives agree with the nouns in gender and number. Here's an example:

0. Los muebles y las paredes son _____. (*white*)

A. blancos

11. Las ensaladas y el queso son _____. (*delicious*)

12. La cantante y el actor son _____. (*famous*)

13. Los libros y las ciudades son _____. (*interesting*)

14. Las pediatras y los doctores son _____. (*intelligent*)

15. Los zapatos y las guías son _____. (*necessary*)

16. Los parques y las ciudades son _____. (*beautiful*)

17. Los hombres y las mujeres son _____. (*combative*)

18. Las chicas y los chicos son _____. (*talkative*)

19. El profesor y las profesoras son _____. (*professional*)

20. Las abogadas y los pediatras son _____. (*expensive*)

Using two or more adjectives with one noun

Sometimes you may want to use two or more adjectives to describe one noun. In such cases, the following rules come into play:

> ✔ To use two adjectives to describe one noun, place both adjectives after the noun and join them with **y** (*and*). Here are two examples:

>> **una película famosa y buena** (*a famous and good movie*)

>> **unas ciudades maravillosas y modernas** (*some marvelous and modern cities*)

✔ To emphasize one adjective over the other, don't place the **y** (and) between the two adjectives. Instead, put the adjective that you want to emphasize last, as shown here:

> Writing **unos escritores modernos mexicanos** (*some modern Mexican writers*) places the emphasis on *Mexican* out of all the modern writers.

> Writing **unos escritores mexicanos modernos** (*some modern Mexican writers*) places the emphasis on *modern* out of all the Mexican writers.

✔ To use three or more adjectives with one noun, place the adjectives after the noun, separate all of them except the last two with commas, and add **y** (*and*) between the last two. Here's an example: **un vestido caro, rojo y blanco** (*an expensive, red and white dress*).

✔ When you want to use more than one adjective and the usual placement of one of them is in front of the noun, keep it before the noun and place the other adjective(s) after the noun, as shown in the following examples. (See the later section "Putting Adjectives in Their Proper Place" for the full scoop on adjective position.)

> **cierto libro interesante** (*a certain interesting book*)

> **otra cantante excelente** (*another excellent singer*)

> **ningunas mujeres preguntonas** (*not any inquisitive women*)

> **pocos hombres generosos** (*few generous men*)

Using a past participle as an adjective

In English, *past participles* are verb forms that end in **-ed** or **-en,** such as *laughed* and *spoken*. You use them to form perfect and passive tenses, but you can also use most of them as adjectives. The same is true in Spanish.

To form a regular past participle in Spanish, drop the **-ar**, **-er**, or **-ir** ending and add **-ado** to **-ar** verbs and **-ido** to **-er** and **-ir** verbs (see Chapter 21 for more details). Here are a few regular past participles:

> **comprado** (*bought*)

> **comido** (*eaten*)

> **pedido** (*ordered, asked*)

Some past participles are irregular, meaning you don't follow a basic formula to form them. Unfortunately, you just have to memorize them. Table 4-5 lists a few common irregular past participles.

Table 4-5		Some Irregular Past Participles	
Verb	*Meaning*	*Past Participle*	*Meaning*
abrir	*to open*	abierto	*opened*
cubrir	*to cover*	cubierto	*covered*
decir	*to say, to tell*	dicho	*said, told*
escribir	*to write*	escrito	*written*

Verb	Meaning	Past Participle	Meaning
hacer	to do, to make	hecho	done, made
morir	to die	muerto	dead
poner	to place, to put	puesto	placed, put
resolver	to resolve	resuelto	resolved
romper	to break	roto	broken
ver	to see	visto	seen
volver	to return	vuelto	returned

As you can see in Table 4-5, these past participles are presented in the masculine singular form. To use a past participle as an adjective, you must make it agree with the noun it modifies in both gender and number. So to use a past participle to describe a feminine noun, simply change the **-o** to **-a.** To make any past participle plural, just add **-s** to the singular masculine or feminine form. Check out the following examples:

> **un camión reparado** (*a repaired van*)
>
> **un carro usado** (*a used car*)
>
> **un examen escrito** (*a written exam*)
>
> **un libro perdido** (*a lost book*)
>
> **el viernes pasado** (*last Friday*)
>
> **una actriz pagada** (*a paid actress*)
>
> **una casa pintada** (*a painted house*)
>
> **una ciudad descubierta** (*a discovered city*)
>
> **unos problemas resueltos** (*some solved problems*)
>
> **unas ventanas rotas** (*some broken windows*)
>
> **una piscina llenada** (*a filled swimming pool*)

Give the correct form of the past participle for each verb in parentheses to modify the corresponding noun. Check out the following example:

Q. **un trabajo** (*finished*) _____

A. **terminado**

21. **un editorial** (*written*) _____

22. **el miércoles** (*past*) _____

23. **un camión** (*used*) _____

24. **los anteojos** (*repaired*) _____

25. **el autobús** (*painted*) _____

26. **las tijeras** (*lost*) _____

27. **la cantante** (*paid*) _____

28. **el problema** (*resolved*) _____

29. **los poetas** (*dead*) _____

30. **el portal** (*opened*) _____

Putting Adjectives in Their Proper Place

Positioning adjectives correctly is just as important as making them agree with the nouns they modify (I discuss this topic earlier in this chapter). In English, an adjective precedes the noun it modifies. In Spanish, the opposite is true: In most cases, you place the adjective *after* the noun it modifies. Interesting, right? Of course, Spanish has a few additional rules for placing adjectives, including exceptions for when you actually do place them *before* the nouns they modify. The following sections get you up to speed on these rules.

Placing an adjective after a noun

If an adjective adds information about or describes qualities related to the noun it modifies, place it after the noun. Here are some examples of adjectives that appear after the nouns they modify:

el collar bonito (*the pretty necklace*)

el alambre nuevo (*the new wire*)

el equipaje viejo (*the old luggage*)

el cine grande (*the large cinema*)

la cama pequeña (*the small bed*)

los programas interesantes (*the interesting programs*)

los días largos (*the long days*)

los niños inteligentes (*the intelligent children*)

las clases buenas (*the good classes*)

Placing an adjective before a noun

Of course, Spanish has exceptions to the rule that adjectives come after the nouns they modify. Here are some instances when the adjective comes *before* the noun:

✔ **Adjectives that describe inherent traits:** These adjectives don't add new information. They simply emphasize certain inherent qualities, as in this example: **el pegajoso jarabe** (*the sticky syrup*).

✔ **Possessive adjectives:** These adjectives indicate ownership, as in this example: **tus zapatos** (*your shoes*). See the later section "Belonging with possessive adjectives" for more about possessive adjectives.

✔ **Demonstrative adjectives:** These adjectives point out the location of the nouns they describe and include *this*, *that*, and *these* in English. Here's an example: **este disfraz** (*this disguise*). For more about demonstrative adjectives, see the section "Noting location with demonstrative adjectives."

✔ **Limiting adjectives:** These adjectives indicate an amount or number, as in these examples: **más arroz** (*more rice*) or **cinco hombres** (*five men*). Table 4-6 lists a few useful limiting adjectives, most of which have four forms.

✔ **Comparative adjectives that express an opinion:** If you're expressing a subjective opinion, place the comparative adjectives **mejor** (*better*) and **peor** (*worse*) before the nouns they modify as in the following examples:

> **un mejor camión** (*a better truck*)
>
> **un peor guía** (*a worse guide*)

Table 4-6		Limiting Adjectives That Describe Quantity		
Masculine Singular	*Feminine Singular*	*Masculine Plural*	*Feminine Plural*	*English Translation*
algún	alguna	algunos	algunas	*some*
bastante	bastante	bastantes	bastantes	*enough*
mucho	mucha	muchos	muchas	*many*
ningún	ninguna	ningunos	ningunas	*no, not any*
poco	poca	pocos	pocas	*few*
suficiente	suficiente	suficientes	suficientes	*sufficient*
tanto	tanta	tantos	tantas	*as much*
		varios	varias	*various*

Translate the following expressions into Spanish. Here's an example:

Q. some girls = _____

A. **algunas chicas**

31. some customs = _____

32. many horses = _____

33. no concert = _____

34. a sufficient disguise = _____

35. many lawyers = _____

36. various dilemmas = _____

37. *some bakers* = _____

38. *not any archeologists* = _____

39. *a beautiful flower* = _____

40. *enough classes* = _____

Shortening and changing the meaning of some adjectives based on their position

In Spanish, some adjectives drop a letter or two depending on how you use them in a sentence, and other adjectives change their meaning depending on where you place them. The following sections explain the rules that govern these changes and demonstrate how the rules apply in specific expressions.

Using adjectives that shorten their form

The adjectives of quantity **uno** (*one*), **alguno** (*some*), and **ninguno** (*no, not any*) drop the **-o** when they modify a masculine singular noun, as shown in the following examples:

> **un dentista** (*one dentist*)
>
> **algún turista** (*some tourist*)
>
> **ningún atleta** (*no athlete*)

Note: As you can see, you have to add an accent to **algún** and **ningún** when you drop the **-o.** This addition is a result of the rule that states that any word that ends in **-n**, **-s**, or a vowel has the stress placed on the second-to-last syllable. When you omit the **-o,** you must add a written accent mark to make sure that the last syllable is stressed. (See Chapter 2 for more on stress and accents.)

The adjective **ciento** (*one hundred*) drops the **-to** when it modifies a masculine or feminine noun. You use **ciento** only for the numbers 101 (one hundred and one) through 199 (one hundred and ninety-nine). Following are two examples:

> **cien papeles** (*one hundred papers*)
>
> **ciento veinticinco camiones** (*one hundred and twenty-five trucks*)

If you're expressing a subjective opinion, place the adjectives **bueno** (*good*) and **malo** (*bad*) before the nouns they modify. Be sure to drop the final **-o** from **bueno** and **malo** when you place them in front of masculine singular nouns. (Note that you replace the final **-o** with **-a** when you place them in front of feminine singular nouns.) Check out the following examples:

> **un buen chico** (*a good boy*)
>
> **una buena chica** (*a good girl*)
>
> **un mal chico** (*a bad boy*)
>
> **una mala chica** (*a bad girl*)

A couple of other useful adjectives that shorten their endings are **cualquiera** (*any*) and **grande** (*large*). When you place it in front of a masculine or feminine singular noun, **cualquiera** shortens to **cualquier** and **grande** shortens to **gran**. When you place the adjective **grande** in front of a noun, you not only shorten its form but also change its meaning from *large* to *great*. (In the next section, you find out more about adjectives that change their meaning.) Consider the following examples:

cualquier pediatra (*any pediatrician*)

un gran hombre (*a great man*)

Changing the meaning of an adjective

Some adjectives change their meanings based on whether you place them before or after the nouns they modify. Table 4-7 provides some examples.

Table 4-7	Adjectives That Change Meaning in Different Positions	
Adjective	**Meaning When Placed before the Noun**	**Meaning When Placed after the Noun**
antiguo (*former* or *ancient*)	**mi antigua casa** (*my former house*)	**el castillo antiguo** (*the ancient castle*)
cierto (*certain* or *true*)	**cierto libro** (*a certain book*)	**un amigo cierto** (*a sure friend, a true friend*)
cualquier (*any* or *any old*)	**cualquier hombre** (*any man*)	**un camión cualquiera** (*any old truck*)
diferentes (*various* or *different*)	**diferentes mujeres** (*various women*)	**mujeres diferentes** (*different women*)
grande (*great* or *large*)	**un gran presidente** (*a great president*)	**una casa grande** (*a large house*)
medio (*half* or *average*)	**medio salvaje** (*half savage*)	**el niño medio** (*the average child*)
mismo (*the same* or *himself/ herself*)	**la misma cosa** (*the same thing*)	**mi padre mismo** (*my father himself*)
nuevo (*another* or *new*)	**un nuevo día** (*another day*)	**unos zapatos nuevos** (*some new shoes*)
pobre (*unfortunate* or *poor*)	**la pobre madre** (*the unfortunate mother*)	**la madre pobre** (*the poor mother*)
simple (*just* or *simple*)	**un simple dosis** (*just a dose*)	**un personaje simple** (*a simple character*)
única (*only* or *unique*)	**la única hija** (*the only daughter*)	**una hija única** (*a unique daughter*)

Translate the following adjective/noun combinations into Spanish. Here's an example:

Q. *a unique story* = _____

A. **un cuento único**

41. *a good book* = _____

42. *one hundred dollars* = _____

43. *the only heir* = _____

44. *the same problem* = _____

45. *any woman* = _____

46. *the unfortunate family* = _____

47. *a new life* = _____

48. *a bad movie* = _____

49. *just a swallow* = _____

50. *a great year* = _____

Dealing with Possessive and Demonstrative Adjectives

Possessive and demonstrative adjectives tend to march to the beat of a different drummer. The following sections introduce you to these two types of adjectives and explain how to use them properly to describe the nouns they modify.

Belonging with possessive adjectives

When you want to say that a certain thing or group of things belongs to a particular person or group of people, you need to use a *possessive adjective*. The list of possessive adjectives is as long as the list of subject pronouns, because they represent exactly the same people. Table 4-8 shows the subject pronouns to the left with their corresponding possessive adjectives to the right. (Flip to Chapter 9 for full details on subject pronouns.)

Table 4-8		Possessive Adjectives	
Subject Pronoun	**English Translation**	**Possessive Adjective**	**English Translation**
yo	*I*	**mi/mis**	*my*
tú	*you* (singular, informal)	**tu/tus**	*your*
él/ella/usted	*he, she, you* (singular, formal)	**su/sus**	*his, her, hers, your*

Subject Pronoun	English Translation	Possessive Adjective	English Translation
nosotros/nosotras	we	nuestro/nuestros/ nuestra/nuestras	our
vosotros/vosotras	you (plural, informal)	vuestro/vuestros/ vuestra/vuestras	your
ellos/ellas/ustedes	they, you (plural, formal)	su/sus	their, your

All the possessive adjectives have singular and plural forms. The **nosotros** and **vosotros** forms have masculine and feminine forms, as well. Like all adjectives, the possessive adjectives must agree in number and gender with the nouns they modify, as in the following examples:

Es mi carro. (*It is my car.*)

Son tus carros. (*They are your* [singular, informal] *cars.*)

Son sus libros. (*They are her books.*)

Es nuestra casa. (*It is our house.*)

Esas son vuestras maletas. (*Those are your* [plural, informal] *suitcases.*)

Son sus vestidos nuevos. (*They are your new dresses.*)

Fill in the appropriate possessive adjective to say that the given items belong to the people indicated. Here's an example:

Q. (mi madre) _____ **cartas**

A. **sus**

51. (Felipe) _____ **casa**

52. (nosotros) _____ **libros**

53. (ella) _____ **idea**

54. (yo) _____ **vestido**

55. (Ana y Luisa) _____ **relojes**

56. (vosotros) _____ **banco**

57. (ustedes) _____ **documentos**

58. (ellos) _____ **amigos**

59. (usted) _____ **camas**

60. (tú) _____ **jardín**

Noting location with demonstrative adjectives

Demonstrative adjectives describe the location of an item in relationship to the speaker(s) and the person(s) being spoken to. English uses the words *this*, *that*, *these*, and *those* as demonstrative adjectives. As usual, Spanish has a few more words because it breaks demonstrative adjectives into masculine, feminine, singular, and plural forms to agree with the nouns they modify. Table 4-9 lists the Spanish demonstrative adjectives along with their English counterparts. Each demonstrative adjective has all four forms.

Table 4-9		Demonstrative Adjectives			
Masculine Singular	**Feminine Singular**	**English Translation**	**Masculine Plural**	**Feminine Plural**	**English Translation**
este	esta	*this (here)*	estos	estas	*these (here)*
ese	esa	*that (there)*	esos	esas	*those (there)*
aquel	aquella	*that (over there)*	aquellos	aquellas	*those (over there)*

Demonstrative adjectives precede the nouns they modify and always agree with those nouns in number and gender.

Here are a few examples to give you an idea of how demonstrative adjectives work:

Me gustan estos zapatos. (*I like these shoes.*)

Ese libro es muy interesante. (*That book is very interesting.*)

Esas mesas están sucias. (*Those tables are dirty.*)

Aquellos niños están jugando en el parque. (*Those children [over there] are playing in the park.*)

Fill in the appropriate demonstrative adjectives to modify the following nouns. Make sure the demonstrative adjective matches the noun it modifies in number and gender. Here's an example:

0. (this [here]) _____ mesa

A. **esta mesa**

61. (that [over there]) _____ **puerta**

62. (those [there]) _____ **flores**

63. (these [here]) _____ **diccionarios**

64. (this [here]) _____ **plato**

65. (those [over there]) _____ **muchachas**

66. *(that [there])* _____ **lápiz**

67. *(those [over there])* _____ **muchachos**

68. *(this [here])* _____ **blusa**

69. *(those [there])* _____ **anillos**

70. *(these [here])* _____ **carpetas**

Identifying Nationality with Adjectives

Adjectives that describe nationality are a mixed bag in terms of the type of ending they have. But generally speaking, they follow these rules:

- ✔ If the masculine form of an adjective of nationality ends in **-o**, change the **-o** to **-a** to form the feminine. To form the plural, add **-s**.
- ✔ If the masculine form of an adjective of nationality ends in a consonant, add **-es** to pluralize and **-a** to make it feminine. Then add **-s** to pluralize the feminine form.

Table 4-10 lists a few of the Spanish adjectives of nationality that follow these rules. (Notice that Spanish adjectives of nationality aren't initial-capped as they are in English.)

Table 4-10		**Adjectives of Nationality**		
Masculine Singular	*Feminine Singular*	*Masculine Plural*	*Feminine Plural*	*English Translation*
africano	africana	africanos	africanas	*African*
alemán	alemana	alemanes	alemanas	*German*
chileno	chilena	chilenos	chilenas	*Chilean*
chino	china	chinos	chinas	*Chinese*
español	española	españoles	españolas	*Spanish*
francés	francesa	franceses	francesas	*French*
inglés	inglesa	ingleses	inglesas	*English*
japonés	japonesa	japoneses	japonesas	*Japanese*
mexicano	mexicana	mexicanos	mexicanas	*Mexican*
norteamericano	norteamericana	norteamericanos	norteamericanas	*North American or just American*

Note that if a word has an accent mark on the final syllable and then you add another syllable that ends in **-n**, **-s**, or a vowel to make it feminine or plural, you also have to drop the accent. (Find out more about stress and accents in Chapter 2.)

Naturally, Spanish has some exceptions to the basic rules. Some adjectives of nationality that end in **-a**, **-án**, **-ense**, and **-í** are both masculine and feminine. To pluralize these adjectives, just add **-s**, as in the following examples:

- **belga(s)** (*Belgian*)
- **canadiense(s)** (*Canadian*)
- **catalán(es)** (*Catalan*)
- **estadounidense(s)** (*American, from the United States*)
- **iraní(s)** (*Iranian*)
- **iraquí(s)** (*Iraqui*)
- **israelí(es)** (*Israeli*)
- **kuwaití(s)** (*Kuwaiti*)
- **nicaragüense(s)** (*Nicaraguan*)
- **australiano/a(s)** (*Australian*)
- **vietnamita(s)** (*Vietnamese*)

Following are some examples that use adjectives of nationality to describe people or things (note that these adjectives typically go after the nouns they describe):

una pintura japonesa (*a Japanese painting*)

un hombre kuwaití (*a Kuwaiti man*)

un pintor norteamericano (*an American painter*)

un arquitecto mexicano (*a Mexican architect*)

el idioma francés (*the French language*)

un atleta australiano (*an Australian athlete*)

unos jugadores israelís (*some Israeli players*)

unas mujeres chinas (*some Chinese women*)

Using Adjectives as Nouns

In Spanish, you can use an adjective as a noun. To do so, simply precede the adjective with a definite article (**el, la, los,** and **las**), an indefinite article (**un, una, unos,** and **unas**), a number (**dos, tres, cuatro,** and so on), or a limiting adjective (see the earlier section "Placing an adjective before a noun" for some examples of limiting adjectives). Such expressions translate into English using words such as *one* or *thing*. Here are a few examples:

El pequeño es precioso. (*The little one is precious.*)

Unos pobres no son contentos. (*Some poor aren't happy.*)

Tres verdes son suficientes. (*Three green ones are sufficient.*)

Muchos jóvenes son habladores. (*Many young people are talkative.*)

You can also use adjectives of nationality (see the preceding section) as nouns in Spanish. Used as a noun, an adjective of nationality can refer to the name of the language or the people of a particular nationality. You need an article in front of an adjective of nationality when you use it as a noun and as the subject of a sentence. Here are some examples:

Él es francés. (*He is a Frenchman.*)

Mi madre habla español. (*My mother speaks Spanish.*)

Los mexicanos son amables. (*The Mexicans are nice.*)

Ellos son alemanes. (*They are Germans.*)

Answer Key

1 inteligente	**25** pintado	**49** un simple trago
2 marrón	**26** perdidas	**50** un gran año
3 fuertes	**27** pagada	**51** su
4 optimista	**28** resuelto	**52** nuestros
5 fáciles	**29** muertos	**53** su
6 difícil	**30** abierto	**54** mi
7 radiantes	**31** algunas costumbres	**55** sus
8 interesante	**32** muchos caballos	**56** vuestro
9 brillante	**33** ningún concierto	**57** sus
10 importantes	**34** un suficiente disfraz	**58** sus
11 deliciosos	**35** muchos abogados	**59** sus
12 famosos	**36** varios dilemas	**60** tu
13 interesantes	**37** algunos panaderos	**61** aquella puerta
14 inteligentes	**38** ningunos arqueólogos	**62** esas flores
15 necesarios	**39** una hermosa flor	**63** estos diccionarios
16 hermosos	**40** bastantes clases	**64** este plato
17 peleadores	**41** un buen libro	**65** aquellas muchachas
18 habladores or charlatanes	**42** cien dólares	**66** ese lápiz
19 profesionales	**43** el único heredero	**67** aquellos muchachos
20 caros	**44** el mismo problema	**68** esta blusa
21 escrito	**45** cualquier mujer	**69** esos anillos
22 pasado	**46** la pobre familia	**70** estas carpetas
23 usado	**47** una nueva vida	
24 reparados	**48** una mala película	

Chapter 5

Dealing with Numbers, Dates, and Time

....

In This Chapter

▶ Counting to one billion

▶ Using ordinal numbers like first, second, and third

▶ Naming the days of the week, the months of the year, and more

▶ Talking about time

....

Regardless of which language you use to communicate, you need to dabble in numerology to some extent; that is, you need to deal with numbers. You have to count things (when order doesn't matter); label things first, second, third, and so on (when order does matter); talk about the days of the week, the months of the year, and the actual year itself; and use numbers to tell the time. Short of introducing mathematical operations, this chapter explains just about everything you need to know about numbers to get you through an average day in Spanish.

Counting from Zero to a Billion: Cardinal Numbers

If you can count **uno, dos, tres** but you start to get a little fuzzy at **cuatro,** take a quick peek at Table 5-1, which brings you up to speed on the Spanish *cardinal* (counting) numbers from zero to a billion.

Table 5-1		Counting from Zero to One Billion	
Number	*Spanish*	*Number*	*Spanish*
0	cero	*8*	ocho
1	uno	*9*	nueve
2	dos	*10*	diez
3	tres	*11*	once
4	cuatro	*12*	doce
5	cinco	*13*	trece
6	seis	*14*	catorce
7	siete	*15*	quince

(continued)

Table 5-1 *(continued)*

Number	Spanish	Number	Spanish
16	dieciséis	80	ochenta
17	diecisiete	90	noventa
18	dieciocho	100	cien (ciento)
19	diecinueve	101	ciento uno
20	veinte	200	doscientos
21	veintiuno	300	trescientos
22	veintidós	400	cuatrocientos
23	veintitrés	500	quinientos
24	veinticuatro	600	seiscientos
25	veinticinco	700	setecientos
26	veintiséis	800	ochocientos
27	veintisiete	900	novecientos
28	veintiocho	1,000	mil
29	veintinueve	1,001	mil uno
30	treinta	10,000	diez mil
31	treinta y uno	100,000	cien mil
40	cuarenta	1,000,000	un millón
50	cincuenta	10,000,000	diez millones
60	sesenta	100,000,000	cien millones
70	setenta	1,000,000,000	mil millones

Here are some rules for using cardinal numbers in Spanish:

✔ English speakers generally write the number 1 in one short, downward stroke. In the Spanish-speaking world, however, the number 1 has a little hook on top, which makes it look a little like a 7. To distinguish a 1 from a 7, put a line through the 7 like so: 7.

✔ Spanish uses periods in place of commas and commas in place of periods (the decimal point), so 1,234.56 in English is 1.234,56 in Spanish.

✔ You use **y** (*and*) between the tens and ones units for numbers between 31 and 99. For example:

> **treinta y cinco** (*35*)
>
> **cuatrocientos cincuenta y dos** (*452*)

✔ If a noun is preceded by a number that ends in **uno** (*one*), the number has to agree in gender with the noun. So you drop the **-o** from **uno** when it comes in front of a masculine noun (**uno** becomes **un**), and you change the **-o** to **-a** when it comes in front of a feminine noun (**uno** becomes **una**). Here are some examples:

> **un libro** (*one book*)
>
> **una moneda** (*one coin*)
>
> **veintiún estudiantes** (*twenty-one students*) (Note the addition of an accent to the **-u** in **veintiún**. Flip to Chapter 2 for an introduction to accents in Spanish.)
>
> **treinta y una mujeres** (*thirty-one women*)

✔ The numbers 200, 300, 400, 500, 600, 700, 800, and 900 also agree in gender with the nouns that they precede, as shown in the following examples:

> **cuatrocientos dólares** (*four hundred dollars*)
>
> **novecientas vacas** (*nine hundred cows*)

✔ Instead of **ciento** (*100*), you use **cien** in front of nouns of either gender and **mil** (*thousand*), **un millón** (*a million*), or **millones** (*millions*) to express the number, quantity, or amount, as shown in the following examples:

> **cien dólares** (*one hundred dollars*)
>
> **cien cartas** (*one hundred letters*)
>
> **cien mil millas** (*one hundred thousand miles*)
>
> **cien millones de personas** (*one hundred million people*) (**Note:** The preposition **de** (*of*) comes after **millón** or **millones** when it precedes a noun unless another number comes between **millón** or **millones** and the noun that follows it, as in **diez millones cien personas** [*ten million one hundred people*].)

Write out the number shown in parentheses. Here's an example:

0. (*118*) _____

A. **ciento dieciocho**

1. (*1,674*) _____

2. (*47*) _____

3. (*35*) _____

4. (*10,815,211*) _____

5. (*7,023*) _____

6. (*61*) _____

7. (*752*) _____

8. (*151*) _____

9. (*999*) _____

10. (*83*) _____

Putting Things in Order with Ordinal Numbers

You use *ordinal numbers* to express position or sequence, such as who finished first, second, and third in a race. Ordinal numbers function as adjectives when you use them in front of nouns and as pronouns when you use them alone. Here are the ordinal numbers from first to tenth (masculine/feminine):

- **primero/primera** (*first*)
- **segundo/segunda** (*second*)
- **tercero/tercera** (*third*)
- **cuarto/cuarta** (*fourth*)
- **quinto/quinta** (*fifth*)
- **sexto/sexta** (*sixth*)
- **séptimo/séptima** (*seventh*)
- **octavo/octava** (*eighth*)
- **noveno/novena** (*ninth*)
- **décimo/décima** (*tenth*)

To represent positions higher than tenth, use cardinal numbers and place the numbers *after* the nouns they modify, as in this example: **Es nuestra reunión veintiuno.** (*It is our 21st reunion.*)

Here are a few other things you need to remember when using ordinal numbers:

- When you use an ordinal number as an adjective in front of a noun, make the number agree with the noun's gender, as in the following examples:

    Es la quinta vez que veo esta película. (*It's the fifth time that I'm seeing this movie.*)

    Él es el octavo amigo que llega. (*He is the eighth friend who arrives.*)

- Drop the **-o** from **primero** (*first*) and **tercero** (*third*) when you use them as adjectives in front of masculine nouns, as in these two examples:

    Es el primer libro en la trilogía. (*It is the first book in the trilogy.*)

    Él es el tercer muchacho en la línea. (*He is the third boy in the line.*)

- You can use the following abbreviated forms of the ordinal numbers when writing them (masculine/feminine):

    $1^{o}/1^{a}$ (*1st*)

    $2^{o}/2^{a}$ (*2nd*)

    $3^{o}/3^{a}$ (*3rd*)

    $4^{o}/4^{a}$ (*4th*)

5°/5ª (*5th*)

6°/6ª (*6th*)

7°/7ª (*7th*)

8°/8ª (*8th*)

9°/9ª (*9th*)

10°/10ª (*10th*)

Choose the appropriate ordinal number to modify each noun. Spell out the number instead of using the abbreviated form and be sure that the number agrees in gender with the noun. (***Note:*** Nouns preceded by **el** are masculine, and nouns preceded by **la** are feminine. See Chapter 3 for more on masculine and feminine articles and nouns.) Here's an example:

O. la _____ vez (*7th*)

A. séptima

11. la _____ hora (*1st*)

12. el _____ muchacho (*9th*)

13. la _____ clase (*4th*)

14. el _____ vuelo (*6th*)

15. la _____ cita (*5th*)

16. el _____ año (*10th*)

17. el _____ corredor (*3rd*)

18. el _____ mes (*2nd*)

19. la _____ semana (*8th*)

20. la _____ muchacha (*7th*)

Talking about Days, Months, Seasons, and Dates

To talk about dates in Spanish, you need to know more than just numbers. You also have to know how to say the days of the week and the months of the year. I discuss all these topics in the following sections, along with the four seasons.

Days of the week

In Spanish, the days of the week are *not* capitalized (unless they appear at the beginning of a sentence), and the week itself starts with Monday, not Sunday. Table 5-2 shows you what the week looks like in Spanish.

Table 5-2	Days of the Week
Spanish	*English*
lunes	*Monday*
martes	*Tuesday*
miércoles	*Wednesday*
jueves	*Thursday*
viernes	*Friday*
sábado	*Saturday*
domingo	*Sunday*

Keep in mind the following guidelines when you talk about days of the week:

✔ Use the article **el** for *on* to say that something happens on a particular day. Here's an example: **Voy a su casa el miércoles.** (*I go to his house on Wednesday.*)

✔ Use the plural article **los** with the day of the week to express the idea that an action takes place habitually on a certain day. Then write the day in its plural form, as shown in the following examples. (*Note:* You add an **-s** only to **sábado** and **domingo** to pluralize them. The other days don't change form in the plural.)

   Voy a este restaurante los domingos. (*I go to this restaurant on Sundays.*)

   Voy a la ópera los martes. (*I go to the opera on Tuesdays.*)

Months and seasons of the year

Table 5-3 lists the 12 months of the year in Spanish and English. As with the days of the week (see the preceding section), you capitalize the first letter of a month's name in Spanish only if the month appears at the beginning of a sentence.

Table 5-3	Months of the Year
Spanish	*English*
enero	*January*
febrero	*February*
marzo	*March*
abril	*April*
mayo	*May*

Spanish	English
junio	June
julio	July
agosto	August
septiembre (sometimes spelled setiembre)	September
octubre	October
noviembre	November
diciembre	December

The months of the year are all masculine; however, you very rarely use articles with months in Spanish. Here are examples of instances when you would use an article with one of the months of the year:

> **El diciembre es mi mes favorito.** (*December is my favorite month.*)

> **Aquí el junio es un mes muy caluroso.** (*June is a very hot month here.*)

In Spanish, all the seasons are masculine except for spring:

- ✔ **el invierno** (*the winter*)
- ✔ **la primavera** (*the spring*)
- ✔ **el verano** (*the summer*)
- ✔ **el otoño** (*the autumn or fall*)

Specific dates

Expressing the date in Spanish is quite simple. All you have to do is follow this formula:

> day + **el** + number + **de** + month

For example: **Hoy es martes el diez de octubre.** (*Today is Tuesday the tenth of October.*)

The one trick is remembering that Spanish uses cardinal (counting) numbers for all the days of the month *except* the first. So when you want to say it's the first of the month, use the ordinal number **primero,** as in this example: **Hoy es domingo el primero de enero.** (*Today is Sunday the first of January.*)

Here are a couple of other things to keep in mind when expressing the date in Spanish:

- ✔ If you want to say the year with the date, simply add another **de** and then the year, as in the following examples:

    > **Hoy es viernes el once de octubre de dos mil doce.** (*Today is Friday the eleventh of October of 2012.*)

    > **Ella nació martes el veinte de abril de mil novecientos noventa y tres.** (*She was born Tuesday the twentieth of April of 1993.*)

✔ You can write an abbreviated form of the date, just as in English, *except* that the order is slightly different. In English, you write abbreviated dates as month/day/year, but Spanish speakers write theirs as day/month/year. So June 20, 2013, looks like this: 20/6/13.

The following expressions may come in handy when you're talking about dates. (Of course, you can substitute any day, month, and date into the following examples.)

¿Qué fecha es hoy? (*What's today's date?*)

¿Cuál es la fecha de hoy? (*What's today's date?*)

Hoy es el quince de mayo. (*Today is May 15th.*)

¿Cuál es la fecha de mañana? (*What's tomorrow's date?*)

Mañana es el veinte de junio. (*Tomorrow is June 20th.*)

¿Qué día es hoy? (*What day is today?*)

Hoy es martes. (*Today is Tuesday.*)

¿Qué día es mañana? (*What day is tomorrow?*)

Mañana es sábado. (*Tomorrow is Saturday.*)

a principios de junio (*at the beginning of June*)

a mediados de diciembre (*in the middle of December*)

a finales de abril (*at the end of April*)

Write out the following dates in Spanish. Although Spanish writers usually write the number in number form, for the sake of practice, write out the words for the numbers. Here's an example:

0. *Sunday, June 2nd*

A. **domingo el dos de junio**

21. *Wednesday, July 13th*

_____

22. *Monday, April 25th*

_____

23. *Thursday, August 15th*

_____

24. *Friday, December 1st*

_____

25. *Saturday, September 7th*

_____

26. *Tuesday, January 11th*

_____

27. *Sunday, May 4th*

_____

28. *Monday, February 28th*

_____

29. *Wednesday, March 19th*

_____

30. *Friday, October 31st*

_____

Telling Time

After you master numbers in Spanish (with help from the info I provide earlier in this chapter), put your new knowledge to work by using some of those numbers to tell time.

To ask someone for the time, say **¿Qué hora es?** (Literally: *What hour is it?*). For 1:00, say **Es la una**. For all the other hours, say **Son las . . .**, as in the following examples:

Son las dos. (*It's 2:00.*)

Son las tres. (*It's 3:00.*)

Son las cuatro. (*It's 4:00.*)

Son las cinco. (*It's 5:00.*)

Son las seis. (*It's 6:00.*)

Son las siete. (*It's 7:00.*)

Son las ocho. (*It's 8:00.*)

Son las nueve. (*It's 9:00.*)

Son las diez. (*It's 10:00.*)

Son las once. (*It's 11:00.*)

Son las doce. (*It's 12:00.*)

Here are a few other important rules for telling time in Spanish:

- To talk about time *after* the hour (that is, 1 to 30 minutes after the hour), use **y** (*and*), as in these examples:

  Es la una y diez. (*It's 1:10.*)

  Son las dos y veinte. (*It's 2:20.*)

- To talk about time *before* the hour (that is, 31 to 59 minutes after the hour), use **menos** (*minus*). Subtract the number of minutes from 60 and then say that it's the next hour **menos** (*minus*) that many minutes, as in these examples:

  Es la una menos cinco. (*It's 12:55.*)

  Son las dos menos diez. (*It's 1:50.*)

- To talk about 15 minutes after or 15 minutes before the hour, use **cuarto**, as in these examples:

  Son las tres y cuarto. (*It's 3:15. It's a quarter after three.*)

  Son las ocho menos cuarto. (*It's 7:45. It's a quarter 'til eight.*)

- To talk about half past the hour, use **media** (*half*). Here are two examples:

  Es la una y media. (*It's 1:30. It's half past one.*)

  Son las cuatro y media. (*It's 4:30. It's half past four.*)

- To clarify whether the time is a.m. or p.m., use the following phrases based on whether it's morning, afternoon, or evening:

  . . . de la mañana (*a.m.*): Morning, from 12:00 a.m. until 11:59 a.m.

  . . . de la tarde (*p.m.*): Afternoon, from 12:00 p.m. until 5:59 p.m.

  . . . de la noche (*p.m.*): Night, from 6:00 p.m. until 11:59 p.m.

  Note that these time divisions aren't etched in stone, so don't worry if you hear some slight variations . . . within reason of course.

  Here are a few examples of how to use these time indicators to clarify whether you're talking about a.m. or p.m.:

  Son las siete de la mañana. (*It's 7:00 a.m.*)

  Son las cinco y cuarto de la tarde. (*It's 5:15 p.m.*)

  Son las ocho y diez de la noche. (*It's 8:10 p.m.*)

- To talk about when something happens, use **a**. To ask when something is going to happen, say **¿A qué hora (es)?** (Literally: *At what hour [is]?*). See the following examples:

  ¿A qué hora es la fiesta? (*What time is the party?*)

  La fiesta es a las ocho y media de la noche. (*The party is at 8:30 p.m.*)

  ¿A qué hora empieza la película? (*What time does the movie start?*)

  La película empieza a las tres y cuarto de la tarde. (*The movie starts at 3:15 p.m.*)

✔ For official times, such as train, bus, or plane schedules, use the 24-hour clock. Doing so eliminates the need to clarify a.m. or p.m. Here are the main points you need to know about the 24-hour clock:

- The minutes are counted after the hour from 1 to 59.
- Use **quince** for *quarter after* and **cuarenta y cinco** for *quarter 'til* (rather than **cuarto**).
- Instead of using **media** for *half past,* use **treinta**.
- Follow the time with **horas** (*hours*).

Here are some examples of time using the 24-hour clock:

Son las diez y treinta horas. (*It's 10:30 a.m.*)

Son las catorce y quince horas. (*It's 2:15 p.m.*)

Son las veinte y cincuenta horas. (*It's 8:50 p.m.*)

Write the following times out in Spanish, using words. Do not use the 24-hour clock.

0. *It's 9:08 p.m.*

A. **Son las nueve y ocho de la noche.**

31. *It's 2:25 p.m.*

_____

32. *It's 3:30 a.m.*

_____

33. *It's 7:00 p.m.*

_____

34. *It's 1:07 p.m.*

_____

35. *It's 5:15 a.m.*

_____

36. *It's 1:55 p.m.*

_____

37. *It's 6:45 p.m.*

_____

38. *It's 10:10 p.m.*

_____

39. *It's 4:13 a.m.*

_____

40. *It's 8:29 a.m.*

_____

Answer Key

1 mil seiscientos setenta y cuatro

2 cuarenta y siete

3 treinta y cinco

4 diez millones ochocientos quince doscientos once

5 siete mil veintitrés

6 sesenta y uno

7 setecientos cincuenta y dos

8 ciento cincuenta y uno

9 novecientos noventa y nueve

10 ochenta y tres

11 primera

12 noveno

13 cuarta

14 sexto

15 quinta

16 décimo

17 tercer

18 segundo

19 octava

20 séptima

21 miércoles el trece de julio

22 lunes el veinticinco de abril

23 jueves el quince de agosto

24 viernes el primero de diciembre

25   sábado el siete de septiembre

26   martes el once de enero

27   domingo el cuatro de mayo

28   lunes el veintiocho de febrero

29   miércoles el diecinueve de marzo

30   viernes el treinta y uno de octubre

31   Son las dos y veinticinco de la tarde.

32   Son las tres y media de la mañana.

33   Son las siete de la noche.

34   Es la una y siete de la tarde.

35   Son las cinco y cuarto de la mañana.

36   Son las dos menos cinco de la tarde.

37   Son las siete menos cuarto de la noche.

38   Son las diez y diez de la noche.

39   Son las cuatro y trece de la mañana.

40   Son las ocho y veintinueve de la mañana.

Part II

Constructing Simple Sentences and Asking Questions

The 5th Wave   By Rich Tennant

"When making small talk in Spanish, remember 'The Five Ws'—who, what, when, where, and why me?"

In this part . . .

Words may be the building blocks of any language, but to be able to use a language, you need to know how to string those words together to form sentences that make sense. This part explains how to do just that. Here, you find out how to construct basic subject-verb sentences in the present tense; express your state of being with the verbs **ser** and **estar;** ratchet up your verb repertoire with the present progressive tense; replace nouns with pronouns so that you don't have to keep repeating yourself; express what you like and dislike with the verb **gustar;** and formulate and answer questions.

If you think that sounds like a lot, you're right! It is. But if you can wrap your brain around the concepts in this part and put them to use, you'll be well on your way to mastering Spanish grammar.

Chapter 6

Writing in the Present Tense

A verb in the *present tense* describes action that's happening right now, is habitual, or is a fact about someone or something. Here are a few examples in English:

✔ *The teacher talks to her class.*

✔ *They always go out to eat on Saturdays.*

✔ *She speaks Spanish and Italian.*

To communicate in the present tense, you need to know how to *conjugate* (or form) the verb in a sentence so that it conveys the present tense and agrees in person and number with the *subject* of the sentence (whoever or whatever is performing the action). This chapter introduces you to Spanish verb fundamentals, explains how to conjugate regular and irregular verbs in the present tense, and then shows you how to use those verbs to construct basic and compound sentences.

Grasping Spanish Verb Fundamentals

All sentences have a subject and a predicate. The subject performs the action, while the predicate is the action the subject performs. No matter what tense you're communicating in, you need to conjugate the verb so that it does the following two things:

✔ Indicates whether the action is occurring, has occurred, or will occur

✔ Agrees in person and number with the subject of the sentence

In the following sections, I explain a few verb fundamentals you need to know before you start conjugating verbs in Spanish.

Introducing infinitives

The infinitive form of a verb is pure action, meaning that nobody's doing it. In English, you form the infinitive by adding the word *to* before the verb, as in *to run, to skip,* and *to jump.* In

Spanish, the infinitive forms end in **-ar, -er,** or **-ir,** as in the verbs **cantar** (*to sing*), **beber** (*to drink*), and **vivir** (*to live*).

You often use the infinitive directly after another conjugated verb in a Spanish sentence. For example, **Quiero leer su libro** (*I want to read his book*). In this case, **quiero** (*I want*) is the conjugated verb followed by the infinitive **leer** (*to read*).

Conjugating verbs to agree with subjects

In Spanish, subject pronouns reflect person and number; Table 6-1 lists the Spanish subject pronouns. When you conjugate verbs, you have to make them agree with the subject of the sentence in both number and person.

Table 6-1	Subject Pronouns in Spanish
Singular	*Plural*
yo (*I*)	**nosotros/nosotras** (*we*)
tú (*you* singular, informal)	**vosotros/vosotras** (*you* plural, informal)
él/ella/usted (*he/she/you* singular, formal)	**ellos/ellas/ustedes** (*they/you* plural, formal)

Note: Spanish has masculine and feminine forms for *we, you* (plural and informal), and *they*. You use the masculine form for males and groups of males and females and the feminine form for females. See Chapter 9 for more details.

Spanish has no equivalent for the English word *it*. If *it* is the subject of the sentence, then it's implied by the third person, singular form of the verb and the context of the sentence. For example: **Es muy difícil.** (*It is very difficult.*)

In most languages, including English, you conjugate verbs to reflect the *tense* (when the action occurred, is occurring, or will occur) and to agree with the subject in person and number. In English, for example, you conjugate the present tense of the verb *to go* like so:

I go	*we go*
you (singular) *go*	*you* (plural) *go*
he/she/it goes	*they go*

Note how the verb form changes from *go* to *goes* for the third person singular; you use *go* for all the other subjects in the present tense.

Unlike English, Spanish conjugates all verbs into six forms or conjugations in the present tense. You can see an example in the following table. (Don't worry if you're unfamiliar with these specific endings right now; I give you the details on how to conjugate a regular **-ar** verb later in this chapter.)

nadar (*to swim*)	
yo **nado**	nosotros/nosotras **nadamos**
tú **nadas**	vosotros/vosotras **nadáis**
él/ella/usted **nada**	ellos/ellas/ustedes **nadan**

Conjugating Regular Verbs

Forming the present tense of regular **-ar, -er,** and **-ir** verbs is easy. You simply drop the verb ending from the infinitive and then add the appropriate present tense ending to the verb stem. Because these regular verbs follow a regular pattern, you need to memorize only one set of endings for each verb type and you're good to go:

Infinitive Ending	*Present Tense Endings*
-ar	**-o, -as, -a, -amos, -áis, -an**
-er	**-o, -es, -e, -emos, -éis, -en**
-ir	**-o, -es, -e, -imos, -ís, -en**

Following are some examples of conjugations for the three different types of regular verbs:

cantar (*to sing*)	
yo **canto**	nosotros/nosotras **cantamos**
tú **cantas**	vosotros/vosotras **cantáis**
él/ella/usted **canta**	ellos/ellas/ustedes **cantan**

beber (*to drink*)	
yo **bebo**	nosotros/nosotras **bebemos**
tú **bebes**	vosotros/vosotras **bebéis**
él/ella/usted **bebe**	ellos/ellas/ustedes **beben**

vivir (*to live*)	
yo **vivo**	nosotros/nosotras **vivimos**
tú **vives**	vosotros/vosotras **vivís**
él/ella/usted **vive**	ellos/ellas/ustedes **viven**

When using the present tense, certain time words and expressions come into play. Here are some of the words and expressions commonly used with the present tense:

Spanish Expression	Translation
a la una	*at one*
a las dos, a las tres, and so on	*at two, at three,* and so on
casi siempre	*almost always*
casi nunca	*almost never*
el lunes, el martes, and so on	*on Monday, on Tuesday,* and so on
los lunes, los martes, and so on	*on Mondays, on Tuesdays,* and so on
esta tarde	*this afternoon*
esta noche	*tonight*
hoy	*today*
nunca	*never*
siempre	*always*
cada día	*every day*
todos los días	*every day*

Conjugate the verbs in parentheses into the correct present tense form according to the subject of the sentence. Here's an example to get you started:

0. Yo _____ (caminar) en el parque.

A. camino

1. Ellos _____ (hablar) por teléfono todos los días.

2. Nosotros _____ (comer) pizza los sábados.

3. Ella _____ (escribir) muchas cartas.

4. Juan _____ (tocar) la guitarra.

5. Tú _____ (bailar) muy bien.

6. Vosotros _____ (leer) un libro muy interesante.

7. Susana _____ (subir) al taxi.

8. Yo _____ (desayunar) en un restaurante muy bueno.

9. Él _____ (beber) un refresco.

10. Los estudiantes _____ (estudiar) mucho.

Conjugating Regular Stem-Changing Verbs

Stem-changing verbs are just what they sound like — verbs whose stems change when you conjugate them. The three basic types of stem-changing verbs change vowels in all the conjugated forms except the **nosotros/nosotras** and **vosotros/vosotras** forms. The vowels that change are

✔ e → i

✔ e → ie

✔ o → ue

Note: Dictionaries and verb lists usually show these stem changes in parentheses next to the verb. Here's an example: **empezar (ie).**

Sometimes the conjugation format of stem-changing verbs is called *the boot.* Why? Well, if you draw a dark box around the forms that have a stem change, you get a shape that looks a lot like a boot. Figure 6-1 shows you what I'm talking about with the verb **dormir.**

In the following sections, I talk about regular **-ar, -er,** and **-ir** verbs that require different types of stem changes. (I list endings for regular verbs earlier in this chapter.)

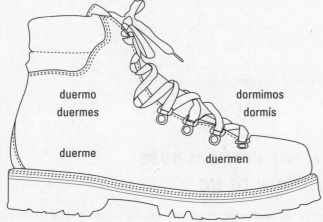

Figure 6-1: The conjugation of a stem-changing verb looks like a boot.

duermo   dormimos
duermes   dormís

duerme   duermen

Regular -ar and -er verbs whose stems change from e to ie

Following are two examples of regular **-ar** and **-er** verbs in which the vowel in the stem changes from **e** to **ie:**

empezar *(to begin, to start)*	
yo **empiezo**	nosotros/nosotras **empezamos**
tú **empiezas**	vosotros/vosotras **empezáis**
él/ella/usted **empieza**	ellos/ellas/ustedes **empiezan**

entender (*to understand*)	
yo **entiendo**	nosotros/nosotras **entendemos**
tú **entiendes**	vosotros/vosotras **entendéis**
él/ella/usted **entiende**	ellos/ellas/ustedes **entienden**

Here are some other **-ar** and **-er** verbs that follow the **e** to **ie** stem-changing pattern. (***Note:*** The verbs that have **-se** after the verb ending are reflexive verbs. See Chapter 14 for details about reflexive verbs.)

✔ **comenzar** (*to begin, to start*)

✔ **defender** (*to defend*)

✔ **despertarse** (*to wake up*)

✔ **pensar** (*to think*)

✔ **perder** (*to lose*)

✔ **querer** (*to want*)

✔ **recomendar** (*to recommend, to commend*)

✔ **sentarse** (*to sit down*)

Regular -ar and -er verbs whose stems change from o to ue

Following are two examples of **-ar** and **-er** verbs in which the vowel in the stem changes from **o** to **ue**:

encontrar (*to encounter, to find, to meet*)	
yo **encuentro**	nosotros/nosotras **encontramos**
tú **encuentras**	vosotros/vosotras **encontráis**
él/ella/usted **encuentra**	ellos/ellas/ustedes **encuentran**

poder (*to be able*)	
yo **puedo**	nosotros/nosotras **podemos**
tú **puedes**	vosotros/vosotras **podéis**
él/ella/usted **puede**	ellos/ellas/ustedes **pueden**

Here are some other **-ar** and **-er** verbs that follow the **o** to **ue** stem-changing pattern. (***Note:*** The verbs that have **-se** after the verb ending are reflexive verbs. See Chapter 14 for the low-down on reflexive verbs.)

- **acordar** (*to agree [upon]*)
- **acordarse** (*to remember*)
- **acostarse** (*to go to bed*)
- **almorzar** (*to eat lunch*)
- **colgar** (*to hang [up]*)
- **doler** (*to ache, to hurt*)
- **probar** (*to test, to prove*)
- **probarse** (*to try on [clothes]*)
- **recordar** (*to remember, to remind*)
- **sonar** (*to ring, to sound*)
- **soñar** (*to dream*)
- **volar** (*to fly*)
- **volver** (*to return, to go back*)

An unusual stem-changing -ar verb: Jugar in the present tense

One verb, **jugar** (*to play [a game or a sport]*), has a strange stem change from **u** to **ue**, but luckily, its conjugated verb endings are regular. So you just have to remember the stem change. The following table shows what **jugar** looks like in the present tense:

jugar (*to play [a game or a sport]*)	
yo **juego**	nosotros/nosotras **jugamos**
tú **juegas**	vosotros/vosotras **jugáis**
él/ella/usted **juega**	ellos/ellas/ustedes **juegan**

Regular -ir verbs whose stems change from e to i

The following table shows an example of a regular **-ir** verb whose stem changes from **e** to **i**:

pedir (*to ask for*)	
yo **pido**	nosotros/nosotras **pedimos**
tú **pides**	vosotros/vosotras **pedís**
él/ella/usted **pide**	ellos/ellas/ustedes **piden**

Here are some other **-ir** verbs that follow this stem-changing pattern. (*Note:* The verbs that have **-se** after the verb ending are reflexive verbs. See Chapter 14 for details on reflexive verbs.)

- ✔ **desvestirse** (*to undress*)
- ✔ **medir** (*to measure, to weigh*)
- ✔ **repetir** (*to repeat*)
- ✔ **servir** (*to serve*)
- ✔ **vestirse** (*to get dressed*)

Regular -ir verbs whose stems change from e to ie

Here's an example of a regular **-ir** verb whose stem changes from **e** to **ie:**

sentir (*to regret*)	
yo **siento**	nosotros/nosotras **sentimos**
tú **sientes**	vosotros/vosotras **sentís**
él/ella/usted **siente**	ellos/ellas/ustedes **sienten**

Following are some other **-ir** verbs that follow this stem-changing pattern. (*Note:* The verbs that have **-se** after the verb ending are reflexive verbs. See Chapter 14 for the skinny on reflexive verbs.)

- ✔ **advertir** (*to advise, to give warning*)
- ✔ **divertirse** (*to enjoy oneself, to have a good time*)
- ✔ **herir** (*to harm, to wound*)
- ✔ **mentir** (*to lie*)
- ✔ **preferir** (*to prefer*)
- ✔ **sentirse** (*to feel [well, ill], to suffer*)

Regular -ir verbs whose stems change from o to ue

The only two regular **-ir** verbs whose stems change from **o** to **ue** are **dormir** (*to sleep*) and **morir** (*to die*). This table shows the conjugated forms of **dormir:**

dormir (*to sleep*)	
yo **duermo**	nosotros/nosotras **dormimos**
tú **duermes**	vosotros/vosotras **dormís**
él/ella/usted **duerme**	ellos/ellas/ustedes **duermen**

Choose one of the following verbs to complete each sentence. Conjugate the verb into the correct form according to the subject of the sentence. I provide an example after the verb list.

colgar   pedir

dormir   pensar

empezar   poder

entender   querer

jugar   volver

0. Mi madre _____ la ropa en el armario.

A. cuelga

11. Ella _____ una hamburguesa.

12. Él _____ que el problema es muy difícil.

13. Yo siempre _____ los pantalones después de lavarlos.

14. Ellos _____ al fútbol.

15. Yo _____ hasta las diez.

16. Nosotros _____ hablar español.

17. Rafael _____ salir temprano.

18. Vosotros _____ mañana.

19. Tú _____ alemán.

20. La fiesta _____ a las ocho.

Dealing with Regular Spelling-Changing Verbs

Spanish is a completely phonetic language, meaning that it sounds exactly like it looks. Because spoken language came before written language, the sound of a word was determined even before it was spelled. Fortunately, Spanish has a straightforward alphabet with consonants and vowels that don't vary in their pronunciation. Therefore, if a word sounds a certain way, its spelling must match that pronunciation.

When you conjugate a verb to match the number and gender of the subject, sometimes you have to change the spelling of that verb to maintain the proper pronunciation. In other words, some spelling changes, also called *orthographic changes,* occur in verbs when the conjugated form changes the sound of a particular letter or throws off where the stress is placed. These spelling changes occur in more than the present tense, but I focus on the present in this chapter. In the following sections, I talk about regular **-ar, -er,** and **-ir** verbs that require unusual spelling changes. (I provide endings for regular verbs earlier in this chapter.)

Verbs that end in a consonant plus -cer or -cir

For verbs that end in a consonant + **-cer** or **-cir,** change the **c** to **z** in the **yo** form in the present tense, as in the following examples. All the other present tense forms follow the regular pattern (see the earlier section "Conjugating Regular Verbs" for details).

vencer (*to overcome, to conquer*)	
yo **venzo**	nosotros/nosotras **vencemos**
tú **vences**	vosotros/vosotras **vencéis**
él/ella/usted **vence**	ellos/ellas/ustedes **vencen**

esparcir (*to scatter, to spread*)	
yo **esparzo**	nosotros/nosotras **esparcimos**
tú **esparces**	vosotros/vosotras **esparcís**
él/ella/usted **esparce**	ellos/ellas/ustedes **esparcen**

Following are some other verbs that end in a consonant and **-cer** or **-cir** and that follow this spell-changing rule:

- ✔ **coercer** (*to constrain, to restrict*)
- ✔ **convencer** (*to convince*)
- ✔ **ejercer** (*to practice [a profession]*)
- ✔ **zurcir** (*to darn, to mend*)

Verbs that end in a vowel plus -cer or -cir

For verbs that end in a vowel + **-cer** or **-cir,** change the **c** to **zc** in the **yo** form in the present tense, as in the following examples. All the other present tense forms follow the regular pattern (see the earlier section "Conjugating Regular Verbs" for details).

ofrecer (*to offer*)	
yo **ofrezco**	nosotros/nosotras **ofrecemos**
tú **ofreces**	vosotros/vosotras **ofrecéis**
él/ella/usted **ofrece**	ellos/ellas/ustedes **ofrecen**

producir (*to produce, to cause*)	
yo **produzco**	nosotros/nosotras **producimos**
tú **produces**	vosotros/vosotras **producís**
él/ella/usted **produce**	ellos/ellas/ustedes **producen**

Here are a few additional examples that follow this change in spelling:

- ✔ **aparecer** (*to appear*)
- ✔ **complacer** (*to please*)
- ✔ **conducir** (*to drive*)
- ✔ **conocer** (*to know a person, to be familiar with a place*)
- ✔ **crecer** (*to grow*)
- ✔ **establecer** (*to establish*)
- ✔ **permanecer** (*to remain*)
- ✔ **reconocer** (*to recognize*)
- ✔ **traducir** (*to translate*)

Verbs that end in -ger or -gir

For verbs that end in **-ger** or **-gir,** change the **g** to **j** in the **yo** form in the present tense, as in the following examples. All the other present tense forms follow the regular pattern (see the earlier section "Conjugating Regular Verbs" for details).

escoger (*to choose*)	
yo **escojo**	nosotros/nosotras **escogemos**
tú **escoges**	vosotros/vosotras **escogéis**
él/ella/usted **escoge**	ellos/ellas/ustedes **escogen**

fingir (*to pretend*)	
yo **finjo**	nosotros/nosotras **fingimos**
tú **finges**	vosotros/vosotras **fingís**
él/ella/usted **finge**	ellos/ellas/ustedes **fingen**

Here are some other verbs that end in **-ger** or **-gir** and follow this spell-changing rule:

✔ **coger** (*to grasp, to grab*)

✔ **dirigir** (*to direct*)

✔ **exigir** (*to demand*)

✔ **proteger** (*to protect*)

✔ **recoger** (*to gather, to collect*)

✔ **sumergir** (*to submerge*)

Verbs that end in -guir

For verbs that end in **-guir,** change the **gu** to **g** in the **yo** form in the present tense, as in the following examples. All the other present tense forms follow the regular pattern that I describe earlier in this chapter.

distinguir (*to distinguish*)	
yo **distingo**	nosotros/nosotras **distinguimos**
tú **distingues**	vosotros/vosotras **distinguís**
él/ella/usted **distingue**	ellos/ellas/ustedes **distinguen**

seguir (*to follow, to pursue, to continue*)	
yo **sigo**	nosotros/nosotras **seguimos**
tú **sigues**	vosotros/vosotras **seguís**
él/ella/usted **sigue**	ellos/ellas/ustedes **siguen**

Following are some other verbs that end in **-guir:**

✔ **conseguir** (*to get, to obtain*)

✔ **extinguir** (*to extinguish*)

✔ **perseguir** (*to persecute, to pursue*)

✔ **proseguir** (*to continue, to proceed*)

Verbs that end in -iar or -uar

For some verbs that end in **-iar** or **-uar,** add an accent mark to the **i** or to the **u** in all the conjugated forms except the **nosotros/nosotras** and the **vosotros/vosotras,** as shown in the following examples. Because **i** and **u** are weak vowels, you have to add an accent mark to have the stress fall on the correct syllable. (For more about pronunciation rules, see Chapter 2.)

esquiar (*to ski*)	
yo **esquío**	nosotros/nosotras **esquiamos**
tú **esquías**	vosotros/vosotras **esquiáis**
él/ella/usted **esquía**	ellos/ellas/ustedes **esquían**

actuar (*to act*)	
yo **actúo**	nosotros/nosotras **actuamos**
tú **actúas**	vosotros/vosotras **actuáis**
él/ella/usted **actúa**	ellos/ellas/ustedes **actúan**

Here are some other verbs that end in **-iar** or **-uar** and that conjugate like the preceding examples:

- ✔ **acentuar** (*to accent, to emphasize*)
- ✔ **confiar (en)** (*to rely [on], to confide [in]*)
- ✔ **criar** (*to raise*)
- ✔ **desafiar** (*to challenge, to dare*)
- ✔ **efectuar** (*to carry out*)
- ✔ **evaluar** (*to evaluate*)
- ✔ **guiar** (*to guide, to lead*)
- ✔ **rociar** (*to sprinkle, to spray*)
- ✔ **variar** (*to vary*)

Verbs that end in -uir

For verbs that end in **-uir** (except those that end in **-guir;** see the earlier section on this verb ending), add a **y** right after the **u** before you add the conjugated endings in all the forms except the **nosotros/nosotras** and the **vosotros/vosotras.** Here's an example:

incluir (*to include*)	
yo **incluyo**	nosotros/nosotras **incluimos**
tú **incluyes**	vosotros/vosotras **incluís**
él/ella/usted **incluye**	ellos/ellas/ustedes **incluyen**

Following are some other verbs that end in **-uir** and, thus, follow this spell-changing rule:

- ✔ **concluir** (*to conclude*)
- ✔ **construir** (*to build*)

> ✔ **contribuir** (*to contribute*)
>
> ✔ **distribuir** (*to distribute*)
>
> ✔ **destruir** (*to destroy*)
>
> ✔ **huir** (*to flee*)
>
> ✔ **influir** (*to influence*)
>
> ✔ **sustituir** (*to substitute*)

Give the correct form of the following verbs according to the subject given. Here's an example to help you get started:

0. ella/sumergir: _____

A. sumerge

21. Luisa y María/concluir: _____

22. tú/zurcir: _____

23. ustedes/conocer: _____

24. yo/seguir: _____

25. ellos/vencer: _____

26. Luisa/conducir: _____

27. ella/escoger: _____

28. usted/fingir: _____

29. nosotros/esquiar: _____

30. vosotros/actuar: _____

Examining Irregular Verbs

Irregular verbs don't follow the usual pattern for conjugations that I describe earlier in this chapter. Some irregular verbs change irregularly in the stem, and some of them don't have regular endings. Some are irregular only in the **yo** form, and some are irregular in all the conjugated forms. The following sections group irregular verbs according to their particular irregularity.

Verbs that are irregular only in the yo form

The following verbs are irregular only in the **yo** form of the present tense. Because these verbs are regular in all the other present tense forms, this list provides only the **yo** form of the verb rather than the entire verb conjugation. (**Note:** This list doesn't include verbs that have a **yo** form irregularity due to a regular spelling change, which I describe earlier in this chapter.)

Spanish Verb	Translation	Conjugation in the Yo Form
caber	*to fit*	**yo quepo**
caer	*to fall*	**yo caigo**
dar	*to give*	**yo doy**
hacer	*to do, to make*	**yo hago**
poner	*to place, to put*	**yo pongo**
saber	*to know something*	**yo sé**
salir	*to leave*	**yo salgo**
traer	*to bring*	**yo traigo**
valer	*to be worth*	**yo valgo**
ver	*to see*	**yo veo**

Some commonly used compound verbs follow the same irregular **yo** form as **hacer, poner,** and **traer:**

Spanish Verb	Translation	Conjugation in the Yo Form
componer	*to compose*	**yo compongo**
deshacer	*to undo*	**yo deshago**
distraer	*to distract*	**yo distraigo**
proponer	*to propose*	**yo propongo**
rehacer	*to remake*	**yo rehago**
suponer	*to suppose*	**yo supongo**

Verbs that are irregular in most or all of their present tense conjugations

The following verbs are irregular in most or all of their present tense conjugations. (*Note:* The verbs **ser** and **estar** are particularly special in Spanish; check out Chapter 7 for the scoop.)

estar *(to be [describing location or temporary conditions])*	
yo **estoy**	nosotros/nosotras **estamos**
tú **estás**	vosotros/vosotras **estáis**
él/ella/usted **está**	ellos/ellas/ustedes **están**

ir *(to go)*	
yo **voy**	nosotros/nosotras **vamos**
tú **vas**	vosotros/vosotras **vais**
él/ella/usted **va**	ellos/ellas/ustedes **van**

oír (*to hear*)	
yo **oigo**	nosotros/nosotras **oímos**
tú **oyes**	vosotros/vosotras **oís**
él/ella/usted **oye**	ellos/ellas/ustedes **oyen**

ser (*to be [describing, age, profession, origin, and permanent qualities]*)	
yo **soy**	nosotros/nosotras **somos**
tú **eres**	vosotros/vosotras **sois**
él/ella/usted **es**	ellos/ellas/ustedes **son**

tener (*to have*)	
yo **tengo**	nosotros/nosotras **tenemos**
tú **tienes**	vosotros/vosotras **tenéis**
él/ella/usted **tiene**	ellos/ellas/ustedes **tienen**

venir (*to come*)	
yo **vengo**	nosotros/nosotras **venimos**
tú **vienes**	vosotros/vosotras **venís**
él/ella/usted **viene**	ellos/ellas/ustedes **vienen**

decir (*to say, to tell*)	
yo **digo**	nosotros/nosotras **decimos**
tú **dices**	vosotros/vosotras **decís**
él/ella/usted **dice**	ellos/ellas/ustedes **dicen**

Translate the following subjects and irregular verbs into Spanish. Here's an example:

Q. *she says* _____

A. **ella dice**

31. *I fall* _____

32. *you* (plural, formal) *suppose* _____

33. *you* (plural, informal) *have* _____

34. *we are* (referring to location) _____

35. *I see* _____

36. *she is* (referring to profession) _____

37. *I come* _____

38. *they hear* _____

39. *you* (singular, informal) *go* _____

40. *I leave* _____

Building Basic Sentences

A subject and a verb are all you really need to create a bona fide sentence: **Yo canto** (*I sing; I am singing*). That's a sentence in both Spanish and English. In Spanish, though, you can even drop the subject when its meaning is understood from the verb ending: **Canto** (*I sing; I am singing*). Now that's one short sentence!

Of course, if you walk around Spain or Mexico or some other Spanish-speaking country, expressing yourself in one-word sentences, you'll come across as being a little odd. Most of the time, you want to convey a little (or a lot) more information in your sentences. For example, you may want to indicate when something happened, why it happened, who performed the action, and what the action was being performed on.

When you have more to say, you can turn to some other parts of speech, such as adjectives (see Chapter 4), adverbs (see Chapter 12), direct objects (see Chapter 9), and prepositional phrases (see Chapter 13). By putting a subject, verb, and a few other select words together, you can begin to express yourself in Spanish.

Use the elements given to construct basic sentences. Be sure to conjugate the verb to agree with the subject of the sentence. All the verbs listed are regular in the present tense, except for **entender,** which has a stem change of **e** to **ie**. Here's an example:

0. **vosotros/hablar/francés**

A. **Vosotros habláis francés.**

41. **yo/ayudar/en la casa**

_____

42. ellos/bailar/en la fiesta

_____

43. ustedes/estudiar/cada día

_____

44. él/entender/el inglés

_____

45. vosotros/correr/en el parque

_____

46. nosotros/mirar/la televisión

_____

47. ella/describir/la foto

_____

48. ellos/prohibir/comer en la sala

_____

49. usted/limpiar/la casa

_____

50. tú/abrir/la puerta

_____

Constructing Compound Sentences with Conjunctions

A *compound sentence* is a sentence with two independent clauses joined by a coordinating conjunction, such as *and* in English. An *independent clause* contains a subject and a verb and expresses a complete thought. Table 6-2 lists some of the more popular coordinating conjunctions in Spanish.

Table 6-2	Coordinating Conjunctions in Spanish
Spanish Expression	*Translation*
y (or **e** in front of a word that begins with **i** or **hi**)	*and*
no . . . ni . . . ni	*nor*
pero	*but*
no . . . sino	*rather*
o (or **u** in front of a word that begins with **o** or **ho**)	*or*
porque	*because*
para que	*so that, in order that*
que	*that*
por eso	*so*

When using these conjunctions, keep in mind the following points:

✔ **Y** and **e** (*and*) and **ni** (*nor*) connect independent clauses that both express a similar or the same thought. Here are some examples:

Vamos de compras, y después vamos a comer. (*We're going shopping, and later we're going to eat.*)

Ella no va a esperar ni aquí, ni en su casa. (*She is not going to wait here, nor at her house.*)

Vosotros podéis venir a nuestra casa, e iremos al cine juntos. (*You can come to our house, and we'll go to the cinema together.*)

✔ **Pero** (*but*) and **no . . . sino** (*rather*) indicate opposition between the independent clauses they connect. Here are two examples:

Me gusta viajar pero no me gusta volar. (*I like traveling, but I don't like flying.*)

No me gusta descansar sino trabajar. (*I don't like to rest; I'd rather work.*)

See Chapter 10 for details on using the verb **gustar**.

✔ **O** and **u** (*or*) join independent clauses that express different or conflicting alternatives, as in these examples:

¿Prefieres hablar del problema ahora, u olvidarlo? (*Do you prefer to talk about the problem now, or forget it?*)

¿Va el tren a llegar atrasado, o va a llegar antes de tiempo? (*Is the train going to arrive late, or is it going to arrive ahead of schedule?*)

✔ **Porque** (*because*) introduces a clause that's subordinate to the main clause. For example: **Vamos temprano porque es difícil conseguir boletos.** (*We go early because it is difficult to get tickets.*)

✔ **Para que** (*so that*) introduces an independent clause that expresses the purpose of the main verb action. For example: **Llamamos para que no olvides venir.** (*We call so that you don't forget to come.*)

✔ **Que** (*that*) subordinates one independent clause to another. For example: **Por favor explica a su hermano que no me gustan sus bromas.** (*Please explain to your brother that I don't like his jokes.*)

✔ **Por eso** (*so*) introduces an independent clause that results from another independent clause. For example: **Ella no va, por eso no vamos tampoco.** (*She's not going, so we're not going either.*)

Use one of the conjunctions that follow to complete the sentences correctly. An example follows the list of conjunctions.

y	por eso
o	porque
pero	

Q. Él necesita más dinero, _____ va a buscar otro trabajo.

A. por eso

51. Mi padre visita Alaska, _____ necesita un abrigo.

52. Nosotros vamos a un restaurante, _____ vamos a un café.

53. Yo limpio la casa, _____ lavo la ropa.

54. Él es un buen jugador, _____ no es un buen cantante.

55. Ellos viven muy cerca, _____ vamos a la misma escuela.

56. Ella come su almuerzo ahora, _____ tiene hambre.

57. Vosotros podéis visitar en agosto, _____ podéis visitar en diciembre.

58. Los estudiantes estudian mucho, _____ pasan el examen.

59. Mi madre va al supermercado, _____ compra la comida.

60. Podemos ir en carro, _____ tomar el autobús.

Answer Key

1. hablan

2. comemos

3. escribe

4. toca

5. bailas

6. leéis

7. sube

8. desayuno

9. bebe

10. estudian

11. pide

12. piensa

13. cuelgo

14. juegan

15. duermo

16. podemos

17. quiere

18. volvéis

19. entiendes

20. empieza

21. concluyen

22 zurces

23 conocen

24 sigo

25 vencen

26 conduce

27 escoge

28 finge

29 esquiamos

30 actuáis

31 yo caigo

32 ustedes suponen

33 vosotros tenéis

34 nosotros estamos

35 yo veo

36 ella es

37 yo vengo

38 ellos oyen

39 tú vas

40 yo salgo

41 Yo ayudo en la casa.

42 Ellos bailan en la fiesta.

43 Ustedes estudian cada día.

44 Él entiende el inglés.

45 Vosotros corréis en el parque.

46 Nosotros miramos la televisión.

47   **Ella describe la foto.**

48   **Ellos prohiben comer en la sala.**

49   **Usted limpia la casa.**

50   **Tú abres la puerta.**

51   **por eso**

52   **o**

53   **y**

54   **pero**

55   **por eso**

56   **porque**

57   **o**

58   **por eso**

59   **y**

60   **o**

Chapter 7

Expressing a State of Being with Ser and Estar

In This Chapter

▶ Noting what's similar and different between **ser** and **estar**

▶ Using **ser** and **estar** correctly

▶ Changing an adjective's meaning with **ser** and **estar**

*1*n English, conveying a state of being is as easy as saying, "To be or not to be." One verb — *to be* — conveys the state of being. In Spanish, just being isn't so easy. Spanish uses two different verbs to express a state of being: **ser** and **estar**. Although they both translate as *to be,* they're not interchangeable, so you have to distinguish between the two different ways to be. Generally, you describe permanent qualities with the verb **ser** and temporary conditions with **estar**. So you can't just say *I am* or *you are* or *he is.* You have to think about the nature of the state of being you're describing.

But don't worry. In this chapter, I walk you through the nuances of these two verbs so you aren't intimidated to talk about who is and who isn't.

Comparing Ser and Estar

Ser and **estar** are similar in that they both describe being, but they're different in terms of the type of being they describe:

✔ **Ser describes permanent being.** Use **ser** to describe the essence of a thing, such as the roundness of a ball.

✔ **Estar describes transitory being.** Use **estar** to describe the temporary state of a thing, such as the location of a ball.

Ser and **estar** are both irregular verbs; the following tables list their present tense conjugations.

ser (*to be*)	
yo **soy**	nosotros/nosotras **somos**
tú **eres**	vosotros/vosotras **sois**
él/ella/usted **es**	ellos/ellas/ustedes **son**

estar (*to be*)	
yo **estoy**	nosotros/nosotras **estamos**
tú **estás**	vosotros/vosotras **estáis**
él/ella/usted **está**	ellos/ellas/ustedes **están**

Give the correct conjugated form of either **ser** or **estar** according to the subject given. Here's an example:

0. yo (estar) = _____

A. estoy

1. ellos (ser) = _____

2. nosotros (estar) = _____

3. tú (estar) = _____

4. vosotros (ser) = _____

5. él (estar) = _____

6. ella (ser) = _____

7. vosotros (estar) = _____

8. tú (ser) = _____

9. yo (ser) = _____

10. ustedes (estar) = _____

Knowing When to Use Ser

When you need to describe *what* something is, use the verb **ser.** This verb captures the essence of being, including all of the following:

- A person's profession, hometown, and relationship to another person
- What something is made of
- Specific times, dates, and days of the week
- Who owns a particular item

Notice the common thread in these descriptions: They all deal with unchanging characteristics.

Follow these three rules of thumb to help you use the verb **ser** correctly:

✔ Use **ser** when a noun rather than an adjective describes the subject: **Adrián es un abogado.** (*Adrián is a lawyer.*)

✔ Use **ser** when you're talking about where someone or something is from rather than where it is right now: **Elena es de España.** (*Elena is from Spain.*)

✔ Use **ser** when you want to describe when or where an event takes place: **La fiesta es el sábado.** (*The party is Saturday.*)

The following sections provide additional guidance to help you decide when to use **ser**.

Identifying a person, place, or thing

The verb **ser** describes the basic essence of something, which is exactly what you're describing when you identify a person, place, or thing. Here are a few examples:

Él es mi padre. (*He is my father.*)

Ella es mi tía. (*She is my aunt.*)

Es la estación de tren. (*It is the train station.*)

Es una pelota. (*It is a ball.*)

El 5 de mayo es el día de la independencia de Francia para los mexicanos. (*The fifth of May is the day of independence from France for the Mexicans.*)

Noting profession, origin, and essential qualities

When you introduce yourself or someone else to another person, you generally share a little bit of basic information, such as your name, your profession, and your hometown. Use the verb **ser** to present this kind of information, as in the following examples:

Mucho gusto, soy María. (*Pleased to meet you. I am María.*)

Soy la amiga de Juan. (*I am Juan's friend.*)

Los dos somos de la misma puebla pequeña. (*We are both from the same small town.*)

Su padre es de Alemania. (*His father is from Germany.*)

Juan es un amigo fenomenal. (*Juan is a wonderful friend.*)

Soy dentista. (*I am a dentist.*)

In addition to describing the essential qualities of people, **ser** describes the essential qualities of things, as in the following examples:

El edificio es de adobe. (*The building is constructed of adobe.*)

La fortaleza es fuerte. (*The fort is strong.*)

La chaqueta es de lana. (*The jacket is made of wool.*)

Describing physical appearance and personality

Even though physical appearance and personality are subject to change, you use the verb **ser** to describe them because they're considered to be inherent and mostly unchanging. After all, physical appearance and personality traits typically change very gradually over the course of a lifetime. Nationality and religion also fall into this category. Here are some examples:

El señor Escobar es guapo. (*Mr. Escobar is handsome.*)

Mi amiga Susana es muy divertida. (*My friend Susana is very fun.*)

Mi hermano y mi padre son altos. (*My brother and my father are tall.*)

Esteban es muy trabajador. (*Esteban is very hardworking.*)

Clarisa es habladora. (*Clarisa is talkative.*)

Fabián es fuerte. (*Fabian is strong.*)

El señor García es venezolano. (*Mr. Garcia is Venezuelan.*)

Él es amable. (*He is very kind.*)

Usted es muy amable. (*You are very kind.*)

Su pelo es rizado. (*His hair is curly.*)

Rafaela es católica. (*Rafaela is Catholic.*)

Table 7-1 lists several more adjectives that are commonly used with **ser** to describe physical appearance, personal qualities, and personality. (For more on adjectives, see Chapter 4.)

Table 7-1	Adjectives Used with Ser to Describe Appearance, Qualities, and Personality
Adjective	*English Translation*
agradable	*pleasant*
bajo/baja	*short (a person)*
corto/corta	*short (a thing or duration of time)*
delgado/delgada	*thin*
inteligente	*intelligent*
interesante	*interesting*
perezoso/perezosa	*lazy*
popular	*popular*

Note that you change the adjectives that end in **-o** to the feminine form by changing the **-o** to **-a.** For the adjectives that end in **-e,** you use the same form to modify both masculine and feminine nouns. You add **-s** to adjectives that end in a vowel to pluralize them. To pluralize an adjective that ends in a consonant, add **-es.** (See Chapter 4 for more details.)

Expressing the time, date, or days of the week

Use the verb **ser** to express the time, the date, and the days of the week, as in the following examples:

> **Son las dos.** (*It is two o'clock.*)
>
> **Hoy es el primero de septiembre.** (*Today is the first of September.*)
>
> **Hoy es viernes.** (*Today is Friday.*)

Flip to Chapter 5 for the full scoop on times and dates.

Showing possession

When you want to describe something as belonging to someone, use **ser,** as in the following examples:

> **Este es mi carro.** (*This is my car.*)
>
> **El carro es de ella.** (*The car is hers.*)

Read the following sentences with **ser** and decide whether the verb and the adjective have been used correctly. If the sentence is correct, write *correct as is*. If the sentence is incorrect, rewrite it, making the required corrections. ***Note:*** Be sure to check the verb conjugations as well as adjective agreement.

Q. La mujer son muy alta.

A. La mujer es muy alta.

11. El libro es interesantes.

_____

12. Mi padre es abogado.

_____

13. Tú es mi mejor amigo.

_____

14. Su casa es muy bonito.

_____

15. Vosotros son muy amables.

_____

16. Los bailes siempre somos muy divertidos.

_____

17. Su país es muy lejos.

_____

18. Nosotros sois con ellos.

_____

19. Yo soy su prima.

_____

20. Emilio y Dorotea es los tíos de Emiliano.

_____

Knowing When to Use Estar

Certain aspects of being are variable, meaning that they change from day to day (or sometimes from moment to moment). For instance, you may be happy one day and sad the next. A friend may be sick this week but get better by next Saturday. Your aunt may be vacationing in Italy for a couple of weeks, but she doesn't live there. These aspects of being don't define a person's inherent nature or permanent state of being. Instead, they define temporary conditions typically affected by outside influences. When you want to describe the changing nature of a person, place, or thing, such as its health, feelings, or location, you use the verb **estar.**

Follow these three rules of thumb to help you use **estar** correctly:

✔ Use **estar** when an adjective that describes how someone is feeling follows the verb: **Margarita está triste.** (_Margarita is sad._)

✔ Use **estar** when an adjective that describes a temporary condition follows the verb: **Adrián está enfermo.** (_Adrián is sick._)

✔ Use **estar** when you want to talk about where someone or something is located right now: **Elena está en casa.** (_Elena is at home._)

The following sections provide additional guidance to help you decide when to use **estar.**

Putting feelings into words

Use the verb **estar** to describe how someone is feeling as the result of some outside stimulus. Such feelings are temporary; for example, you may be upset that you got a bad grade in a class, but eventually, the sadness will pass. Here are some examples of how to describe feelings with **estar:**

Andrés está nervioso. (*Andrés is nervous.*)

Yo estoy lleno. (*I am full.*)

Esperanza está alegre. (*Esperanza is happy.*)

Tomás está adolorido. (*Tomás is sore.*)

Aureliano está inquieto. (*Aureliano is anxious.*)

Nosotros estamos enfadados. (*We are angry.*)

See Table 7-2 for several other adjectives that tend to accompany **estar.** (For more on adjectives, see Chapter 4.)

Table 7-2	Adjectives Used with Estar to Describe Feelings
Adjective	*English Translation*
abrumado/abrumada	*overwhelmed*
agradecido/agradecida	*grateful*
caliente	*hot*
deprimido/deprimida	*depressed*
enojado/enojada	*angry*
feliz	*happy*
frustrado/frustrada	*frustrated*
mojado/mojada	*wet*
preocupado/preocupada	*worried*
sorprendido/sorprendida	*surprised*

Note that you change the adjectives that end in **-o** to the feminine form by changing the **-o** to **-a.** For the adjectives that end in **-e,** you use the same form to modify both masculine and feminine nouns. You add **-s** to adjectives that end in a vowel to pluralize them. Adjectives that end in a consonant pluralize with **-es.** Adjectives that end in **-z** change the **-z** to **-c** and then add **-es.** (See Chapter 4 for more about pluralizing adjectives.)

Describing temporary conditions or traits

You use **estar** with adjectives that describe a condition that's only temporary, such as being sick or being hot or cold. Here are some examples:

Emiliana está atenta. (*Emiliana is attentive.*)

Reynaldo está cansado. (*Reynaldo is tired.*)

Ellos están sucios. (*They are dirty.*)

La sopa está fría. (*The soup is cold.*)

Él está callado. (*He is being quiet.*)

Read the following sentences with **estar** and decide whether the verb and the adjective have been used correctly. If the sentence is correct, write *correct as is*. If the sentence is incorrect, rewrite it, making the required corrections. *Note:* Be sure to check the verb conjugations as well as adjective agreement.

0. Franco está lista.

A. Franco está listo.

21. Las chicas estáis buenas.

_____

22. Emilio estás aburrido.

_____

23. Ellas están preocupadas.

_____

24. Aurelio y yo estamos sorprendido.

_____

25. Ella está frustrado.

_____

26. Nosotros estamos deprimido.

_____

27. Elicia está cansada.

_____

28. Vosotros están callados.

_____

29. Él estoy agradecido.

_____

30. Francisco y Elena están sucias.

_____

Establishing the location of a person, place, or thing

When you talk about where someone or something is, you're talking about location. Because people tend to move around during the day, location is considered a temporary state of being. So you need to use the verb **estar** whenever you ask or tell where someone or something is.

You use the verb **estar** to describe the location of towns, buildings, parks, and so on. You may think of these things as being permanent, but because you're talking about their location, you use **estar**, not **ser**.

Here are some examples of using **estar** to establish location:

> **Bernardo está en la playa.** (*Bernardo is at the beach.*)
>
> **El cine está al lado del restaurante mexicano.** (*The cinema is next to the Mexican restaurant.*)
>
> **Felipa está en el cine.** (*Felipa is at the cinema.*)
>
> **¿Estás tú en el parque?** (*Are you at the park?*)
>
> **El libro está en la mesa.** (*The book is on the table.*)
>
> **Vosotros estáis en el aeropuerto.** (*You are at the airport.*)
>
> **Ella está en su casa.** (*She is at her house.*)

Using estar with present participles

One common use for the verb **estar** is to describe what a person or thing is doing. To do so, you use the verb **estar** with the present participle of the verb whose action is being performed. The following examples use **estar** with the present participles of the verbs **leer** (*to read*) and **abrir** (*to open*):

> **Ellos están leyendo en la biblioteca ahora.** (*They are reading in the library now.*)
>
> **Los estudiantes están abriendo sus libros.** (*The students are opening their books.*)

Check out Chapter 8 for more on how to use present participles.

Using estar with past participles

One way to describe the condition of something or someone that is the result of a previous action is to use the verb **estar** with the action verb (which describes the past condition) in the past participle. When used in this type of structure, the past participle of the verb is functioning as an adjective and has to agree in number and gender with the noun that it modifies. Here are a few examples:

> **La puerta está abierta.** (*The door is open.*)
>
> **El edificio está abandonado.** (*The building is abandoned.*)
>
> **Ellos están casados.** (*They are married.*)

For more about forming past participles, see Chapter 21.

Based on the different uses for **ser** and **estar**, fill in the blanks in the following sentences with the correct form of **ser** or **estar**. Here's an example:

0. Juanita _____ de México.

A. Juanita es de México.

31. Ezequiel _____ mi amigo.

32. Mis hijos _____ enfermos.

33. Tú _____ de Italia.

34. Ahora nosotros _____ en Nueva York.

35. Este programa _____ muy interesante.

36. Nosotros _____ tristes.

37. La señora Zapata _____ una maestra con mucho talento.

38. Lola _____ italiana.

39. Vosotros _____ bajos.

40. Tú _____ en la playa.

Discovering How an Adjective's Meaning Can Change with Ser and Estar

As the preceding sections illustrate, specific rules govern when to use **ser,** when to use **estar,** and which adjectives typically accompany each verb, but some adjectives work with either verb. In these cases, the adjective's meaning changes depending on which verb it accompanies. Table 7-3 lists some of the most common adjectives that you can use with either **ser** or **estar** and the different meanings they convey based on which verb you use them with.

Table 7-3	Adjectives That Change Meaning with Ser and Estar	
Adjective	**Meaning When Used with Ser**	**Meaning When Used with Estar**
aburrido/aburrida	boring	bored
bueno/buena	a good person	behaving well
listo/lista	clever	ready
malo/mala	bad (a bad person)	ill
orgulloso/orgullosa	conceited, vain	proud
pálido/pálida	fair complexioned	pale
rico/rica	rich	tasty (food or drink)
seguro/segura	safe	sure, certain
viejo/vieja	old	seeming old

Note: When you use the adjectives **bueno** and **malo** with masculine nouns and you place them in front of those nouns (which is an option with these two adjectives), drop the **-o** from the end of the adjective.

Based on the message being conveyed, underline either **ser** or **estar** to correctly complete the following sentences.

0. Jorge es/está de España.

A. es

41. Los estudiantes en la clase son/están muy buenos, porque siempre saben las respuestas de todas las preguntas.

42. Dorotea es/está lista para salir.

43. Nosotros siempre somos/estamos muy aburridos en su clase porque el profesor es/está muy aburrido.

44. El ladrón que robó todos los bancos es/está un muy mal tipo.

45. Carlos no puede ir a la escuela hoy porque es/está muy malo.

46. Su abuela es/está muy vieja.

47. Conchita es/está muy orgullosa porque siempre habla de sí misma.

48. Vosotros sois/estáis muy ricos.

49. La comida en este restaurante es/está muy buena.

50. Generalmente Jorge tiene mucho color pero hoy es/está muy pálido.

Answer Key

1 son

2 estamos

3 estás

4 sois

5 está

6 es

7 estáis

8 eres

9 soy

10 están

11 El libro es interesante.

12 Correct as is

13 Tú eres mi mejor amigo.

14 Su casa es muy bonita.

15 Vosotros sois muy amables.

16 Los bailes siempre son muy divertidos.

17 Correct as is

18 Nosotros somos con ellos.

19 Correct as is

20 Emilio y Dorotea son los tíos de Emiliano.

21 Las chicas están buenas.

22 Emilio está aburrido.

23 Correct as is

24   Aurelio y yo estamos sorprendidos.

25   Ella está frustrada.

26   Nosotros estamos deprimidos.

27   Correct as is

28   Vosotros estáis callados.

29   Él está agradecido.

30   Francisco y Elena están sucios.

31   es

32   están

33   eres

34   estamos

35   es

36   estamos

37   es

38   es

39   sois

40   estás

41   son

42   está

43   estamos, es

44   es

45   está

46   es

47   es

48 sois

49 es

50 está

Chapter 8

Talking about Action in Progress with the Present Progressive

*I*n English, the *present progressive* is the verb structure you use to describe an action that's happening right now. What makes present progressive different from the present tense? Well, the difference is kind of subtle. If you say that a woman walks her dog, you're using the present tense. But if you say she's walking the dog right now, you're using the present progressive.

Spanish makes a similar distinction between the present tense and present progressive. In this chapter, I describe the basic structure of the present progressive in Spanish, and I explain how to form the present progressive, as well as how to put it into action . . . quite literally. (If you need details on writing in the present tense, flip to Chapter 6.)

Breaking Down the Structure of the Present Progressive

Unlike the present tense, which uses only one verb, the present progressive uses two verbs in both English and Spanish:

▶ In English, you use the conjugated form of the verb *to be* with the present participle of the action verb. For example, *Tom is throwing the tomato at Pete.*

▶ In Spanish, you use the conjugated form of the verb **estar** (*to be*) and the present participle of the action verb, such as **pasear** (*to walk*). For example, **Maria está paseando a su perro.** (*Maria is walking her dog.*)

The present progressive isn't a different tense; it's simply a *verb structure* — a construction comprised of a verb and at least one other element, in this case the present participle.

In a way, the present progressive is a snap. All you need to know is how to conjugate **estar** (and a few other verbs) and how to form the present participle. For details on conjugating **estar**, see Chapter 7. In the rest of this chapter, you find out how to form present participles and then how to use them with **estar** (and some other verbs) to form the present progressive.

Forming Regular Present Participles

In English, the *present participle* is the form of the verb that ends in *ing*. It isn't considered a conjugated form of the verb because it doesn't indicate who or what is performing the action. In the present progressive, the verb *to be* indicates who or what is doing the action because it's the verb you conjugate. Similarly, in the present progressive in Spanish, the verb **estar** (*to be*) indicates who or what is doing the action, while the present participle describes the action itself.

Forming the present participles of regular verbs in Spanish is much like forming them in English. The primary difference is this:

- ✔ In English, you remove the word *to* from the infinitive form of the verb and then add *ing*.
- ✔ In Spanish, you drop the infinitive verb ending (**-ar, -er,** or **-ir**) and add **-ando** for **-ar** verbs or **-iendo** for **-er** and **-ir** verbs.

The following sections present additional explanation and examples for forming present participles out of regular Spanish verbs.

Forming the present participle of regular -ar verbs

Forming the present participle of regular **-ar** verbs in Spanish is very simple. You simply drop the **-ar** ending and add **-ando** to the verb stem. Here are a few examples:

Infinitive Verb	Present Participle
bailar (*to dance*)	**bailando** (*dancing*)
esperar (*to wait for*)	**esperando** (*waiting for*)
formar (*to form*)	**formando** (*forming*)
hablar (*to talk*)	**hablando** (*talking*)
lavar (*to wash*)	**lavando** (*washing*)
llegar (*to arrive*)	**llegando** (*arriving*)
mirar (*to watch*)	**mirando** (*watching*)
organizar (*to organize*)	**organizando** (*organizing*)

Fill in the present participle forms of the following regular **-ar** verbs. Here's an example:

0. **acelerar** (*to accelerate*) _____

A. **acelerando**

1. **aclamar** (*to acclaim*) _____

2. **avanzar** (*to advance*) _____

3. **cortar** (*to cut*) _____

4. **costar** (*to cost*) _____

5. **heredar** (*to inherit*) _____

6. **pronunciar** (*to pronounce*) _____

7. **retirar** (*to retire*) _____

8. **recomendar** (*to recommend*) _____

9. **vaciar** (*to empty*) _____

10. **visitar** (*to visit*) _____

Forming the present participle of regular -er and -ir verbs

One reason why forming the present participle of regular verbs in Spanish is so easy is that **-er** and **-ir** verbs share the same present participle ending. For both **-er** and **-ir** verbs, you drop the infinitive ending and add **-iendo**. Following are some examples:

Infinitive Verb	Present Participle
adquirir (*to acquire*)	**adquiriendo** (*acquiring*)
aplaudir (*to applaud*)	**aplaudiendo** (*applauding*)
comer (*to eat*)	**comiendo** (*eating*)
crecer (*to grow*)	**creciendo** (*growing*)
ejercer (*to exercise*)	**ejerciendo** (*exercising*)
escoger (*to choose*)	**escogiendo** (*choosing*)
romper (*to break*)	**rompiendo** (*breaking*)
sumergir (*to submerge*)	**sumergiendo** (*submerging*)

Fill in the present participle form of the following regular **-er** and **-ir** verbs. Here's an example:

O. **beber** (*to drink*) _____

A. **bebiendo**

11. **abrir** (*to open*) _____

12. **absolver** (*to absolve*) _____

13. **aburrir** (*to annoy*) _____

14. **asistir** (*to attend*) _____

15. **convencer** (*to convince*) _____

16. **escribir** (*to write*) _____

17. **correr** (*to run*) _____

18. **defender** (*to defend*) _____

19. **esparcir** (*to scatter*) _____

20. **salir** (*to leave*) _____

Revealing Stem-Changing and Irregular Present Participles

After you've had some practice with forming regular present participles (which I discuss earlier in this chapter), you're ready to step up to the challenge of forming stem-changing and irregular present participles. (You didn't think the present progressive would be *that* easy, did you?) The following sections provide details about these slightly more difficult formations.

Forming the present participle of verbs with stems that end in a vowel

If you formed the present participle of **-er** and **-ir** verbs that have stems ending in a vowel the same way you do for all other **-er** and **-ir** verbs (by adding **-iendo**), you'd end up with three vowels in succession. For example, the verb **caer** (*to fall*) would become **caiendo** (*falling*) in the present participle. Whoa! That looks awkward! When spoken aloud, this combination of vowels causes the *i* to sound like a *y*. To simplify things, the Spanish language includes a rule specifically for cases like this.

When the stem of an **-er** or **-ir** verb ends in a vowel, you add **-yendo** to form the present participle instead of adding the regular present participle ending **-iendo**. Based on this rule, the present participle of the verb **caer** (*to fall*) becomes **cayendo** (*falling*) rather than **caiendo**. Here are some other commonly used **-er** and **-ir** verbs that follow this rule:

Infinitive Verb	Present Participle
atraer (*to attract*)	**atrayendo** (*attracting*)
construir (*to construct*)	**construyendo** (*constructing*)
contribuir (*to contribute*)	**contribuyendo** (*contributing*)
creer (*to believe*)	**creyendo** (*believing*)
destruir (*to destroy*)	**destruyendo** (*destroying*)
huir (*to flee*)	**huyendo** (*fleeing*)
incluir (*to include*)	**incluyendo** (*including*)
leer (*to read*)	**leyendo** (*reading*)
oír (*to hear*)	**oyendo** (*hearing*)
traer (*to bring*)	**trayendo** (*bringing*)

Complete each of the following sentences by filling in the present participle of the verb from the preceding table that makes sense in the context of the sentence. Use a Spanish-English dictionary for any unfamiliar vocabulary. Here's an example:

0. Él está _____ dinero a la organización.

A. contribuyendo

21. La miel está _____ las moscas.

22. Los obreros están _____ una casa en nuestro barrio.

23. Mi amigo Juan está _____ el postre para la cena.

24. Alfonso está _____ un libro.

25. Yo estoy _____ a todos mis amigos en las invitaciones.

26. Ella está _____ un artículo para el periódico.

27. Las hormigas están _____ las plantas.

28. Nosotros estamos _____ la música.

29. Los estudiantes están _____ todo lo que dice el profesor.

30. Él está _____ del oso grande.

Forming the present participle of stem-changing verbs

As I explain in Chapter 6, *stem-changing verbs* are those verbs whose stems change when they're conjugated in the present tense. When you want to form the present participle of stem-changing verbs, the only verbs you have to worry about are the **-ir** stem-changing verbs. After all, **-ar** and **-er** verbs don't require any stem changes when you form their present participles.

Follow these two simple rules to form the present participle of stem-changing **-ir** verbs:

✔ If an **-ir** verb stem changes from **o** to **u** in the third person form of the preterit tense (see Chapter 18), then the stem has the same change in the present participle form. Here are two common verbs in this category:

dormir (*to sleep*)	**durmiendo** (*sleeping*)
morir (*to die*)	**muriendo** (*dying*)

✔ If an **-ir** verb stem changes from **e** to **i** in the third person form of the preterit tense, then the stem has the same change for the present participle form. Here are some common verbs that follow this rule:

advertir (*to warn*)	**advirtiendo** (*warning*)
competir (*to compete*)	**compitiendo** (*competing*)
conseguir (*to get*)	**consiguiendo** (*getting*)
consentir (*to consent, to agree*)	**consintiendo** (*consenting, agreeing*)
convertir (*to convert*)	**convirtiendo** (*converting*)
decir (*to say, to tell*)	**diciendo** (*saying, telling*)
hervir (*to boil*)	**hirviendo** (*boiling*)
mentir (*to lie*)	**mintiendo** (*lying*)
pedir (*to ask for*)	**pidiendo** (*asking for*)
reír (*to laugh*)	**riendo** (*laughing*)
repetir (*to repeat*)	**repitiendo** (*repeating*)
seguir (*to follow*)	**siguiendo** (*following*)
sentir (*to feel*)	**sintiendo** (*feeling*)
servir (*to serve*)	**sirviendo** (*serving*)
sugerir (*to suggest*)	**sugiriendo** (*suggesting*)
venir (*to come*)	**viniendo** (*coming*)

Write the Spanish equivalents of the following present participles. For example:

Q. *feeling* = _____

A. **sintiendo**

31. *serving* = _____

32. *lying* = _____

33. *sleeping* = _____

34. *laughing* = _____

35. *following* = _____

36. *saying* = _____

37. *warning* = _____

38. *boiling* = _____

39. *repeating* = _____

40. *asking for* = _____

Looking at irregular present participles

Two verbs are truly unique in the way you form their present participles, so grammarians group them together in the category of *irregular present participles*. These two verbs are

- **Ir** (*to go*): Has the present participle of **yendo.** For example, **Nosotros estamos yendo a la playa.** (*We are going to the beach.*) Note that in this sentence, the subject of the sentence (*we*) "is in the process of going" to the beach, not "will be going" at some future time.

- **Poder** (*to be able*): Has the present participle of **pudiendo.** For example, **Yo estoy pudiendo asistir a la fiesta.** (*I am being able to attend the party.*)

Note: You may have guessed that the verb **poder** is rarely used in the present participle form. (*Being able to* does sound pretty strange, doesn't it?) The verbs **estar** (*to be*), **ir** (*to go*), and **venir** (*to come*) are also rarely used.

Using the Present Progressive to Describe an Action in Progress

The entire first half of this chapter explains how to form present participles, but how and when do you use them? In the following sections, you get the chance to use present participles with the conjugated form of the verb **estar** (*to be*) and a few other choice verbs to form the present progressive to describe an action that's happening now.

Forming the present progressive with estar

To express an action in progress (that is, one that's in the present progressive form), you use the appropriate conjugated form of **estar** (*to be*) to say who or what is doing the action, followed by the present participle of the verb that describes the action being performed. The following table lists the present tense forms of the verb **estar** (see Chapter 7 for more details).

estar (*to be*)	
yo **estoy**	nosotros/nosotras **estamos**
tú **estás**	vosotros/vosotras **estáis**
él/ella/usted **está**	ellos/ellas/ustedes **están**

To form the present progressive, simply combine the conjugated form of **estar** with the present participle. Here are some examples:

Yo estoy comiendo. (*I am eating.*)

Tú estás esperando el tren. (*You are waiting for the train.*)

Ella está sirviendo la comida. (*She is serving the meal.*)

Nosotros estamos manejando al campo. (*We are driving to the country.*)

Vosotras estáis hablando por teléfono. (*You are talking on the telephone.*)

Ellos están mirando la televisión. (*They are watching T.V.*)

When you want to use a reflexive pronoun or another object pronoun with the present progressive, you have two options for positioning the pronouns:

- ✔ **In front of the conjugated form of estar:** For example, **Mi amigo los está lavando.** (*My friend is washing them.*)

- ✔ **After and attached to the present participle:** When you place the pronoun after and attached to the present participle, you must add a written accent mark to the originally stressed vowel in the participle. (*Tip:* You can determine which vowel was originally stressed by counting back three syllables from the end of the newly formed participle. You count back three syllables because a word that ends in a vowel is stressed on the second-to-last syllable. So in order to keep the stress on the originally stressed syllable, you must add an accent on the third syllable from the end of the present participle and pronoun combination.) For example, **Mi amigo está lavándolos.** (*My friend is washing them.*)

Chapter 9 introduces object pronouns, Chapter 14 covers reflexive verbs, and Chapter 2 explains how to sound out Spanish words and deal with accents.

Using the correct present participle of the verbs given, convert the following present tense verbs into their present progressive form. Here's an example:

Q. el restaurante sirve _____

A. está sirviendo

41. yo vengo _____

42. vosotros aplaudís _____

43. los niños comen _____

44. la bebé duerme _____

45. tú hablas _____

46. nosotros esperamos _____

47. los estudiantes leen _____

48. yo miento _____

49. el agua hierve _____

50. la maestra sugiere _____

Forming the present progressive with verbs other than estar

Estar isn't the only verb you can use with the present participle to form the present progressive. You can use a few other verbs, such as **andar** (*to walk*) and **venir** (*to come*), that imply motion or continuation of an action. When used with the present participle of the action verb, these verbs emphasize that the action is continuing or ongoing in the present moment. The following tables list the other verbs you can use to form the present progressive, along with each verb's present tense conjugation and an example of its use in the present progressive structure.

When used in the progressive tense, these verbs sometimes change their meaning slightly, such as in the case of the verb **andar.** Its meaning with a present participle becomes *to go around* rather than *to walk*.

andar (*to walk*)	
yo **ando**	nosotros/nosotras **andamos**
tú **andas**	vosotros/vosotras **andáis**
él/ella/usted **anda**	ellos/ellas/ustedes **andan**
Rudolfo anda buscando su perro. (*Rudolfo is going around looking for his dog.*)	

continuar (*to continue*)	
yo **continúo**	nosotros/nosotras **continuamos**
tú **continúas**	vosotros/vosotras **continuáis**
él/ella/usted **continúa**	ellos/ellas/ustedes **continúan**
El bebé continúa durmiendo. (*The baby continues sleeping.*)	

ir (*to go*)	
yo **voy**	nosotros/nosotras **vamos**
tú **vas**	vosotros/vosotras **vais**
él/ella/usted **va**	ellos/ellas/ustedes **van**
Ella va diciendo que ganó. (She's going around saying that she won.)	

seguir (*to continue, to follow*)	
yo **sigo**	nosotros/nosotras **seguimos**
tú **sigues**	vosotros/vosotras **seguís**
él/ella/usted **sigue**	ellos/ellas/ustedes **siguen**
Nosotros seguimos caminando por el bosque. (*We continue walking through the forest.*)	

venir (*to come*)	
yo **vengo**	nosotros/nosotras **venimos**
tú **vienes**	vosotros/vosotras **venís**
él/ella/usted **viene**	ellos/ellas/ustedes **vienen**
Agustín viene montando en su bicicleta. (*Agustín comes riding his bike.*)	

Translate the following sentences from English to Spanish, using the appropriate present progressive verb formations. For each sentence, I've included most of the translation so you can focus on forming the verb. Here's an example:

0. *I continue working for him.*

Yo _____ para él.

A. **sigo trabajando**

51. *She is going around talking about her boyfriend.*

Ella _____ de su novio.

52. *They continue driving.*

Ellos _____.

53. *Antonia continues listening to the lecture.*

Antonia _____ la conferencia.

54. *We are going around riding on horseback.*

Nosotros _____ a caballo.

55. *I continue watching the movie.*

Yo _____ la película.

56. *They continue waiting for the package.*

Ellos _____ el paquete.

57. *Armando is going around looking for the restaurant.*

Armando _____ el restaurante.

58. *They continue believing that he is the best professor at the university.*

Ellos _____ que él es el mejor profesor de la universidad.

59. *She is going around complaining about her job.*

Ella _____ de su trabajo.

60. *Celestina comes singing.*

Celestina _____.

Answer Key

1	aclamando	22	construyendo	43	están comiendo
2	avanzando	23	trayendo	44	está durmiendo
3	cortando	24	leyendo	45	estás hablando
4	costando	25	incluyendo	46	estamos esperando
5	heredando	26	contribuyendo	47	están leyendo
6	pronunciando	27	destruyendo	48	estoy mintiendo
7	retirando	28	oyendo	49	está hirviendo
8	recomendando	29	creyendo	50	está sugiriendo
9	vaciando	30	huyendo	51	anda/va hablando
10	visitando	31	sirviendo	52	continúan/siguen manejando
11	abriendo	32	mintiendo	53	continúa/sigue escuchando
12	absolviendo	33	durmiendo	54	andamos/vamos montando
13	aburriendo	34	riendo	55	continúo/sigo mirando
14	asistiendo	35	siguiendo	56	continúan/siguen esperando
15	convenciendo	36	diciendo	57	anda/va buscando
16	escribiendo	37	advirtiendo	58	continúan/siguen creyendo
17	corriendo	38	hirviendo	59	anda/va quejando
18	defendiendo	39	repitiendo	60	viene cantando
19	esparciendo	40	pidiendo		
20	saliendo	41	estoy viniendo		
21	atrayendo	42	estáis aplaudiendo		

Chapter 9

Replacing Nouns with Pronouns

· ·

In This Chapter

▶ Replacing the subject of a sentence with a pronoun

▶ Identifying and using the direct object pronouns

▶ Using an indirect object pronoun in place of an indirect object

· ·

*I*n Spanish and other languages, you often replace names or nouns in a sentence with pronouns, such as *he, him, she, her, it, they,* or *them,* to avoid the monotony of repeating the names or nouns. The use of pronouns in Spanish is very similar to pronoun use in English, but Spanish does have some significant differences. For example, in English, a sentence requires a stated subject (a name, noun, or pronoun), whereas Spanish doesn't because the verb implies the subject (*I, you, he, she, it, we,* or *they*), as I explain in Chapter 6. This chapter introduces you to Spanish pronouns and explains when and how to use them.

Summoning Subject Pronouns

A *subject pronoun* stands in for the person or thing that's performing the action in a sentence. For example, instead of saying, "The rock fell," you can say, "It fell." *It* is the subject pronoun substituting for *The rock.* The following sections introduce you to the Spanish subject pronouns and explain how to use them and where to place them.

In English and Spanish, the infinitive form of a verb means that no one is doing the action, so you don't need a subject or subject pronoun to accompany it. In Spanish, the infinitive has an **-ar, -er,** or **-ir** ending, as in **cantar** (*to sing*), **comer** (*to eat*), and **vivir** (*to live*). I cover infinitives and other verb basics in Chapter 6.

Introducing the subject pronouns

Spanish has nine subject pronouns, as listed here with their English counterparts:

▶ **yo** (*I*)

▶ **tú** (*you* singular, informal)

▶ **usted** (*you* singular, formal)

✔ **él** (*he*)

✔ **ella** (*she*)

✔ **nosotros/nosotras** (*we*)

✔ **vosotros/vosotras** (*you* plural, informal)

✔ **ustedes** (*you* plural, formal)

✔ **ellos/ellas** (*they*)

Spanish rarely uses a subject pronoun for *it*. **Ello** is a Spanish pronoun that means *it*, but **ello** isn't used to refer to a named object. **Él** may be used for a masculine noun and **ella** may be used for a feminine noun when needed for clarification.

When deciding which subject pronoun to use, refer to the following table, which arranges the subject pronouns by their singular and plural and first, second, and third person forms:

Person	Singular	Plural
1st	yo	nosotros/nosotras
2nd	tú	vosotros/vosotras
3rd	él/ella/usted	ellos/ellas/ustedes

Usted and **ustedes** are actually second person subject pronouns (meaning *you* formal), but consider them third person pronouns in Spanish for the purpose of conjugating verbs.

Following are some additional points to keep in mind when using subject pronouns in Spanish:

✔ English has only one word for *you* for the singular and plural. For example, *How are you* (singular)*?* and *You* (plural) *have football practice tonight.* Spanish has four forms of *you*:

- **tú** (singular, informal) for a friend or a family member

- **usted** (singular, formal) for a formal acquaintance or a stranger

- **vosotros/vosotras** (plural, informal) for friends and family

- **ustedes** (plural, formal) for formal acquaintances or strangers

Of course, English speakers in the United States do have the casual expressions *you guys* for the plural *you* in the North and *ya'll* in the South.

✔ **Usted** is usually abbreviated to **Ud.**, and **ustedes** is usually abbreviated to **Uds.** These abbreviations are capitalized regardless of whether they're at the beginning of a sentence. (The full words **usted** and **ustedes** are capitalized only when they're at the beginning of a sentence.)

✔ Spanish has masculine and feminine forms for *we*, *you* (plural, informal), and *they*. For example, **nosotros** (*we*) is masculine, whereas **nosotras** (*we*) is feminine. However, if a group has a mix of male and female members, you use the masculine **nosotros**, **vosotros**, or **ellos** to refer to the group, even if it has a hundred girls and only one boy.

✔ **Vosotros/vosotras** (*you* plural, informal) is used almost exclusively in Spain. In its place, other Spanish-speaking countries use **ustedes (Uds.)** and the corresponding form of the verb.

Choose the appropriate Spanish subject pronoun to replace the following nouns or names. Here's an example:

A. the children _____

Q. ellos

1. my parents _____

2. Sue and Bob _____

3. she _____

4. Tom and I _____

5. you (a friend) _____

6. Alejandra _____

7. your dad _____

8. you (a group of friends, all girls) _____

9. you (a couple that you just met) _____

10. the girls _____

Placing subject pronouns in statements and questions

The placement of subject pronouns in Spanish statements is almost the same as it is in English. In Spanish, you place the subject pronoun

- In front of the verb in a positive statement: **Él juega al fútbol.** (*He plays soccer.*)
- In front of *no* in a negative statement: **Él no juega al fútbol.** (*He doesn't play soccer.*)
- After **sí** (*yes*) in a positive answer: **Sí, yo vivo en Dallas.** (*Yes, I live in Dallas.*)
- Between the two *no's* in a negative answer: **No, yo no vivo en Dallas.** (*No, I don't live in Dallas.*)

The placement of subject pronouns in questions in Spanish is also very similar to English. The rule is to place the subject pronoun after the verb in a question. Here are some examples:

¿Vives tú en Dallas? (*Do you live in Dallas?*)

¿Son ellos tus primos? (*Are they your cousins?*)

¿Es ella la profesora nueva? (*Is she the new teacher?*)

¿Tiene él un carro rojo? (*Does he have a red car?*)

Deciding when to use a subject pronoun

How you use subject pronouns in Spanish is fairly similar to how you use them in English. The main difference is when you use subject pronouns in the first place. The following sections provide guidance on when using a subject pronoun is necessary or useful and when you can safely omit it.

English requires either a subject or a subject pronoun in all statements, except commands (like "*Come here!*"), in which the subject (*you*) is implied. Spanish isn't so cut and dried. Keep reading to find out when to use subject pronouns in Spanish.

Clarifying the subject

Whenever the subject of the sentence is unclear, you must state the subject with either a name or a noun. As in English, you can use a subject pronoun in place of a name or a noun as long as you've already established who (or what) the subject is. Here are some examples of sentences that require a stated subject:

> **Canta muy bien.** (*He/she/you sing(s) really well.*) This sentence uses the third person singular form of the verb. Hence, the subject could be any one of a million singular people. In a case like this, you must clarify the subject with a name, noun, or subject pronoun. For example: **Juan canta muy bien.**

> **Van al cine.** (*They/you go to the movies.*) In this sentence, the third person plural form is ambiguous because the subject could be **ellos/ellas** (*they*) or **ustedes** (*you* plural). In other words, it could be any group of two or more people. So you have to clarify who (or what) the subject is. For example: **Ellos van al cine.**

Emphasizing who the subject is

Sometimes the subject is clear from the verb form, but you may still want to state the subject to emphasize it. The following example shows such an instance:

> **Yo voy a España.** (*I am going to Spain.*) In this sentence, the use of the subject pronoun **yo** (*I*) emphasizes that *I* am the one going, not someone else. The subject pronoun here is only for emphasis; it isn't necessary for clarity.

Emphasizing the action

When you want to emphasize the action (or state of being) that your sentence conveys, you can state your subject even when doing so is unnecessary for clarity's sake. You can also add **sí** (*yes*) before the verb. Here are a couple of examples:

> **Él sí trabaja aquí.** (*He does work here.*)

> **Soy yo.** (*It is I.*)

Contrasting subjects

When you're talking about two different people or groups of people in the same sentence, you usually need to state the subjects to clarify who did what, as in the following examples:

> **José mira la televisión, y ella lee una novela.** (*José is watching the TV, and she is reading a novel.*)

> **Mis amigos tienen un perro, pero ellos tienen tres gatos.** (*My friends have a dog, but they have three cats.*)

In each of these sentences, the contrast between the subjects would be confusing if you didn't state the subjects.

Showing respect with usted or ustedes

You address people with **usted** or **ustedes** when you first meet them or when you want to convey respect. So even when you've already established the subject or when whomever you're talking to knows you're speaking to them, you may continue to use the subject pronoun as a title of respect. Here are a couple of examples:

> **Señor, usted se sienta aquí.** (*Sir, you sit here.*)

> **Señora, tenga usted su cambio.** (*Ma'am, here's your change.*)

Omitting subject pronouns in certain instances

In certain types of expressions, you can safely omit the subject pronoun. Following are some guidelines to help you decide when omitting the pronoun is okay:

- ✔ **When you're referring to yourself with certain verbs that clarify that you're the subject:** For example, **Estoy bien.** (*I am fine.*) You use the verb **estoy** only when **yo** (*I*) is the subject of the sentence, so the subject is clear.

- ✔ **When you're addressing someone directly:** For example, **¿Cómo estás?** (*How are you?*) Whenever you address someone directly, **tú** (*you*) is implied, so unless you want to show respect with **usted** or **ustedes** (see the preceding section), you can omit the subject.

- ✔ **When you've already established what or whom you're talking about:** For example, **Susana es mi mejor amiga. Vive cerca de aquí.** (*Susana is my best friend. She lives close to here.*) In the first sentence, you use the name *Susana,* so you don't need the pronoun in the second sentence.

- ✔ **In common phrases that start with *It*:** For example, **Llueve.** (*It is raining.*)

Choose the subject pronoun that matches the verb in each statement, question, or answer. Then rewrite the sentence, placing the subject pronoun appropriately. If the sentence has more than one possible subject, choose one, but be sure to watch for clues in the sentence. Here's an example:

Q. **No queremos ir a la playa.**

A. **Nosotros no queremos ir a la playa.**

11. **No, no van a la tienda los viernes.**

_____

12. **¿Cómo estás?**

_____

13. **Tengo cinco dólares.**

_____

14. Es mi hermano.

_____

15. Sí, bailáis muy bien.

_____

16. Comes mucho.

_____

17. ¿Dónde están?

_____

18. Nadamos en el verano.

_____

19. No, no quiere una hamburguesa.

_____

20. Es una profesora.

_____

Replacing Direct Objects with Pronouns

In both English and Spanish, you can use a *direct object pronoun* (DOP) in place of a *direct object* — whatever's being acted on in a sentence. For example, if you ask, "Who kicked the ball?," the word *ball* is the direct object. If I answer, "He kicked it," the word *it* is the DOP substituting for *the ball*. You already know that you're talking about *the ball,* so you replace *the ball* with the pronoun *it.*

The following sections introduce you to the DOPs used in Spanish and explain how to use them properly in a sentence.

Introducing the direct object pronouns

Spanish has eight DOPs. Here they are with their English counterparts:

- **me** (*me*)
- **te** (*you* singular, informal)
- **lo** (*him, it,* or *you* masculine, singular, formal)

✔ **la** (*her, it,* or *you* feminine, singular, formal)

✔ **nos** (*us*)

✔ **os** (*you* plural, informal)

✔ **los** (*them* masculine or mixed group of males and females or *you* plural, formal)

✔ **las** (*them* feminine or *you* plural, formal)

Keep in mind the following important points when you use the Spanish DOPs:

✔ **Lo, la, los,** and **las** replace both people and things.

✔ **Lo, la, los,** and **las** substitute for *you* (both singular and plural) as well as *him, her,* and *them.*

✔ In Spain, **le** sometimes replaces the direct object **lo** when referring to people.

✔ When a person is the direct object of a verb in Spanish, you must place the word **a** (called the *personal* **a**) in front of the person's name or the pronoun that refers to that person.

✔ You have to watch out for collective nouns, such as **la clase** (*the class*). A class typically has more than one person in it, so you may consider it plural, but in both English and Spanish, **la clase** (*the class*) is considered singular. For example, **Enseño a la clase. La enseño.** (*I teach the class. I teach it.*)

Underline the direct objects in the following sentences. Then write the DOP you would use to replace it. (Hey, I just used one!) Here's an example:

0. **Nosotros compramos la casa.**

A. **Nosotros compramos <u>la casa</u>. (la)**

21. **Raúl tiene el libro.** _____

22. **Ellos miran a ti.** _____

23. **Yo necesito el carro.** _____

24. **Alejandra escribe las cartas.** _____

25. **Ellas compran los vestidos.** _____

26. **La profesora enseña a vosotros.** _____

27. **La madre viste a los niños.** _____

28. **El Señor Martínez come la pizza.** _____

29. **María ve a nosotros.** _____

30. **Nosotros tenemos las tarjetas.** _____

Placing direct object pronouns

In English, the DOP usually comes after the verb. In Spanish, the DOP usually comes just before the verb, but the exact placement depends on how the verb that's associated with the DOP is structured. The following sections explain how to place DOPs in Spanish sentences.

With a single conjugated verb

When a sentence has just one verb, place the DOP directly before the conjugated verb, as in the following examples:

> **Ella tiene la pelota.** (*She has the ball.*) → **Ella la tiene.** (*She has it.*)
>
> **Ella no tiene la pelota.** (*She doesn't have the ball.*) → **Ella no la tiene.** (*She doesn't have it.*)
>
> **¿Tienes la pelota?** (*Do you have the ball?*) → **¿La tienes?** (*Do you have it?*)
>
> **¿Quién tiene la pelota?** (*Who has the ball?*) → **¿Quién la tiene?** (*Who has it?*)

You can't always translate from Spanish to English word for word. If you do, you may come up with some incorrect (not to mention, funny-sounding) translations. For example, try translating the following Spanish sentence literally:

> **Ella la tiene.** (*She it has.*)

See what I mean?

With a verb plus an infinitive

In a sentence with two verbs, when the first verb is conjugated and the second verb is in the infinitive form, either place the DOP before the conjugated verb or place it after the infinitive verb and attach it to the infinitive. For example, you have two options for using a DOP in place of the direct object in the sentence **Ellos quieren comprar el carro blanco** (*They want to buy the white car*):

> **Ellos lo quieren comprar.** (*They want to buy it.*) In this instance, the DOP **lo** comes before the conjugated verb **quieren.**
>
> **Ellos quieren comprarlo.** (*They want to buy it.*) In this instance, the DOP comes after and is attached to the infinitive **comprar.**

In English, the DOP always comes after the infinitive, as you can see in the preceding examples.

Rewrite each of the following sentences, replacing the direct object with its corresponding DOP. Here's an example:

Q. **Ellos comen la pizza.**

A. **Ellos la comen.**

31. **Ella no tiene la blusa verde.**

32. Nosotros queremos pagar la cuenta.

_____

33. Luisa compra el papel.

_____

34. Ana bebe la limonada.

_____

35. Él paga los gastos.

_____

36. Ellas miran a ti.

_____

37. Marco busca a vosotros.

_____

38. ¿Quién tiene las bicicletas?

_____

39. Ellos oyen a nosotros.

_____

40. Vosotros ofrecéis devolver el dinero.

_____

Replacing Indirect Objects with Pronouns

Like English, Spanish lets you use an _indirect object pronoun_ (IOP) in place of an _indirect object_ — whoever is on the receiving end of the action. The IOP answers the question, "To whom or for whom was the action performed?" In English, if I say, "Sally gave the ball to Tommy," _the ball_ is the direct object (being acted on) and _Tommy_ is the indirect object because he's receiving the ball. (Sentences that have indirect objects generally have direct objects, too.) To substitute the IOP for the indirect object, you'd say, "Sally gave the ball to him."

The following sections introduce you to the IOPs used in Spanish and explain how to use them in a sentence.

Introducing the indirect object pronouns

Spanish has six IOPs. Here they are with their English versions:

- ✔ **me** (*to/for me*)
- ✔ **te** (*to/for you* singular, informal)
- ✔ **le** (*to/for him, her,* or *you* singular, formal)
- ✔ **nos** (*to/for us*)
- ✔ **os** (*to/for you* plural, informal)
- ✔ **les** (*to/for them* masculine, feminine or *you* plural, formal)

The following tidbits may help you remember and use the Spanish IOPS more easily:

- ✔ **Me, te, nos,** and **os,** the first and second person singular and plural forms of the IOPs, are the same as the direct object pronouns.
- ✔ You use **le** and **les** for both masculine and feminine indirect objects.

Choose the appropriate IOP to replace the following indirect objects. Here's an example:

Q. nosotros _____

A. nos

41. la Señora Ramos _____

42. los jugadores _____

43. los estudiantes _____

44. vosotros _____

45. ti _____

46. los Señores Gonzalez _____

47. Ramona _____

48. la camarera _____

49. mí _____

50. los jóvenes _____

Placing indirect object pronouns

In Spanish sentences, the preposition **a** (*to*) or **para** (*for*) generally precedes the indirect object, as shown in these examples:

Traigo la comida a la familia. (*I am bringing the meal to the family.*)

Ramón compró unos regalos para los niños. (*Ramon bought some gifts for the children.*)

In the first example, **la comida** (*the meal*) is what's being brought, so it's the direct object. The meal is being brought **a la familia** (*to the family*), so **la familia** is the indirect object. In the second example, **unos regalos** (*some gifts*) are what Ramon bought, so it's the direct object. Ramon bought the gifts **para los niños** (*for the children*), so **los niños** is the indirect object.

In the following sections, I explain how to replace indirect objects with IOPs in Spanish sentences.

In most cases

After you decide to replace an indirect object with an IOP, you have to figure out where to place it. In most cases, the IOP goes directly in front of the conjugated verb, as shown in the following examples:

Explico el problema a los chicos. (*I explain the problem to the boys.*) → **Les explico el problema.** (*I explain the problem to them.*)

Yo no compro la muñeca para mi hermana. (*I'm not buying the doll for my sister.*) → **Yo no le compro la muñeca.** (*I'm not buying the doll for her.*)

¿Dan ellos el dinero a Paco? (*Are they giving the money to Paco?*) → **¿Le dan ellos el dinero?** (*Are they giving him the money?*)

¿Quién explica el problema a los chicos? (*Who explains the problem to the boys?*) → **¿Quién les explica el problema?** (*Who explains the problem to them?*)

When the direct and indirect objects are both pronouns

When the direct object and the indirect object in a sentence are both pronouns, place them both before the conjugated verb with the IOP before the DOP. Here are a couple of examples:

Raul no explica el problema a nosotros. (*Raul doesn't explain the problem to us.*) → **Raul no nos lo explica.** (*Raul doesn't explain it to us.*)

Él no compró el carro para ti. (*He didn't buy the car for you.*) → **Él no te lo compró.** (*He didn't buy it for you.*)

When a third person IOP (**le** or **les**) precedes a third person DOP (**lo, la, los,** or **las**), the IOP form changes to **se**. For example:

Yo no doy la muñeca a mi hermana. (*I don't give the doll to my sister.*) → **Yo no se la doy.** (*I don't give it to her.*)

¿Quién explica el problema a los chicos? (*Who explains the problem to the boys?*) → **¿Quién se lo explica?** (*Who explains it to them?*)

Here's a list of verbs that commonly have both a DOP and an IOP:

- ✔ **contar** (*to recount, to tell*)
- ✔ **dar** (*to give*)
- ✔ **decir** (*to tell, to say*)

- ✔ **devolver** (*to return*)
- ✔ **enseñar** (*to teach*, *to show*)
- ✔ **entregar** (*to turn over*, *to hand in*)
- ✔ **escribir** (*to write*)
- ✔ **explicar** (*to explain*)
- ✔ **mandar** (*to send*)
- ✔ **ofrecer** (*to offer*)
- ✔ **regalar** (*to gift*)
- ✔ **traer** (*to bring*)
- ✔ **vender** (*to sell*)

With a verb plus an infinitive

In a sentence with two verbs, when the first verb is conjugated and the second verb is in the infinitive form, either place the IOP before the conjugated verb or place it after the conjugated verb and attach it to the infinitive. For example, you have two options for using an IOP in place of the indirect object in the sentence **Ella quiere dar el regalo a Miguel** (*She wants to give the gift to Miguel*):

Ella le quiere dar el regalo. (*She wants to give him the gift.*) In this instance, the IOP comes before the conjugated verb **quiere.**

Ella quiere darle el regalo. (*She wants to give him the gift.*) In this instance, the IOP comes after the verb **quiere** and is attached to the infinitive **dar.**

If you want to use pronouns for both the indirect object and the direct object in the preceding example, you simply place the pronouns together with the IOP before the DOP, regardless of whether you place them in front of the conjugated verb or after the conjugated verb and attached to the infinitive. For example:

Ella se lo quiere dar. (*She wants to give it to him.*)

Ella quiere dárselo. (*She wants to give it to him.*)

Identify the indirect objects in the following sentences and rewrite the sentences, replacing the indirect objects with the appropriate IOPs. Here's an example:

Q. **Federico compra la revista para su esposa.**

A. **Federico le compra la revista.**

51. **La profesora da los papeles a los estudiantes.**

_____

52. **El mecánico repara su carro para ellos.**

_____

53. El camarero sirve la comida a los clientes.

_____

54. La vendedora vende los zapatos a Laura.

_____

55. El médico dice la verdad a ti.

_____

For the next five sentences, identify the indirect object *and* the direct object and replace them both with the appropriate IOP and DOP. Here's an example:

Q. Federico compra la revista para su esposa.

A. Federico se la compra.

56. La maestra lee los libros a los niños.

_____

57. Pilar muestra la casa a mí.

_____

58. Vosotros dais el televisor a Francisco.

_____

59. Ellos traen la pizza a vosotros.

_____

60. Tú explicas la lección a ella.

_____

Answer Key

1 ellos

2 ellos

3 ella

4 nosotros

5 tú

6 ella

7 él

8 vosotras

9 ustedes (Uds.)

10 ellas

11 No, ellos/ellas/ustedes (Uds.) no van a la tienda los viernes.

12 ¿Cómo estás tú?

13 Yo tengo cinco dólares.

14 Él es mi hermano.

15 Sí, vosotros/vosotras bailáis muy bien.

16 Tú comes mucho.

17 ¿Dónde están ellos/ellas/ustedes (Uds.)?

18 Nosotros/Nosotras nadamos en el verano.

19 No, él/ella/usted (Ud.) no quiere una hamburguesa.

20 Ella es una profesora.

21 Raúl tiene <u>el libro</u>. (lo)

22 Ellos miran <u>a ti</u>. (te)

23 Yo necesito <u>el carro</u>. (lo)

24 Alejandra escribe <u>las cartas</u>. (las)

25 **Ellas compran <u>los vestidos</u>. (los)**

26 **La profesora enseña <u>a vosotros</u>. (os)**

27 **La madre viste <u>a los niños</u>. (los)**

28 **El Señor Martínez come <u>la pizza</u>. (la)**

29 **María ve <u>a nosotros</u>. (nos)**

30 **Nosotros tenemos <u>las tarjetas</u>. (las)**

31 **Ella no la tiene.**

32 **Nosotros la queremos pagar. or Nosotros queremos pagarla.**

33 **Luisa lo compra.**

34 **Ana la bebe.**

35 **Él los paga.**

36 **Ellas te miran.**

37 **Marco os busca.**

38 **¿Quién las tiene?**

39 **Ellos nos oyen.**

40 **Vosotros lo ofrecéis devolver. or Vosotros ofrecéis devolverlo.**

41 **le**

42 **les**

43 **les**

44 **os**

45 **te**

46 **les**

47 **le**

48 **le**

49 **me**

50 les

51 La profesora les da los papeles.

52 El mecánico les repara su carro.

53 El camarero les sirve la comida.

54 La vendedora le vende los zapatos.

55 El médico te dice la verdad.

56 La maestra se los lee.

57 Pilar me la muestra.

58 Vosotros se lo dais.

59 Ellos os la traen.

60 Tú se la explicas.

Chapter 10

Expressing Likes and Dislikes

· ·

In This Chapter

▶ Combining an indirect object pronoun with **gustar** to express likes

▶ Saying what you like and dislike

▶ Being more specific by adding prepositional pronouns

▶ Asking what someone else likes or dislikes

▶ Familiarizing yourself with other verbs that work like **gustar**

· ·

To express a like in English, you'd say *I like ice cream*, but in Spanish, you'd say **Me gusta el helado** (*The ice cream is pleasing to me*) (Literally: *To me is pleasing the ice cream*). In other words, in English, whoever's doing the liking is the subject of the sentence, and whatever's being liked is the object receiving the action. Spanish is the complete opposite: The object being liked is the subject of the sentence, and the person doing the liking becomes the object that receives the action (in other words, you need to use indirect object pronouns; see Chapter 9 for details).

In this chapter, I explain how to talk about likes and dislikes with the verb **gustar** (*to be pleasing*), and I show you other verbs that work like **gustar.** Before you know it, you may start to think that the way English speakers express likes and dislikes is strange!

Using Indirect Object Pronouns with the Verb Gustar

Simply stated, a *pronoun* replaces a noun. Suppose you say *Sally rides her bike. Later she falls.* In the second sentence, the pronoun *she* replaces the noun *Sally.* That's an example of a subject pronoun, but English and Spanish both use two other types of pronouns, too:

✔ **Direct object pronoun (DOP):** A DOP is a person or object being acted upon. If you kick a ball to me and I kick it back, *it* is a pronoun because *it* replaces the noun *ball,* and *it* is also a direct object because *it* is being acted upon.

✔ **Indirect object pronoun (IOP):** An IOP indicates to whom or for whom an action is performed. For example, if I kick a ball to you, *the ball* is the direct object and *you* are the IOP because *you* are the person to whom the action is performed.

You always use an IOP with the verb **gustar** (*to be pleasing*). In fact, you might say that the verb **gustar** couldn't survive without IOPs. Hence, the following sections cover IOPs in a little more detail so that you can use them with **gustar.** (For the full scoop on all types of pronouns, including IOPs, see Chapter 9.)

Noting the indirect object pronouns

Because the verb **gustar** always uses an IOP, you need to be familiar with the Spanish IOPs before you can talk about what you (or someone else) likes. Here are the Spanish IOPs with their English counterparts:

- ✔ **me** (*to/for me*)
- ✔ **te** (*to/for you* singular, informal)
- ✔ **le** (*to/for him, her,* or *you* singular, formal)
- ✔ **nos** (*to/for us*)
- ✔ **os** (*to/for you* plural, informal)
- ✔ **les** (*to/for them* or *you* plural, formal)

The IOPs **le** and **les** are ambiguous because each one represents more than one possibility. **Le** may represent *you* (singular, formal) or *him* or *her,* and **les** may represent *you* (plural, formal) or *them.* To remedy this ambiguity, you may use a prepositional phrase to clarify whom the pronoun refers to; see the later section "Clarifying and Emphasizing Pronouns with Prepositional Phrases" for details.

Placing indirect object pronouns with the verb gustar

To use an IOP in a sentence, you place it in front of the conjugated verb, as I explain in Chapter 9. In the case of the verb **gustar,** you use only the third person singular and third person plural forms of the verb because the subject of the sentence is always either a singular person or thing or a plural person or thing. In the case of a verb infinitive being the subject of **gustar**, you use the third person singular form, as I explain in the next section. So when you use an IOP with **gustar,** place it before the third person singular or plural form of the verb **gustar**, as in the following examples:

Me gusta/gustan (*I like*)

Te gusta/gustan (*you* singular, informal *like*)

Le gusta/gustan (*he* or *she likes* or *you* singular, formal *like*)

Nos gusta/gustan (*we like*)

Os gusta/gustan (*you* plural, informal *like*)

Les gusta/gustan (*They* or *you* plural, formal *like*)

Suppose you want to say *I like salad*. Here's what you'd say in Spanish:

Me gusta la ensalada.

Literally, this means *To me is pleasing the salad* or, if you disregard word order, *The salad is pleasing to me.*

Applying a Few Rules for Expressing Likes with the Verb Gustar

No doubt about it — **gustar** is a pretty unusual verb. To conjugate the verb **gustar**, follow these rules:

✔ If you like just one thing or person, use the third person singular form, **gusta,** as in these examples:

Te gusta Chicago. (*You like Chicago.*) (*Chicago is pleasing to you.*)

Le gusta la pizza. (*He likes pizza.*) (*Pizza is pleasing to him.*)

Nos gusta la música. (*We like music.*) (*Music is pleasing to us.*)

Les gusta la televisión. (*They like television [programs].*) (*The television [programs] are pleasing to them.*)

Le gusta el profesor nuevo. (*She likes the new professor.*) (*The new professor is pleasing to her.*)

In the middle three examples, Spanish uses the definite article **la,** which English doesn't require. See Chapter 3 for everything you need to know about articles.

✔ If you like two or more things or people, use the third person plural form, **gustan,** as in these examples:

Me gustan las fresas. (*I like strawberries.*) (*Strawberries are pleasing to me.*)

Te gustan los carros rojos. (*You like red cars.*) (*Red cars are pleasing to you.*)

Le gustan los gatos. (*He likes cats.*) (*Cats are pleasing to him.*)

Les gustan los caballos. (*They like horses.*) (*Horses are pleasing to them.*)

Nos gustan los bailarines. (*We like ballet dancers.*) (*Ballet dancers are pleasing to us.*)

✔ To talk about things that you like to do, use a verb infinitive with the third person singular form of **gustar,** as in the following examples:

Me gusta leer. (*I like to read.*) (*Reading is pleasing to me.*)

Te gusta pescar. (*You like to fish.*) (*Fishing is pleasing to you.*)

Le gusta cantar. (*She likes to sing.*) (*Singing is pleasing to her.*)

Nos gusta montar a caballo. (*We like to ride horses.*) (*Riding horses is pleasing to us.*)

English uses a *gerund* (the *ing* form of the verb used as a noun) as the subject of the sentence, whereas Spanish uses the infinitive form of the verb. For example, **Le gusta cantar** literally means *To sing is pleasing to her.*

Stick with the third person singular form of **gustar** even if you like multiple activities. For example, **Me gusta ir de compras y pasear con mis amigos.** (*I like to shop and to stroll with my friends.*) (*Going shopping and strolling with my friends are pleasing to me.*)

✔ To say you really like something, add the adverb **mucho** (*a lot, really, very much*) after the conjugated form of **gustar**. Here are some examples:

Me gustan mucho los restaurantes mexicanos. (*I really like Mexican restaurants.*) (*Mexican restaurants are really pleasing to me.*)

Te gustan mucho las frambuesas. (*You really like raspberries.*) (*Raspberries are very pleasing to you.*)

Nos gusta mucho el helado. (*We really like ice cream.*) (*Ice cream is really pleasing to us.*)

Les gusta mucho patinar. (*You* [plural] *really like to skate.*) (*Skating is really pleasing to you* [plural].)

Translate the following sentences into Spanish. Use an English-Spanish dictionary to look up any words you don't know. Here's an example:

0. *We like to ski.*

A. **Nos gusta esquiar.**

1. *You* (singular, formal) *like summer.*

_____

2. *I really like to travel.*

_____

3. *She likes to sew.*

_____

4. *We like to play soccer.*

_____

5. *You* (singular, informal) *like to cook.*

_____

6. *You* (plural, informal) *like Italian food.*

_____

7. *They really like concerts.*

_____

8. *She likes to clean.*

_____

9. *I like dogs.*

_____

10. *You* (plural, formal) *really like old houses.*

_____

Clarifying and Emphasizing Pronouns with Prepositional Phrases

When you use the third person IOPs (**le** and **les**) with **gustar,** the person or people who like something can be a little murky. To clarify or emphasize exactly who likes something, you can add a prepositional phrase with **a** (*to*) to the beginning of your sentence. I provide guidelines for how to do so in the following sections.

As I explain in Chapter 13, prepositional phrases typically go at the end of a sentence, but in the case of **gustar,** you're dealing with a flip-flop sentence structure that puts the object at the beginning and the subject at the end. So the fact that you also flip flop the prepositional phrase makes sense.

Clarifying ambiguous pronouns

The only two object pronouns that are ambiguous are **le** (*he, she,* or *you* singular, formal) and **les** (*they* or *you* plural, formal), so they're the only ones you need to worry about clarifying. Here's an example of an ambiguous statement with **le** and **gustar** that you can clarify with a prepositional phrase:

✔ **Ambiguous: Le gustan las películas románticas.** (*She likes romantic movies.*) (*Romantic movies are pleasing to her.*)

✔ **Clear: A Clara le gustan las películas románticas.** (*Clara likes romantic movies.*) (*Romantic movies are pleasing to her to Clara.*)

The prepositional phrase **a Clara** (*to Clara*) clarifies that the IOP **le** (*to her*) means *to Clara.* The first translation of the clear version notes the way you express this statement in English. The second, literal translation highlights the repetition added by the prepositional phrase.

If you've already established the identity of the person you're talking about, you don't have to repeat the person's name. You can replace the name with a prepositional pronoun, as in the following example:

> **A él le gusta montar a motocicleta.** (*He likes to ride a motorcycle.*) (*Riding a motorcycle is pleasing to him to him.*)

Note: The prepositional pronouns for **él** (*him*) and **ella** (*her*) are the same as the subject pronouns **él** (*he*) and **ella** (*she*).

Because you don't need the prepositional phrase for clarification when you've already established whom you're talking about, you use this kind of repetition to emphasize that *he* (not someone else) is the one who likes riding a motorcycle. Admittedly, the repetition *to him to him* seems really weird when translated literally to English. Keep in mind that all languages are different in the way they view the world and how they express that view. Avoid the temptation to judge a language just because you don't understand some of the expressions. Trust me, English is also very unusual to foreigners when they learn it.

Emphasizing certain pronouns

You can also use prepositional phrases to stress that a particular person likes something, even when the IOPs **me** (*to/for me*), **te** (*to/for you* singular, informal), **nos** (*to/for us*), and **os** (*to/for you* plural, informal) have only one possible object. By using the prepositional phrase with these IOPs, you're simply showing emphasis (as in *I am* the one who likes it); you're not clarifying who's doing the liking. The following examples show how this emphasis works:

> **A mí me gusta salir con mis amigos.** (*I like to go out with my friends.*) (*Going out with my friends is pleasing to me to me.*)

> **A ti te gusta ir de compras.** (*You like to go shopping.*) (*Shopping is pleasing to you to you.*)

> **A nosotros nos gusta ir a Chicago.** (*We like to go to Chicago.*) (*Going to Chicago is pleasing to us to us.*)

> **A vosotros os gustan mucho las cerezas.** (*You really like cherries.*) (*Cherries are really pleasing to you to you.*)

The first translation in each of the preceding examples represents the way you'd express the statement in English. The second, literal translation demonstrates the repetition added by the prepositional phrase.

Translate the following sentences into Spanish, using prepositional phrases to clarify or emphasize. Use an English-Spanish dictionary for any words you don't know. Here's an example:

0. *My mother likes to cook.*

A. **A mi madre le gusta cocinar.**

11. *Tomás likes hamburgers.*

12. *Susana likes to listen to the radio.*

_____

13. *You (plural, informal) like computers.*

_____

14. *We like to go to the beach.*

_____

15. *You (singular, informal) like weekends.*

_____

16. *She likes to study Spanish.*

_____

17. *I like to write poetry.*

_____

18. *Raul likes to read.*

_____

19. *He likes horror movies.*

_____

20. *You (plural, formal) like to swim.*

_____

Talking about What You Don't Like

Expressing what you don't like is nearly as easy as expressing what you do like. All you do is insert the word **no** before the IOP, and voilà you've got it! Here's an example:

> **No me gusta bailar.** (*I don't like to dance.*) (*Dancing is not pleasing to me.*)

To add emphasis or clarity, do exactly what you do for positive statements (see the preceding section): Add a prepositional phrase starting with **a** before the word **no**. Here are a couple of examples:

> **A mí no me gusta bailar.** (*I don't like to dance.*) (*Dancing is not pleasing to me to me.*)

> **A Clara no le gusta lavar los platos.** (*Clara doesn't like to wash dishes.*) (*Washing dishes is not pleasing to her to Clara.*)

Translate the following expressions of dislike. Be sure to place a **no** in front of the IOP in the sentence. Use prepositional phrases with **a** at the beginning of the sentences for clarity or emphasis. Use an English-Spanish dictionary for words you don't know. Here's an example:

0. *Enrique doesn't like pizza.*

A. **A Enrique no le gusta la pizza.**

21. *You* (singular, informal) *don't like to dance.*

_____

22. *We don't like to play basketball.*

_____

23. *They don't like pizza.*

_____

24. *I don't like ice cream.*

_____

25. *You* (plural, informal) *don't like dogs.*

_____

26. *Rafael doesn't like to wash the dishes.*

_____

27. *You* (plural, formal) *don't like to work.*

_____

28. *Marisol doesn't like algebra.*

_____

29. *She doesn't like to cook.*

_____

30. *The students don't like crossword puzzles.*

_____

Asking What Someone Else Likes

One-sided conversations can get rather dull and are actually quite impolite, so you have to know how to ask others about their likes and dislikes (and not just focus on your own). The good news is that doing so is easy. All you have to do is change the intonation in your voice to turn the statement you want to ask about into a question. In other words, your pitch needs to rise toward the end of the question (instead of staying level as it does when you make a statement). See Chapter 2 for more about intonation.

Ask the following questions, using a questioning tone in your voice:

¿Te gusta comer pizza? (*Do you like to eat pizza?*) (*Is eating pizza pleasing to you?*)

¿A Juan le gusta montar a bicicleta? (*Does Juan like to ride bikes?*) (*Is riding a bike pleasing to Juan?*)

¿A Adelina y Paco les gustan las manzanas? (*Do Adelina and Paco like apples?*) (*Are apples pleasing to Adelina and Paco?*)

Introducing Other Verbs That Work Like Gustar

In the realm of Spanish verbs, **gustar** is peculiar, but it's not alone. In fact, it's a member of an exclusive group of verbs that use only the third person singular and plural forms and take an indirect object. Table 10-1 lists other verbs that work like **gustar.**

Table 10-1	Verbs like Gustar	
Spanish Verb	*Figurative Translation*	*Literal Translation*
disgustar	*to hate*	*to be repugnant to*
encantar	*to love*	*to be enchanting to*
faltar	*to need*	*to be lacking to*
fascinar	*to love, to adore*	*to be fascinating to*
importar	*to care about*	*to be important to*
interesar	*to be interested by*	*to be interesting to*
molestar	*to be bothered by*	*to bother*
parecer	*to seem to, to appear to*	*to seem, to appear*

When you conjugate the verbs in Table 10-1, follow the same rules that you follow for **gustar** (see the rest of this chapter for details). The following examples show these verbs in action:

A mí me disgustan las anchoas. (*I hate anchovies.*) (*Anchovies are repugnant to me to me.*)

A Tomás le encanta mirar la televisión. (*Tomás loves to watch television [programs].*) (*Watching television [programs] is enchanting to him to Tomás.*)

A Juana le falta papel para clase. (*Juana needs paper for class.*) (*Paper is lacking for class for her for Juana.*)

A nosotros nos fascina la ópera. (*We adore the opera.*) (*The opera is fascinating to us to us.*)

A Sara le importa recibir notas buenas. (*It is important to Sara to get good grades.*) (*Getting good grades is important to her to Sara.*)

A ellos les interesan las telenovelas. (*They are interested in soap operas.*) (*Soap operas are interesting to them to them.*)

A ti te molesta el comercialismo. (*You are bothered by commercialism.*) (*Commercialism is bothersome to you to you.*)

A Adriana le parecen caras las botas. (*Adriana thinks the boots seem expensive.*) (*The boots seem expensive to her to Adriana.*)

Note that these verbs use only the third person singular and plural endings. The **-ar** verbs use **-a** or **-an,** and the verb **parecer,** which is the only **-er** verb, uses **-e** or **-en.** In the last example in the preceding list, the adjective comes before the noun because the sentence is expressing that the boots *seem expensive,* not that they actually are *expensive.*

Using the verbs in Table 10-1 and the verb **gustar,** translate the following sentences into Spanish. Use an English-Spanish dictionary for words you don't know. Here's an example:

0. The Spanish teacher loves to travel.

A. **A la maestra de español le encanta viajar.**

31. You (plural, informal) *are interested in chess.*

_____

32. Birds fascinate them.

_____

33. The students need books.

_____

34. The Italian restaurant seems very good to us.

_____

35. It is very important to me to work a lot.

_____

36. The boys like to play soccer.

_____

37. You (singular, informal) *need money in order to go to Europe.*

_____

38. *My father loves classical music.*

_____

39. *Lola is bothered by her younger brothers every day.*

_____

40. You (plural, formal) *hate the opera.*

_____

Answer Key

1 Le gusta el verano.

2 Me gusta mucho viajar.

3 Le gusta coser.

4 Nos gusta jugar al fútbol.

5 Te gusta cocinar.

6 Os gusta la comida italiana.

7 Les gustan mucho los conciertos.

8 Le gusta limpiar.

9 Me gustan los perros.

10 Les gustan mucho las casas viejas.

11 A Tomás le gustan las hamburguesas.

12 A Susana le gusta escuchar la radio.

13 A vosotros os gustan las computadoras.

14 A nosotros nos gusta ir a la playa.

15 A ti te gustan los fines de semana.

16 A ella le gusta estudiar español.

17 A mí me gusta escribir poesía.

18 A Raul le gusta leer.

19 A él le gustan las películas de terror.

20 A ustedes (Uds.) les gusta nadar.

21 A ti no te gusta bailar.

22 A nosotros no nos gusta jugar al baloncesto (al básquetbol).

23 A ellos no les gusta la pizza.

24 A mí no me gusta el helado.

25. A vosotros no os gustan los perros.

26. A Rafael no le gusta lavar los platos.

27. A ustedes no les gusta trabajar.

28. A Marisol no le gusta el álgebra.

29. A ella no le gusta cocinar.

30. A los estudiantes no les gustan los crucigramas.

31. A vosotros os interesa el ajedrez.

32. A ellos les fascinan los pájaros.

33. A los estudiantes les faltan libros.

34. A nosotros nos parece muy bueno el restaurante italiano.

35. A mí me importa trabajar mucho.

36. A los muchachos les gusta jugar al fútbol.

37. A ti te falta dinero para ir a Europa.

38. A mi padre le encanta la música clásica.

39. A Lola le molestan sus hermanos menores todos los días.

40. A ustedes (Uds.) les disgusta la ópera.

Chapter 11

Handling Questions and Exclamations

Curious minds are constantly asking questions, whether they're simple yes or no questions (like "Did you go to the store yesterday?" and "Did you go with Steve?") or more detailed *interrogative* questions (like "Where did you go?" and "When did you arrive?").

Questions (and their answers) are a big part of most people's lives. For example, when you visit a foreign country, you have to know how to ask questions to get where you're going, to get what you want to eat and drink, to find out your new friend's name, to find lodging, and so on. Of course, you also have to know how to interpret the answers you get in response. And you need to know how to answer questions that other people ask you and how to form exclamatory statements to stress your point or convey your enthusiasm.

This chapter explains how to compose and answer yes or no and interrogative questions, as well as how to use exclamatory sentences. If you still have questions after you finish this chapter, at least you'll know how to ask them!

Composing Yes or No Questions

Yes or no questions are very direct in that they cut down your answer options to just two. You either do or you don't. You either are or you aren't. You either know or you don't. (You get the picture.)

Such directness can be very effective, such as when a lawyer asks a witness on the stand a yes or no question to which only two answers are acceptable. Yes or no questions can be equally effective in the classroom when a teacher asks a student, "Did you do your homework?" The student has only two ways to respond — yes or no.

In English, when you ask a yes or no question in the present tense, you often begin with either *do* or *does*. For example, "Do you like yogurt?" and "Does she live near here?" When you want to ask a yes or no question in Spanish, however, you don't have to add anything, except a couple of funky punctuation marks (¿ and ?). But you do have to choose one of three methods to ask your question. Each of the questions in the following sections asks the exact same thing, yet each one is composed slightly differently, depending on the method used.

Sticking with a statement and adding question marks

In Spanish, the easiest way to form a question is to start with a statement, add an inverted question mark at the beginning, and replace the period at the end with a regular question mark, like so:

> **Roberto tiene un perro.** (*Roberto has a dog.*)
>
> **¿Roberto tiene un perro?** (*Does Roberto have a dog?*)

The question marks tell you to raise the intonation of your voice at the end of the sentence, just as you do when asking a question in English.

Adding a tag question to a statement

If you want to do a little more than just add question marks, you may opt for the *tag question method*. To form a yes or no question with this method, you just add a tag question to the end of the statement. (A *tag question* is a short question tacked on to the end of a statement to convert the statement into a question.) Here are a couple of examples:

> **Roberto tiene un perro, ¿verdad?**
>
> *Roberto has a dog, right? (or isn't that right?)*
>
> **Roberto tiene un perro. ¿No?**
>
> *Roberto has a dog. Doesn't he?*

Trying variations of the inversion method

The textbook method of forming a question is the *inversion method*. To use this method, simply follow these steps:

1. **Start with a statement.**

   Roberto tiene un perro. (*Roberto has a dog.*)

2. **Invert the subject and the verb.**

   Tiene Roberto un perro. (*Has Roberto a dog.*)

3. **Add an inverted question mark at the beginning and replace the period with a regular question mark at the end.**

   ¿Tiene Roberto un perro? (*Does Roberto have a dog?*)

A less common method for forming a question is a variation of the inversion method. Instead of inverting the subject and verb, you move the subject to the end of the statement and add the inverted and regular question marks, like so:

¿Tiene un perro Roberto? (*Does Roberto have a dog?*)

Transform the following statements into yes or no questions by using the inversion method. Remember to use the upside-down question mark at the beginning of each question. Here's an example:

Q. Diana es una maestra.

A. ¿Es Diana una maestra?

1. Alfredo vive aquí.

_____

2. Carlos prepara la cena.

_____

3. Gabriela trae la paella.

_____

4. Tú tienes bastante arroz.

_____

5. Ellos bailan muy bien.

_____

6. Felipa habla con Ramón todos los días.

_____

7. Vosotros conocéis a sus hermanos.

_____

8. Las calles son muy anchas.

_____

9. Ella quiere un carro nuevo.

_____

10. Federico lee el periódico por la mañana.

_____

Replying to Yes or No Questions

Answering a yes or no question in Spanish obviously requires *yes,* **sí,** or *no,* **no.** You may want to reiterate portions of the question for clarity or emphasis, but the basic yes or no answer is as simple as **sí** or **no.** If you want to clarify what you're answering **sí** or **no** to, you can repeat the essence of the question after answering **sí** or **no:**

✔ To answer a yes or no question affirmatively, open your statement with **sí** and then follow up with the statement that you're supporting.

   For example, to affirmatively answer the question **¿Cocina Laura bien?** (*Does Laura cook well?*), you'd say, **Sí, Laura cocina bien.** (*Yes, Laura cooks well.*)

✔ To answer a yes or no question negatively, start with **No, (subject) no . . .** and then end with the statement that you're negating. (The subject is in parentheses here because you don't always have to include the subject in Spanish if it's clear in context.)

   For example, to negatively answer the question **¿Cocina Laura bien?** (*Does Laura cook well?*), you'd say, **No, Laura no cocina bien.** (*No, Laura doesn't cook well.*)

Note: Spanish speakers often replace the subject's name from the question with a subject pronoun in their answer. For example, in the answers in the preceding list, you could've replaced the name **Laura** with the subject pronoun **ella.** (For details on subject pronouns, see Chapter 9.)

Answer the following questions in the affirmative or negative as specified. Here's an example:

Q. **¿Lava Manolo los platos todos los días?**

A. **Sí, Manolo lava los platos todos los días.**

11. **¿Tienen ellos un carro nuevo?**

   No, _____

12. **¿Canta Susana bien?**

   Sí, _____

13. **¿Va él a la biblioteca ahora?**

   Sí, _____

14. **¿Corre Felipe en el parque todos los días?**

   No, _____

15. **¿Prepara su madre la cena a las seis?**

   No, _____

16. ¿Come Raúl mucha pizza?

Sí, _____

17. ¿Viaja la clase a Europa?

Sí, _____

18. ¿Trabaja Francisca en este restaurante?

No, _____

19. ¿Estudian los estudiantes antes de un examen?

Sí, _____

20. ¿Habla Pilar italiano?

No, _____

Seeking More Specific Information with Interrogatives

Sometimes you need a bit more information than a simple yes or no question is likely to give. When you're seeking more details about a topic, ask *interrogative questions* (also known as *information questions*) instead. Here are just a few examples: Who is she? What does she look like? Where did she go? When did you see her? Why would she do such a thing?

Who, what, where, when, and *why* are often referred to as "The Five Ws." These five *interrogatives,* as they're called, can tell you all the basic information you need to know about a given situation. They bring to mind a police interrogation with the classic bright light shining into the criminal's eyes and the detective trying to extract all the information about a crime that he can. But maybe that's getting a little dramatic. . . .

Anyway, interrogative questions come in handy if you want to be in the know. The following sections tell you what you need to know about Spanish interrogative words and then explain how to use them.

Introducing Spanish interrogatives

Spanish has all the same interrogatives that English does. Table 11-1 presents the Spanish equivalents to "The Five Ws" in English, along with some additional interrogative words.

All Spanish interrogative words have an accent when used in questions, as shown in Table 11-1. *Note:* Interrogative words are sometimes used as relative pronouns in answers or in regular sentences. In these cases, they don't have an accent mark.

Table 11-1	Spanish Interrogative Words
Spanish Interrogative Word	*English Translation*
¿Quién(es) . . . ?	*Who . . . ?*
¿Qué . . . ?	*What . . . ? or Which . . . ?*
¿Dónde . . . ?	*Where . . . ?*
¿Adónde . . . ?	*Where (to) . . . ?*
¿De dónde . . . ?	*Where (from) . . . ?*
¿Cuándo . . . ?	*When . . . ?*
¿Por qué . . . ?	*Why . . . ?*
¿Cuál(es) . . . ?	*Which one(s) . . . ?*
¿Cómo . . . ?	*How . . . ? or What . . . ?*
¿Cuánto/Cuánta . . . ?	*How much . . . ?*
¿Cuántos/Cuántas . . . ?	*How many . . . ?*

Forming questions with interrogatives

To form a question with an interrogative word, follow the inversion method for forming a yes or no question and then just add the appropriate interrogative word to the beginning of the question after the inverted question mark, as shown in the following steps:

1. **Start with a statement.**

   Roberto corre en el parque. (*Roberto runs in the park.*)

2. **Invert the subject and the verb.**

   Corre Roberto en el parque. (*Runs Roberto in the park.*)

3. **Add an inverted question mark at the beginning and replace the period with a regular question mark at the end.**

   ¿Corre Roberto en el parque? (*Does Roberto run in the park?*)

4. **Add the appropriate interrogative word in front of the verb.**

   To find out *when* Roberto runs in the park, use **¿Cuándo?,** as in this example:

   ¿Cuándo corre Roberto en el parque? (*When does Roberto run in the park?*)

   To find out *who* runs in the park, simply omit Roberto's name and rephrase your question with a different interrogative at the beginning:

   ¿Quién corre en el parque? (*Who runs in the park?*)

In an interrogative question, the interrogative word comes first, followed by the verb and then any other information necessary to make your question clear. Note that you don't always have to state the subject in an interrogative question. For example, when you've already established the subject or when the subject is clear from the verb form, you may omit it from your question.

You can also use interrogative words in sentences that state indirect questions. An *indirect question* is a question that the speaker restates after someone else has asked it; the sentence ends in a period rather than a question mark. To form an indirect question, all you have to do is make sure that the interrogative word is accented the same way that it would be if it were in an interrogative question. Here's an example:

> **Ella quiere saber quién es su hermano.** (*She wants to know who his brother is.*)

Choose the appropriate interrogative word to complete the following questions, as in this example:

0. *Where does Adán work?*

A. **¿Dónde trabaja Adán?**

21. *Where is my dictionary?*

¿ _____ **está mi diccionario?**

22. *When do her parents arrive?*

¿ _____ **llegan sus padres?**

23. *Who is his English professor?*

¿ _____ **es su profesor de inglés?**

24. *Why is Pilar here?*

¿ _____ **está Pilar aquí?**

25. *Where is the library?*

¿ _____ **está la biblioteca?**

26. *How is Elena? (feeling)*

¿ _____ **está Elena?**

27. *How much does this dress cost?*

¿ _____ **cuesta este vestido?**

28. *How many guests are coming to the party?*

¿ _____ **invitados vienen a la fiesta?**

29. *What is the special ingredient?*

¿ _____ **es el ingrediente especial?**

30. *When do they eat dinner?*

¿ _____ **cenan ellos?**

Using ¿Cómo? in different ways

The interrogative word **¿Cómo?** has a few different meanings depending on the context in which you use it:

- ✔ **¿Cómo?** means *How?* when you use it with the verb **estar** (*to be*) to describe a temporary condition, as in the question **¿Cómo estás?** (*How are you?*)

- ✔ **¿Cómo?** means *What?* when you use it with the verb **ser** (*to be*) to describe permanent conditions or qualities, as in the question **¿Cómo es el profesor de historia?** (*What's the history professor like?*)

Note: Flip to Chapter 7 for an introduction to the differences between **ser** and **estar.**

You can also use **¿Cómo?** by itself as an utterance when you didn't hear something well or you didn't understand what someone said to you. In this context, **¿Cómo?** means *What?* or *How was that?* and basically says to the person you ask that you need something repeated. In essence, it's a much shorter way to say **Repita, por favor.** (*Please, repeat that.*)

In Spanish, **¿Cómo?** never directly precedes an adjective or an adverb. In English, you may ask, "How heavy is the luggage?" or "How long is the train?" or "How fast does it travel?" But Spanish has a different way to ask for measurements. You use the interrogative word that asks for the information you seek, followed by the noun that describes the kind of measurement you're looking for, such as height, weight, speed, and so on. Here are a few examples:

¿Cuánto pesa el equipaje? (*How heavy is the luggage?*)

¿Cuánto dinero necesito? (*How much money do I need?*)

¿Cuánto pesas? (*How much do you weigh?*)

Determining when to use ¿Cuál? or ¿Qué?

¿Cuál? or **¿Cuáles?** asks the question *Which (one)?* or *Which (ones)?* when your question involves a choice. But if you ask *Which?* and you follow the interrogative with a noun, you need to use the interrogative word **¿Qué?** (*What?* or *Which?*) rather than **¿Cuál?** Here are some examples:

¿Cuál prefiere usted? (*Which [one] do you prefer?*)

¿Cuál es su casa? (*Which [one] is their house?*)

¿Qué libro lees ahora? (*Which book are you reading now?*)

¿Qué carro prefieren ellos? (*Which car do they prefer?*)

Note that you use **¿Cuál?** almost exclusively with the verb **ser** (*to be*) to mean *What?*, except when the question is to distinguish or define something, in which case you use **¿Qué?** Here are some examples of when to use **¿Cuál?**:

¿Cuál es la fecha de hoy? (*What's today's date?*)

¿Cuál es el mes de su cumpleaños? (*What's the month of his/her birthday?*)

¿Cuál es su selección? (*What's his/her selection?*)

¿Cuál es la capital de Chile? (*What's the capital of Chile?*)

¿Cuál es la diferencia? (*What's the difference?*)

¿Cuál es el resultado? (*What's the outcome?*)

Use **¿Qué?** with the verb **ser** to ask for a definition, as in the following examples:

¿Qué es cuadruplicado? (*What is quadruplicate?*)

¿Qué es mixomatosis? (*What is myxomatosis?*)

Now those are some serious questions!

Using prepositions with interrogatives

In Spanish, a preposition may precede an interrogative word if the answer to the question contains a preposition or if the question itself contains a preposition. For example, **¿Para quién es el libro?** (*For whom is the book [intended]?*) In English, the preposition usually comes at the end of such questions, although you do encounter the preposition-first structure more often in the Queen's English, or proper English. Here are some other examples of interrogative questions with prepositions at the beginning:

¿Adónde van? (*Where are they going [to]?*)

¿De dónde vienen? (*Where are they coming from?*)

¿A quién(es) escribes? (*Who are you writing [to]?*)

¿De quién(es) es el regalo? (*Who is the gift from?*)

¿De quien(es) son los zapatos? (*Whose shoes are they?*)

¿Con quién(es) va Ileana? (*Who is Ileana going with?*)

¿Para quién(es) son las flores? (*Who are the flowers for?*)

¿Con qué mide? (*What is he/she measuring with?*)

Be careful when you translate Spanish interrogative questions to modern English. If you translate them literally, you'll end up with some weird-sounding questions. The following table lists some examples.

Question in Spanish	Modern English Translation	Literal English Translation
¿De quién es este libro?	Whose book is this?	Of whom is this book?
¿Con quién vas?	Who are you going with?	With whom are you going?
¿Adónde vas?	Where are you going?	To where are you going?
¿De dónde vienes?	Where are you coming from?	From where are you coming?
¿Para qué?	What for?	For what (purpose)?
¿Por qué?	Why?	For what (reason)?

Note that **¿Para qué?** and **¿Por qué?** mean two different things even though their literal translations are the same. You use **¿Para qué?** to ask for what purpose and **¿Por qué?** to find out a reason. The answer to a **¿Para qué?** question usually begins with **Para . . .** (*In order to . . .*), and the answer to a **¿Por qué?** question usually begins with **Porque . . .** (*Because . . .*), as shown in the following examples:

¿Para qué necesitas una hoja de papel? (*Why [for what purpose] do you need a piece of paper?*)

Para escribir la tarea. (*In order to write the assignment.*)

¿Por qué tienes el dinero? (*Why do you have the money?*)

Porque voy a la tienda. (*Because I'm going to the store.*)

Answering an Interrogative Question

The easiest way to answer an interrogative question is to recycle the material — that is, to rephrase the question as a statement and then add the specific information the interrogator requested. As I explain in the earlier section "Forming questions with interrogatives," you make an interrogative question out of a statement by inverting the subject and verb and then adding the interrogative word to the beginning of the question. To answer an interrogative question, you simply reverse the process by following these three easy steps:

1. **Omit the interrogative word and the question marks from the question.**

   ¿Cuándo prepara Micaela la cena? (*When does Micaela prepare dinner?*) becomes **Prepara Micaela la cena . . . .**

2. **Invert the verb and subject to create a statement.**

   Micaela prepara la cena . . . . (*Micaela prepares the dinner . . .*)

3. **Add the information that gives the answer.**

   Micaela prepara la cena a las siete de la noche. (*Micaela prepares the dinner at 7:00 p.m.*)

Write interrogative questions to ask about the information in the following statements. Use the interrogative word shown in parentheses to begin your question. Here's an example to get you started:

Q. Answer: **Diana es una maestra.**

Question: (**¿Quién . . . ?**) _____

A. **¿Quién es una maestra?**

31. Answer: **Alfredo vive aquí.**

Question: (**¿Dónde . . . ?**) _____

32. Answer: **Carlos prepara la cena.**

Question: (**¿Quién . . . ?**) _____

33. Answer: **Gabriela trae la paella.**

Question: (**¿Qué . . . ?**) _____

34. Answer: **Tú tienes bastante arroz.**

Question: (**¿Qué . . . ?**) _____

35. Answer: **Ellos bailan muy bien.**

Question: (**¿Cómo . . . ?**) _____

36. Answer: **Felipa habla con Ramón todos los días.**

Question: (**¿Cuándo . . . ?**) _____

37. Answer: **Francisco va a la biblioteca los sábados.**

Question: (**¿Cuándo . . . ?**) _____

38. Answer: **Las calles son muy anchas.**

Question: (**¿Cómo . . . ?**) _____

39. Answer: **Susana quiere un carro nuevo.**

Question: (**¿Qué . . . ?**) _____

40. Answer: **Federico lee el periódico por la mañana.**

Question: (**¿Cuándo . . . ?**) _____

Getting Excited with ¡Exclamations!

Have you ever felt so excited you thought you were going to burst? Or so angry you wanted to scream? In such cases, you probably uttered some sort of exclamation, speaking louder than you normally would. When you speak excitedly or with a lot of emotion, you're uttering what are called *exclamatory expressions*.

To show an exclamation in written English, you put an exclamation mark (!) at the end of your statement. In Spanish, you put an upside-down exclamation mark (¡) at the beginning of your exclamation and a regular exclamation mark at the end.

Spanish exclamations often use the same interrogative words that you see in questions (I discuss these words earlier in this chapter). When you use these words in exclamations, you must put an accent mark on the interrogative words just as you do in questions. Here are a few interrogative words you may want to use in exclamations:

- ✔ **¡Cuánto/Cuánta . . . !** (*How much . . . !*)
- ✔ **¡Cuántos/Cuántas . . . !** (*How many . . . !*)
- ✔ **¡Cómo . . . !** (*How . . . !*)
- ✔ **¡Por qué . . . !** (*Why . . . !*)
- ✔ **¡Qué . . . !** (*What . . . !*)
- ✔ **¡Quién(es) . . . !** (*Who . . . !*)

Here are some actual expressions to get you familiar with using interrogative words in exclamations:

¡Cuánto tiempo tengo que esperar! (*How much time do I have to wait!*)

¡Cuánto habla! (*He/she talks so much!*) (Literally: *How much he/she talks!*)

¡Cuántos gatos tienen! (*[Wow!] They have a lot of cats!*) (Literally: *How many cats they have!*)

¡Cuántos zapatos tienes! (*How many shoes you have!*)

¡Por qué no! (*Why not!*)

¡Qué vestido tan feo! (*What an ugly dress!*)

¡Qué color tan horrible! (*What a terrible color!*)

¡Qué rápido va su carro! (*[Wow!] How fast his/her car goes!*)

¡Qué pesado! (*How heavy!*)

¡Qué mala suerte! (*What bad luck!*)

¡Qué buena suerte! (*What good luck!*)

¡No es la verdad! (*It's not true!*)

This exercise presents ten exclamations followed by ten numbered expressions. Next to each numbered expression, write the letter of the exclamation that is the most appropriate response to the statement. Use a Spanish-English dictionary for any words you don't know. An example follows the list of exclamations.

a. **¡Qué barato!**

b. **¡Qué cómico!**

c. **¡Qué interesante!**

d. **¡Qué mala suerte!**

e. **¡Qué buena suerte!**

f. **¡Cuánto dinero!**

g. **¡Cuánto trabajo!**

h. **¡Qué sabrosa!**

i. **¡Cuántas personas!**

j. **¡Qué fácil!**

Q. Ella siempre gana. _____

A. e

41. La cena es muy rica. _____

42. Ellos nunca ganan. _____

43. El Sr. Martinez gana mil dólares cada día. _____

44. La bolsa solamente cuesta cinco dólares. _____

45. Yo sé todas las respuestas del examen. _____

46. Hay veinte clientes en la sala. _____

47. Nosotros ganamos todos los partidos. _____

48. Este libro describe la vida de los indios inca. _____

49. Tengo que escribir veinte informes antes de mañana. _____

50. El mono lleva un vestido. _____

Answer Key

1 ¿Vive Alfredo aquí?

2 ¿Prepara Carlos la cena?

3 ¿Trae Gabriela la paella?

4 ¿Tienes tú bastante arroz?

5 ¿Bailan ellos muy bien?

6 ¿Habla Felipa con Ramón todos los días?

7 ¿Conocéis vosotros a sus hermanos?

8 ¿Son las calles muy anchas?

9 ¿Quiere ella un carro nuevo?

10 ¿Lee Federico el periódico por la mañana?

11 No, ellos no tienen un carro nuevo.

12 Sí, Susana canta bien.

13 Sí, él va a la biblioteca ahora.

14 No, Felipe no corre en el parque todos los días.

15 No, su madre no prepara la cena a las seis.

16 Sí, Raúl come mucha pizza.

17 Sí, la clase viaja a Europa.

18 No, Francisca no trabaja en este restaurante.

19 Sí, los estudiantes estudian antes de un examen.

20 No, Pilar no habla italiano.

21 ¿Dónde . . . ?

22 ¿Cuándo . . . ?

23 ¿Quién . . . ?

24 ¿Por qué . . . ?

25 ¿Dónde . . . ?

26 ¿Cómo . . . ?

27 ¿Cuánto . . . ?

28 ¿Cuántos . . . ?

29 ¿Cuál . . . ?

30 ¿Cuándo . . . ?

31 ¿Dónde vive Alfredo?

32 ¿Quién prepara la cena?

33 ¿Qué trae Gabriela?

34 ¿Qué tienes (tú)?

35 ¿Cómo bailan ellos?

36 ¿Cuándo habla Felipa con Ramón?

37 ¿Cuándo va Francisco a la biblioteca?

38 ¿Cómo son las calles?

39 ¿Qué quiere Susana?

40 ¿Cuándo lee Federico el periódico?

41 h

42 d

43 f

44 a

45 j

46 i

47 e

48 c

49 g

50 b

Part III
Beefing Up Your Sentences with More Description

The 5th Wave   By Rich Tennant

"If you're having trouble with irregular verbs, try using flash cards and taking more fiber."

In this part . . .

Basic subject-verb sentences are great if you're Tarzan picking up a little Spanish from Jane, but they're just a click above grunting and groaning. To become more eloquent, you need to be more descriptive, and this part can help. In these chapters, I explain how to use adverbs to describe verbs, adjectives, and other adverbs; use prepositions and construct prepositional phrases to specify location, direction, points in time, and more; describe actions performed on oneself with the reflexive; employ the passive voice to shed responsibility for performing an action; make comparisons; and add negative words to completely change the meaning of a sentence.

By combining what you know from this part with what you know from Parts I and II, you can say or write just about anything in Spanish — as long as you do it in the present or present progressive.

Chapter 12

Describing Action with Adverbs

In This Chapter

▶ Expressing time, place, process, quantities, and duration

▶ Putting adverbs in the right place in a sentence

▶ Comparing equalities and inequalities

*I*n its most rudimentary form, a sentence merely tells *who* does *what*. For example: *Man talks. Woman walks. Dog barks.* In prehistoric times, such expressions may have been sufficient, but nowadays, people demand details. They want the rest of the story, such as how eloquently or tediously the man talks, how fast the woman walks, and how repetitiously the dog barks. Heck, they may even want to know *where* the action occurred or *how long* it lasted. You provide these details using **adverbios** (*adverbs*) — words or phrases that describe verbs, adjectives, or other adverbs. This chapter presents adverbs and adverbial expressions to help you more clearly describe actions, whatever they may be and wherever and however they may occur.

Telling When, Where, How, How Many, How Much, and How Long

Adverbs give you information on manner (how), place (where), time (when), and quantity (how much or how many). Table 12-1 provides a list of frequently used adverbs grouped by the kind of information they provide.

Table 12-1	Frequently Used Adverbs by Category
Adverb	*English Translation*
Manner	
alegremente	*happily*
bīen	*well*
claramente	*clearly*
cuidadosamente	*carefully*
elegantemente	*elegantly*
inteligentemente	*intelligently*
mal	*badly*

(continued)

Table 12-1 (continued)

Adverb	English Translation
Place	
a la derecha	on the right
a la izquierda	on the left
abajo	down, downstairs
acá	over here
afuera	out, outside
al fondo	in back, at the bottom
al lado	next door, next to it
allá	over there
allí	there
arriba	up, upstairs, above
atrás	behind
cerca	close, nearby
debajo	under
detrás	behind
encima	on top
fuera	outside
lejos	far off, far away
por algún lado	somewhere
por ningún lado	nowhere
Time	
ahora	now
ahora mismo	right now
anteanoche	the night before last
anteayer	the day before yesterday
anteriormente	formerly
antes	before
ayer	yesterday
después	after, later
en seguida	right away
hoy	today
luego	then, later
mucho antes	much before
mucho después	much later
nunca	never
siempre	always
tarde	late

Adverb	English Translation
temprano	*early*
todavía	*still*
ya	*already*
Quantity	
bastante	*enough*
demasiado	*too much*
mucho	*much, a lot*
muy	*very*
poco	*little, not very*
suficiente	*enough*

Complete each sentence with the appropriate adverb from the following list. An example follows the list.

afuera	demasiado
bastante	mal
bien	nunca
cerca	tarde
delante	todavía

0. A veces me despierto _____.

A. tarde

1. El carro va _____ rápido para llegar a tiempo.

2. La tienda está muy _____, podemos ir caminando.

3. La clase no empieza hasta las diez, no tenemos que salir _____.

4. Todos vienen cuando él canta, porque canta tan _____.

5. La maestra está mal de humor porque los estudiantes siempre llegan _____.

6. A veces como _____, y tengo un dolor de estómago.

7. Necesito ir al doctor porque me siento muy _____.

8. El conductor está _____ de la orquesta.

9. Debo poner al perro _____.

10. _____ voy a sus conciertos.

Getting to Know the Forms That Adverbs Take

Adverbs commonly answer the questions *When? Where? How? How many? How much?* and *How long?* But the questions you're probably thinking right now are *What are some common Spanish adverbs?* and *How do I form them?*

Adverbs come in many forms that vary in length and complexity:

- ✔ **Single word:** An adverb may be a single word, such as **abajo** (*downstairs*). For example: **Ellos están abajo.** (*They are downstairs.*)

- ✔ **Compound word:** An adverb may be a compound word, such as **anteanoche** (*the night before last*). For example: **Ella llamó anteanoche.** (*She called the night before last.*)

- ✔ **Compound adjective:** A *compound adjective* is an adverb derived from an adjective. This type of adjective is usually formed with the feminine singular form of an adjective + the suffix **-mente,** which is equivalent to the English *-ly.* For example: **Él camina lentamente.** (*He walks slowly.*)

- ✔ **Adverbial expressions:** An *adverbial expression* is a phrase of two or more words that functions as an adverb. Many adverbial expressions consist of a preposition followed by one or more other parts of speech. Following are a couple of examples:

  • A preposition + an adjective, as in **de nuevo** (*again*): **Tengo que leer el libro de nuevo.** (*I have to read the book again.*)

  • A preposition + a noun, as in **de noche** (*at night*): **Nosotros siempre salimos de noche.** (*We always go out at night.*)

The following sections provide additional details about forming and using adverbs in Spanish.

Forming adverbs that end in -mente (-ly)

To form a *compound adverb* (an adverb derived from an adjective) in Spanish, follow these two easy rules:

- ✔ If the adjective ends in **-e** or a consonant or if it has the same form for both masculine and feminine, just add **-mente,** which is equivalent to the English *-ly,* to the end of it. For example:

    cortés (*polite*) → **cortésmente** (*politely*)

    general (*general*) → **generalmente** (*generally*)

- ✔ In all other cases, take the feminine singular form of the adjective and then add the suffix **-mente.** For example:

    tranquilo (*calm*) → **tranquilamente** (*calmly*)

    flojo (*lazy*) → **flojamente** (*lazily*)

Note: These types of adverbs usually come after the verb they modify. See the later section on adverb placement for details.

If the adjective has a written accent mark, keep the accent mark in place for the adverb form.

Sometimes you need to use more than one adverb to modify a verb or other part of speech. If a sentence has two or more adverbs that end in **-mente** connected by a conjunction such as **y** (*and*), **ni** (*neither*), or **pero** (*but*), add the suffix **-mente** only to the last adverb in the sentence. Here's an example:

Ella baila dramática y elegantemente. (*She dances dramatically and elegantly.*)

Change the following adjectives into compound adverbs, as in the following example:

Q. continuo → _____

A. continuamente

11. triste → _____

12. difícil → _____

13. débil → _____

14. terrible → _____

15. feliz → _____

16. serio → _____

17. nervioso → _____

18. alegre → _____

19. irónico → _____

20. rápido → _____

Meeting some adverbial expressions

Sometimes Spanish uses adverbial expressions rather than single or compound words to answer the questions *When? Where? How? How many? How much?* and *How long?* Table 12-2 presents some of the most commonly used adverbial expressions.

Note: Many adverbial expressions, including all those listed in Table 12-2, consist of a preposition combined with one or more other words. Prepositions followed by other elements or parts of speech can give information that more fully supports the action of the verb in the sentence. (See Chapter 13 for details on prepositions and prepositional phrases.)

Table 12-2	Commonly Used Adverbial Expressions Formed with Prepositions and Other Words
Adverbial Expression	*English Translation*
a menudo	frequently, often
a veces	sometimes
al fin	finally
al mismo tiempo	at the same time
con alegría	happily
con facilidad	easily
con frecuencia	frequently
con rapidez	quickly
con tristeza	sadly
de día	in the daytime
de noche	at night
de nuevo	again
de pronto	suddenly
de repente	suddenly
para atrás	backward, to the back
por aquí	around here
por desgracia	unfortunately
por fin	finally
por suerte	fortunately
por supuesto	of course
por último	finally
sin duda	without a doubt
sin razón	without (a) reason

Fill in the blank with the Spanish adverbial expression that's equivalent to the English adverb in parentheses, as demonstrated in the following example:

0. Ella hace la tarea _____. (*easily*)

A. con facilidad

21. Él trabaja _____. (*in the daytime*)

22. Necesito ir a la tienda _____. (*again*)

23. La familia tiene que mudarse a otra ciudad _____. (*unfortunately*)

24. Ellos van de vacaciones _____. (*happily*)

25. Hay un parque _____. (*around here*)

26. Ganamos el partido _____. (*fortunately*)

27. Ella es la más inteligente _____. (*without a doubt*)

28. Siempre dormimos _____. (*at night*)

29. Mi madre pierde su collar de perlas _____. (*frequently*)

30. Nosotros vamos al centro para ir de compras _____. (*sometimes*)

Table 12-3 presents some of the more commonly used adverbial expressions created with verb forms and other adverbs (rather than prepositions and other words, as is the case in Table 12-2).

Table 12-3	Adverbial Expressions Formed with Verb Forms and Other Adverbs
Adverbial Expression	*English Translation*
acá abajo	*down here*
al anochecer	*at nightfall*
al frente de	*in front of*
al parecer	*apparently*
al salir el sol	*at sunrise*
allá arriba	*up there*
cerca de	*near (to)*
de ahora en adelante	*from now on*
de veras	*really, truly*
de vez en cuando	*once in a while*
desde aquí	*from here*
desde entonces	*since then*
hasta aquí	*to here*
por lo visto	*apparently, evidently*

Translate the following sentences into Spanish, using the adverbial expressions from Table 12-3. Use an English-Spanish dictionary for any words you don't know. Here's an example:

Q. *She is really very beautiful.*

A. **Ella es muy hermosa de veras.**

31. *Once in a while, we work ten hours in one day.*

_____

32. *They usually have the fireworks at nightfall.*

_____

33. *From here you have to drive five more miles.*

_____

34. *From now on, we don't have to work every day.*

_____

35. *Apparently, they really want to win this game.*

_____

36. *From here you can see her house.*

_____

37. *She lives near (to) the library.*

_____

38. *The chalkboard is in front of the class.*

_____

39. *They have the majority of the boxes up there.*

_____

40. *I love to wake up at sunrise.*

_____

Using adjectives as adverbs

As you can see in Table 12-4, adjectives can also function as adverbs in idiomatic expressions. (An *idiomatic expression* is a word or phrase used by native speakers to mean something other than the usual definition of the word or phrase; for example, if you say *time flies* in English, you mean that it passes quickly, not that it literally flies.)

Using adjectives as adverbs in idiomatic expressions is quite common in everyday Spanish speech. When you use an adjective as an adverb, don't change its gender or number. In other words, keep the adjective in its masculine singular form to use it as an adverb. Here are a couple of examples:

> **Él siempre habla alto.** (*He always speaks loudly.*)

> **A veces ella maneja muy rápido.** (*Sometimes she drives very fast.*)

Table 12-4	Adjectives Used as Adverbs
Adjective/Adverb	**English Translation**
alto	loudly
bajo	softly
claro	clearly
directo	directly
duro	hard, intensely
fatal	bad(ly)
fuerte	loudly, strongly
lento	slowly
rápido	quickly

Placing Adverbs in a Sentence

Placing adverbs in a sentence can be a little tricky because the placement rules change depending on the function the adverb serves in the sentence. The only consistent rule for adverb placement is that the adverb should always be near the word it *modifies* (or gives more information about). For example, in the following sentence, the adverbs **siempre** (*always*) and **lentamente** (*slowly*) surround **habla** (*speaks*) on both sides because both adverbs modify that verb:

> **La maestra siempre habla lentamente cuando describe algo importante.** (*The teacher always speaks slowly when she is describing something important.*)

Whether you place the adverb before or after the word it modifies depends on how you use the adverb. I explain more in the next sections.

Adverbs that modify verbs

Adverbs that modify verbs usually come right after the verb, as in this example:

> **Él corre rápidamente.** (*He runs quickly.*)

> **Ella se viste elegantemente.** (*She dresses elegantly.*)

Of course, like most rules in Spanish (and English, for that matter), this rule has a few exceptions:

✔ You can place an adverb that modifies a verb after the direct object of the verb as long as the direct object is just one or two words. For example, you can say **La secretaria llama a muchos clientes diariamente** (*The secretary calls many clients everyday*).

But if more words follow the verb, the adverb can't come afterward. For example, if you add more words to the preceding example, you have to say **La secretaria llama diariamente a muchos clientes para conseguir información** (*The secretary calls many clients to get information daily*). In English, you can place the adverb *daily* at the end of the sentence, but in Spanish, the adverb **diariamente** must be closer to the verb.

✔ You can place the adverb before the verb to add emphasis to the verb, as shown in these examples:

> **Las reglas principalmente se basan en la importancia de respeto en las escuelas.** (*The rules principally are based on the importance of respect in the schools.*)

> **Por fin él llega a tiempo a la reunión.** (*Finally he is arriving on time to the meeting.*)

✔ **No** always precedes the verb that it negates, and other adverbs that negate the verb, such as **nunca** (*never*), frequently go in front of the verb that they negate, as shown in these examples:

> **Ellos no quieren bailar.** (*They don't want to dance.*)

> **Yo nunca hablo con él.** (*I never talk to him.*)

Adverbs that modify other adverbs

Adverbs that modify other adverbs come before the adverbs they modify, as shown in these examples:

> **Mi abuela siempre camina muy lentamente.** (*My grandmother always walks very slowly.*)

> **Cuando quiere él puede correr tan rápidamente como el viento.** (*When he wants he can run as fast as the wind.*)

Adverbs that modify adjectives

Adverbs that modify adjectives come before the adjectives they modify, as shown in these examples:

> **Me siento muy bien.** (*I feel very well.*)

> **Los estudiantes son increíblemente difíciles hoy.** (*The students are incredibly difficult today.*)

Adverbs that modify the entire sentence

An adverb that modifies an entire sentence often comes at the beginning of the sentence, as shown in these examples:

> **De vez en cuando nosotros tenemos mucha suerte.** (*From time to time we have a lot of luck.*)

> **Evidentemente, ellos no están de acuerdo.** (*Evidently, they do not agree.*)

However, an adverb that modifies the whole sentence can also come in the middle of the sentence before the verb or later in the sentence after the verb. The following examples show the same sentence with three different placements for the adverb:

> **Posiblemente, mi madre va a viajar a España.** (*Possibly my mother is going to travel to Spain.*)

> **Mi madre posiblemente va a viajar a España.** (*My mother possibly is going to travel to Spain.*)

> **Mi madre va a viajar posiblemente a España.** (*My mother is going to travel possibly to Spain.*)

Making Comparisons with Adverbs

When describing action, you often draw comparisons, such as *Sally has worked here longer than Tim has* and *She's performing the task much faster today than she did last week.* Like adjectives, adverbs have certain *comparative constructions* that allow you to compare two actions in terms of being equal or unequal. I explain these constructions and more in the following sections. (See Chapter 16 for additional information on comparisons.)

Making comparisons of inequality

To make a comparison of inequality, use the words **más** (*more*) or **menos** (*less*) + the adverb + **que** (*than*). Here are a couple of examples:

> **Desde luego trabajo más que antes.** (*Lately I am working more than before.*)

> **Ahora ella anda menos rápidamente que el año pasado.** (*Now she walks slower [less rapidly] than last year.*)

Making comparisons of equality

To make a comparison of equality, use the words **tan** (*as*) + the adverb + **como** (*as*), as in these examples:

> **Ella maneja tan rápido como su esposo.** (*She drives as fast as her husband.*)

> **Este grupo toca su música tan alto como el otro.** (*This group plays their music as loud as the other one.*)

Answer Key

1 bastante

2 cerca

3 todavía

4 bien

5 tarde

6 demasiado

7 mal

8 delante

9 afuera

10 nunca

11 tristemente

12 difícilmente

13 débilmente

14 terriblemente

15 felizmente

16 seriamente

17 nerviosamente

18 alegremente

19 irónicamente

20 rápidamente

21 de día

22 de nuevo

23 por desgracia

24 con alegría

25   por aquí

26   por suerte

27   sin duda

28   de noche

29   a menudo

30   a veces

31   De vez en cuando, trabajamos diez horas en un día.

32   Generalmente ellos tienen los fuegos artificiales al anochecer.

33   Desde aquí tiene que manejar cinco millas más.

34   De ahora en adelante, no tenemos que trabajar todos los días.

35   Al parecer, ellos quieren ganar este partido mucho.

36   Desde aquí se puede ver su casa.

37   Ella vive cerca de la biblioteca.

38   El pizarrón está al frente de la clase.

39   Ellos tienen la mayoría de las cajas allá arriba.

40   Me encanta despertar al salir el sol.

Chapter 13

Modifying Meaning with Prepositions

In This Chapter

▶ Understanding what prepositions are and how you can use them

▶ Meeting some simple and compound prepositions

▶ Identifying certain verbs that can't live without prepositions

Las preposiciones (*prepositions*) are words that are used before nouns and pronouns to show a relationship between those nouns or pronouns and another part of the sentence. Prepositions are also used with certain verbs to form phrases that more accurately describe actions or express spatial or temporal relationships. Prepositions begin phrases such as *at the mall, outside the gate, before the show,* or *in the box,* which are cleverly called *prepositional phrases.* As the name implies, prepositions are pre-positioned or placed at the beginning of prepositional phrases.

Like in English, you can use Spanish prepositions to link nouns to adjectives, other nouns, or verbs. However, unlike in English, you can also use prepositions to connect two verbs. Prepositional phrases can function as either adjectives or adverbs, depending on which parts of speech they join together. Acting as adjectives, prepositional phrases link nouns or pronouns to other nouns to answer questions like *Which one?* (*the dinosaur with short arms*). Acting as adverbs, propositional phrases link nouns or pronouns to verbs or adjectives to answer questions like *Where?* (*outside the gate*), *When?* (*before the show*), *Why?* (*for the pizza*), and *How?* (*with style*).

This chapter introduces you to common Spanish prepositions and shows you how to use them. Be forewarned that Spanish prepositions can be tricky because of their multiple meanings and uses. The best advice I can give you is to read this chapter a couple of times, taking advantage of the lists of common prepositions and usage examples, and then practice, practice, practice. The more you hear, say, and see a Spanish preposition used in a particular way, the more accustomed to its use you'll become.

Parading Simple Prepositions

A *simple preposition* is called *simple* because it consists of a single word, but the meanings and uses of simple prepositions aren't exactly simple. Table 13-1 lists the most common simple prepositions and an example of how to use each one. The sections that follow the table cover some subtle variations in meaning and usage for a few of the more complicated simple prepositions.

Table 13-1	Simple Prepositions	
Spanish	*English*	*Example*
a	to, at	**Caminamos a la tienda.** (*We are walking to the store.*)
ante	before, in the presence of	**El gobernador va a hablar ante el público.** (*The governor is going to speak before the public.*)
bajo	under	**El perro está bajo la mesa.** (*The dog is under the table.*)
con	with	**Siempre corro con él.** (*I always run with him.*)
contra	against	**Yo estoy contra sus ideas.** (*I am against his ideas.*)
de	of, from	**Ella siempre recibe diez dólares de sus abuelos en su cumpleaños.** (*She always receives ten dollars from her grandparents on her birthday.*)
desde	from, since	**Juan camina desde su casa a la escuela.** (*Juan walks from his house to the school.*)
durante	during	**A veces usamos la computadora durante la clase de ciencias.** (*Sometimes we use the computer during science class.*)
en	at, in, on	**Ellos ponen sus libros en los escritorios.** (*They put the books on the desks.*)
entre	between, among	**La biblioteca está entre unos edificios muy altos.** (*The library is between some very tall buildings.*)
hacia	toward	**Adelita camina hacia el centro.** (*Adelita is walking toward the downtown.*)
hasta	until	**Todos los sábados ellos duermen hasta las diez.** (*Every Saturday they sleep until 10:00.*)
para	for, in order to	**El regalo es para ella.** (*The gift is for her.*)
por	for, by, through	**Para llegar a su oficina él tiene que pasar por el parque.** (*In order to arrive at his office he has to go through the park.*)
según	according to	**Según mi doctor es muy importante comer bien.** (*According to my doctor it is very important to eat well.*)
sin	without	**No se puede entrar sin un boleto.** (*You cannot enter without a ticket.*)
sobre	about, around, over, above	**Miramos un programa sobre el clima.** (*We are watching a program about the climate.*)
tras	after	**Las vacas vienen una tras otra.** (*The cows are coming one after the other.*)

Choose a simple preposition from the following list to complete each sentence, as in the example that follows the list:

a	en
bajo	hasta
con	según
contra	sobre
de	tras
durante	

0. Él va _____ la tienda.

A. a

1. El libro está _____ la silla.

2. _____ la maestra es un libro muy interesante.

3. Los estudiantes vienen por el pasillo uno _____ otro.

4. Ellos tienen que trabajar _____ las ocho.

5. Voy al cine _____ mis amigos todos los viernes.

6. Ella pone toda la ropa _____ el armario.

7. El documental es _____ Chile.

8. Tengo una colección de estampillas _____ España.

9. Ellos están _____ la guerra.

10. Siempre tomo muchos apuntes _____ la clase de inglés.

Contrasting the personal *a* and the prepositional *a*

The uses for the preposition **a** don't end with *at*, *to*, and *toward*. Spanish has a rule that when the direct object of a verb is a person or a pet you must precede the direct object with the *personal a*. When you use the personal **a** in this capacity, it doesn't have a translation in English. See the following examples:

Yo llamo a Miguel los domingos. (*I call Miguel on Sundays.*)

Juan camina a su perro en el parque todos los días. (*Juan walks his dog in the park every day.*)

To an English speaker, the personal **a** seems out of place, but native Spanish speakers are accustomed to using it. As you continue to study and use Spanish, using the personal **a** will become natural to you.

Note: In Spanish, the prepositional **a** (*to, at*) and the personal **a** contract with **el** (*the*) when followed by a masculine singular noun that is preceded by that article, as shown in these examples:

> **Vamos al (a + el = al) mercado.** (*We're going to the market.*)
>
> **Ve al (a + el = al) obrero.** (*He sees the worker.*)

Decide which of the following sentences needs a personal **a**. Add the personal **a** in the space provided. Write an *X* in the space if the sentence doesn't need the personal **a.** Here's an example:

0. Hablo con _____ María.

A. x

11. Voy a la casa de _____ Martín.

12. Llamo _____ mi amigo a las cuatro.

13. Nosotros llegamos a la casa de _____ Ramón tarde.

14. Luisa acaricia _____ su gato.

15. Jorge toca _____ la guitarra.

16. Tú siempre llevas _____ ellos a la escuela en su carro.

17. Carolina besa _____ su novio.

18. Rosa persigue _____ su perro.

19. Vicente y Natalia escriben _____ la tarea.

20. La madre lava _____ la bebé.

Comparing por and para

Por (*by, for, through*) and **para** (*for, in order to*) are both simple prepositions, but getting used to their subtle variations in meaning isn't exactly simple. For example, although both **para** and **por** can equal *for*, you use **para** if you do something *for* someone and **por** if you pay *for* something:

> **Este regalo es para mi madre.** (*This gift is for my mother.*)
>
> **Pago diez dólares por la pizza.** (*I pay ten dollars for the pizza.*)

This is just one of the many nuances in the uses of **por** and **para.** I explain some of the others in the following sections.

Getting to know por

Deciding when to use **por** can be a little tricky. Table 13-2 lists some guidelines to help make your decision a bit easier.

Table 13-2	Uses for por	
English Equivalent	*Use*	*Example(s)*
by	In multiplication and division	**Tres por dos son seis.** (*Three times [by] two equals six.*) **Seis dividido por dos son tres.** (*Six divided by two equals three.*)
	For means of communication or transportation	**Mi padre siempre viaja por avión.** (*My father always travels by plane.*)
	In passive constructions (in which something is done *by* someone or something; see Chapter 15)	**El libro fue escrito por un autor muy famoso.** (*The book was written by a very famous author.*)
during	To describe an undetermined or general time	**Siempre leemos por la tarde.** (*We always read during the afternoon.*)
for	To show gratitude or express apology	**Gracias por el regalo.** (*Thanks for the gift.*) **Lo siento por los problemas.** (*Sorry for the problems.*)
	To mean *in exchange for* when buying or selling	**Ellos pagan veinte dólares por el boleto.** (*They pay twenty dollars for the ticket.*)
	To mean *on behalf of* or *in favor of*	**Él votó por el candidato popular.** (*He voted for the popular candidate.*)
	To express a length of time	**Hablamos por teléfono por dos horas cada fin de semana.** (*We talk on the phone for two hours every weekend.*)
	To show the reason for when used with **ir** (*to go*), **venir** (*to come*), **pasar** (*to pass, to come by*), **mandar** (*to send*), **volver** (*to return*), and **preguntar** (*to ask*)	**Mandan por él a las dos.** (*They send for him at two.*)
	In the case of mistaken identity	**Siempre me confunden por mi hermana.** (*They always confuse me for my sister.*)
in the mood for	To mean *to be in the mood for:* **estar** (*to be*) + **por**	**Estoy por comer comida mexicana.** (*I'm in the mood to eat Mexican food.*)
per	To express speed, frequency, and proportion	**Hablo con Susana tres veces por semana.** (*I talk to Susana three times per week.*)
through	To mean *through, along, by,* or *in the area of*	**Andamos por la sala para llegar a la cocina.** (*We walk through the living room to get to the kitchen.*)
yet to be	To express an action that hasn't yet been completed: **estar** (*to be*) + **por** + **infinitive**	**El almuerzo está por servir.** (*The lunch is yet to be served.*)

Numerous idiomatic expressions, including those in the following table, also use **por**. (*Idiomatic expressions* are words that mean something different in the expression than they do in their literal definition.)

Idiomatic Expression	English Translation
palabra por palabra	word for word
por adelantado	in advance
por ahora	for now
por allí	around there, that way
por amor de Dios	for the love of God
por aquí	around here, this way
por casualidad	by chance
por ciento	percent
por cierto	certainly
por completo	completely
por dentro	inside
por desgracia	unfortunately
por ejemplo	for example
por eso	therefore
por favor	please
por fin	finally
por lo general	generally
por lo menos	at least
por lo tanto	consequently
por lo visto	apparently
por medio de	by means of
por mi parte	as for me
por ningún lado	nowhere
por otra parte	on the other hand
por primera vez	for the first time
por suerte	fortunately
por supuesto	of course
por todas partes	everywhere
por todos lados	on all sides
por último	finally

Getting to know para

Deciding when to use **para** is easier than deciding when to use **por** because **para** has fewer uses. Table 13-3 lists the guidelines for when to use **para**.

Table 13-3	Uses for para	
English Equivalent	*Use*	*Example*
about to	To express an action that is about to be completed: **estar** + **para** = *to be about to*	**Los invitados están para salir.** (*The guests are about to leave.*)
by	To give a deadline or a specific time	**Tengo que terminar para las cuatro.** (*I have to finish by 4:00.*)
for	To indicate a destination	**Él sale para el centro todas las mañanas.** (*He leaves for downtown every morning.*)
	To express the purpose or use of something	**El jarrón es para flores.** (*The vase is for flowers.*)
	To express an idea contrary to what is expected	**Para una muchacha tan joven es muy madura.** (*For such a young girl, she is very mature.*)
	To designate a recipient	**Las flores son para mi madre.** (*The flowers are for my mother.*)
in order to	To mean *for the purpose of*	**Para hacer una piñata, primero necesita mezclar la harina y el agua.** (*In order to make a piñata, first you need to mix the flour and the water.*)

Using por and para correctly

Using **por** when you should've used **para** or vice versa can really change the meaning of a sentence, so be sure to follow the guidelines in Tables 13-2 and 13-3 to make sure you use these prepositions correctly. Here's an example of how using **por** versus **para** can change the meaning of a sentence:

> **Francisca hace el pastel para su madre.** (*Francisca is making the cake for her mother.* In other words, *She is making it for her mother to have.*)

> **Francisca hace el pastel por su madre.** (*Francisca is making the cake for her mother.* In other words, *She is making the cake on behalf of her mother.*)

Por and **para** also have slightly different meanings when used in questions. **¿Por qué?** means *Why?* (*for what reason?*), whereas **¿Para qué?** means *Why?* (*for what purpose?*). See the following examples for clarification:

> **Question: ¿Por qué tienes diez dólares?** (*Why do you have ten dollars?*)

> **Answer: Porque voy al mercado.** (*Because I'm going to the market.*)

> **Question: ¿Para qué tienes diez dólares?** (*Why do you have ten dollars?*)

> **Answer: Para comprar un vestido nuevo.** (*In order to buy a new dress.*)

Fill in the blank for each sentence with either **por** or **para**. Here's an example:

0. La llave no sirve _____ abrir esta puerta.

A. para

21. ¿Cuándo sale el avión _____ Nueva York?

22. Estoy _____ comer pizza.

23. La cena está _____ servir.

24. Ellos van al cine _____ pasar el tiempo.

25. Ella siempre estudia _____ la noche.

26. La clase dura _____ una hora y media.

27. Esta jarra es _____ limonada.

28. Tengo que terminar el proyecto _____ el lunes.

29. Vamos a un restaurante dos veces _____ semana.

30. Voto _____ el candidato republicano.

Designating possession with de

The simple preposition **de** has many uses. One of its most common uses is to mean *of*, but even this use can have different translations, as in **Las paredes son de hormigón** (*The walls are made of concrete*) versus **Él es un hombre de buen carácter** (*He is a man of good character*). Note that **de** contracts with the article **el** to form **del** (*from* or *of the*). Table 13-4 lists some guidelines that can help you decide when and how to use the preposition **de.**

Table 13-4		Uses for de
English Equivalent	*Use*	*Example(s)*
about	To indicate a topic	**Yo sé muy poco de este restaurante.** (*I know very little about this restaurant.*)
from	To indicate motion from a place	**Ellos vienen del centro.** (*They are coming from downtown.*)
	To indicate a place of origin	**Él es de San Francisco.** (*He is from San Francisco.*)
of	To indicate the contents of something or the material of which something is made	**Es una casa de vidrio.** (*It is a glass house [house of glass].*) **Tengo un vaso de jugo.** (*I have a glass of juice.*)

English Equivalent	Use	Example(s)
	To indicate possession (the equivalent of 's in English)	**Es el carro de Carmen.** (*It is Carmen's car [the car of Carmen].*) **¿De quién es este libro?** (*Whose book is this?*)
	To indicate a specific type	**Es la Facultad de Química.** (*It is the Chemistry Department [the Department of Chemistry].*) **Necesito una nueva máquina de lavar.** (*I need a new washing machine [machine of washing].*) **¿Dónde está el cuarto de baño?** (*Where is the bathroom [the room of the bath]?*)
	To indicate the character-istic of a noun	**Ella es una chica de mucho talento.** (*She is a very talented girl [a girl of much talent].*) **Su padre es un hombre de negocios.** (*Her father is a businessman [a man of business].*)
in or *with*	In descriptive expressions	**El techo está cubierto de nieve.** (*The roof is covered with snow.*) **Ella está vestida de blanco.** (*She is dressed in white.*)
as, *in*, or *on*	To indicate the manner in which something is done	**Nos ponemos de pie para cantar.** (*We stand up to sing*). (Literally: *We put ourselves on our feet.*) **A veces hago algo de buena fe.** (*Sometimes I do something in good faith.*) **Ellos están de luto.** (*They are in mourning.*) **Se visten de payasos para la fiesta.** (*They dress up as clowns for the party.*) **De vez en cuando sirvo de intérprete.** (*Every once in a while I serve as an interpreter.*)

You can also use **de** in idiomatic expressions that have no direct translation to English, including these examples:

Idiomatic Expression	English Translation
de corazón	*sincerely*
de acuerdo	*in agreement*
de hoy en adelante	*from today on*
de mal en peor	*from bad to worse*
de modo que	*so that*

Expressing location with en

The Spanish preposition **en** usually translates as *at*, *in*, or *on*, and you use it when you're referring to the location of someone or something. Table 13-5 lists a few guidelines you need to follow when you use **en**.

Table 13-5		Uses for *en*
English Equivalent	*Use*	*Example(s)*
at, *in*, or *on*	To indicate location	**Estoy en la casa.** (*I am in the house.*) **Él está en la fiesta.** (*He is at the party.*) **Siempre pongo mis libros en la mesa.** (*I always put my books on the table.*)
	To indicate an extent of time	**El tren sale en diez minutos.** (*The train is leaving in ten minutes.*) **Ellos tienen que salir en dos horas.** (*They have to leave in two hours.*)
by	To indicate the means by which an action takes place	**Se puede ir a Europa en avión o en barco.** (*You can go to Europe by plane or by boat.*) **Siempre vamos en coche o en tren cuando vamos a su casa.** (*We always go by car or by train when we go to their house.*)

En doesn't translate to anything in English when you use it in some Spanish expressions of manner, such as the following:

> **Hablo en serio.** (*I'm talking seriously.*)

> **Lo dice en broma.** (*He says it as a joke.*)

> **Ellos están en contra el impuesto nuevo.** (*They are against the new tax.*)

To refer to doing something on a specific day of the week in English, you use *on* plus the day of the week, as in, *On Friday I will go to the movies*. Similarly, if you have a habit of doing the same thing every Saturday, you use *on* plus the plural form of the day of the week, as in, *On Saturdays I visit my grandmother*. In Spanish, however, you don't use the preposition *on*. To say that you do something on a particular day of the week, you use **el** plus the day of the week, and to say that you tend to do something on a particular day in general, you use **los** plus the plural form of the day of the week. Here are some examples:

> **Tengo que ir al doctor el viernes.** (*I have to go to the doctor on Friday.*)

> **Voy al mercado los sábados.** (*I go to the market on Saturdays.*)

Of course, **en** also shows up in several Spanish idiomatic expressions, including the ones in the following table:

Idiomatic Expression	*English Translation*
en cambio	*in exchange*
en efecto	*in fact*
en la actualidad	*nowadays*
en realidad	*in reality*
en voz alta	*out loud*
en voz baja	*in a soft voice*

Considering con

The Spanish preposition **con** usually translates as *with* and indicates accompaniment or the means by which something is done. Table 13-6 offers some guidelines for using the preposition **con**.

Table 13-6	Uses of con	
English Equivalent	*Use*	*Example(s)*
with	To indicate accompaniment	**Me gusta el café con leche.** (*I like coffee with milk.*) **Voy al cine con ella.** (*I'm going to the movies with her.*)
	To indicate the means by which something is done	**Cierro la puerta con la llave.** (*I lock the door with the key.*)
	To indicate the contents of a container (For this use, **con** is sometimes used in place of **de** [*of*].)	**Tengo una bolsa con joyas.** (*I have a bag with [of] jewels.*)
in spite of	To indicate that in spite of a certain situation, a person feels a contrary emotion or has a contrary outcome to that which would be logical	**Con todas sus riquezas, todavía no está contento.** (*In spite of his riches, he is still not happy.*) **Con todo lo que hace, todavía no tiene éxito.** (*In spite of everything that he does, he still isn't successful.*)

Presenting Compound Prepositions

A *compound preposition* is a preposition that's made up of more than one word. The last word of a compound preposition is always a simple preposition, so compound prepositions are easy to identify. The following table lists the most commonly used compound prepositions. *Note:* Many of these compound prepositions consist of a directional word and the simple preposition **de**. But if you use the directional word without **de**, it isn't considered a preposition. When a directional word appears without a preposition, it's considered an adverb. (See Chapter 12 for more on adverbs.)

Compound Preposition	*English Translation*
a espaldas de	*behind*
a fines de	*at the end*
a lo largo de	*along*
a partir de	*from (time or date) on, starting (time or date)*
a través de	*through*
abajo de	*underneath*
adentro de	*inside (of)*

Compound Preposition	English Translation
afuera de	outside (of)
al lado de	next to
alrededor de	around
antes de	before
arriba de	above
cerca de	near
debajo de	under
delante de	before (location), in front of
dentro de	in, within, inside of
después de	after (time or order)
detrás de	behind, after
en lugar de	in place of
en vez de	instead of
encima de	on top of, above
enfrente de	in front of
frente a	opposite, facing
fuera de	outside of
lejos de	far from

Recognizing and Using Some Verbs That Require Prepositions

In Spanish, some conjugated verbs always require **a, de,** or another preposition when they're followed by an infinitive; for example, **Nos decidimos a volver a casa** (*We decided to return home*). Other conjugated verbs can be followed directly by an infinitive; for example, **Queremos ir al cine ahora** (*We want to go to the movies now*).

The easiest way to remember which Spanish verbs require which prepositions is to group your verbs according to which preposition they require. However, some verbs can use different prepositions depending on the meaning you're trying to achieve with the verb. For example, **correr** means *to run*, **correr a** means *to run to,* and **correr de** means *to run from.*

The following sections offer some preposition-verb basics, as well as a list that groups verbs according to which prepositions they require.

The basics of verbs that require prepositions

Sometimes you follow up a conjugated verb in Spanish with an infinitive to show that the subject hasn't changed; for example, **Quiero ir de compras** (*I want to go shopping*). As you can see in this example, some Spanish verbs require the use of a preposition in between the conjugated verb and the infinitive when they're directly followed by an infinitive. What makes this issue a little tricky is that the prepositions used in Spanish don't always correspond to the usage in English, such as in this example:

El próximo verano voy a tratar de aprender a nadar. (*Next summer I'm going to try to learn to swim.*)

Some verbs also require the use of a preposition when they're followed by a predicate noun. A *predicate noun* is a noun that follows a linking verb, such as **es** or **está** (*is*) or **son** or **están** (*are*), and is equivalent to the subject. For example, in the sentence **Bill es un líder excelente** (*Bill is an excellent leader*), *leader* is a predicate noun equivalent to the subject, *Bill.*

Here are a few of the prepositions that are commonly used when certain verbs are followed by another verb or a predicate noun:

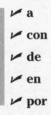

- ✔ **a**
- ✔ **con**
- ✔ **de**
- ✔ **en**
- ✔ **por**

In Spanish, when a verb comes after another verb, the second verb is usually in its infinitive form (*to* + verb). But when you translate the verbs into English, the second verb often translates to its *ing* form. Here's an example:

Él insiste en venir. (*He insists on coming.*) (Literally: *He insists on to come.*)

In some cases, however, the Spanish and English translations are the same, as in this example:

Ella quiere aprender francés. (*She wants to learn French.*)

Sometimes when a verb has a preposition after it, the preposition maintains its meaning, as in this example:

Los estudiantes se cansan de estudiar. (*The students get tired of studying.*)

Other times, the preposition merely introduces the infinitive verb or the noun and isn't translated in English, as in the following example:

Ellos amenazan con salir. (*They are threatening to leave.*)

In this case, the preposition **con** (*with*) is required with the verb **amenazar** (*to threaten*), but it isn't translated into English.

Lists of verbs that require prepositions

The following tables list some of the most commonly used verbs that require prepositions, categorized by the prepositions they use. Note that in many instances, the prepositions used with these verbs either don't translate into English or translate to another preposition in English (see the preceding section for details).

Verbs That Require the Preposition *a*

acercarse a	*to get close to*
acertar a + verb	*to succeed in* + verb
animar a + verb	*to encourage to* + verb
aprender a + verb	*to learn* + verb
asistir a	*to attend*
atreverse a	*to dare to*
ayudar a + verb	*to help* + verb
comenzar a + verb	*to begin* + verb
correr a	*to run to*
cuidar a	*to care for (a person)*
decidirse a + verb	*to decide* + verb
dedicarse a	*to dedicate oneself to*
empezar a + verb	*to begin* + verb
enseñar a + verb	*to teach* + verb
inspirar a + verb	*to inspire* + verb
invitar a	*to invite to*
meterse a	*to take up*
montar a	*to ride*
negarse a + verb	*to refuse* + verb
oponerse a	*to be opposed to*
ponerse a	*to begin to*
probar a + verb	*to try* + verb
resignarse a	*to resign oneself to*
subir a	*to climb, to get on (something), to go up*
venir a	*to come to*
volver a	*to do (something) again*

Verbs That Require the Preposition *con*

casarse con	*to marry*
conformarse con	*to conform to, to make due with*
contar con	*to count on*
encontrarse con	*to meet up with, to run into*
enfadarse con	*to get angry at*
equivocarse con	*to be mistaken about*
preocuparse con	*to worry about*
salir con	*to go out with, to date*
soñar con	*to dream of*

Verbs That Require the Preposition de

acabar de + verb	*to have just* + verb
acordarse de	*to agree about*
alegrarse de	*to be happy about*
cansarse de	*to get tired of*
cuidar de	*to care for (something)*
deber de	*to be obliged to*
dejar de + verb	*to stop* + verb (ing)
depender de	*to depend on*
disfrutar de	*to enjoy*
enamorarse de	*to fall in love with*
gozar de	*to enjoy*
informarse de	*to become aware of*
olvidarse de	*to forget about*
pensar de	*to think of, to have an opinion of*
probar de	*to sample, to try out*
quejarse de	*to complain about*
reírse de	*to laugh about*
salir de	*to leave from*
servir de	*to be useful as*
tratar de + verb	*to try* + verb

Verbs That Require the Preposition en

consentir en + verb	*to consent to* + verb
consistir en	*to consist of*
convertir en	*to become, to change into*
equivocarse en	*to make a mistake about*
fijarse en	*to pay attention to*
insistir en	*to insist on*
pensar en	*to think about (something or someone, not an opinion)*
trabajar en	*to work on, to work at*

Verbs That Require the Preposition por

comenzar por	*to begin by*
interesarse por	*to be interested in*
preocuparse por	*to be worried about*

Choose the appropriate verb + preposition combination to correctly complete the following sentence translations, as shown in this example:

0. *She begins by reading the book.*

Ella _____ leer el libro.

A. **comienza por**

31. *They insist on going.*

Ellos _____ ir.

32. *We worry about leaving on time.*

Nosotros _____ salir a tiempo.

33. *His parents are trying to learn to ski.*

Sus padres _____ aprender a esquiar.

34. *Susana consented to attend the dance with Juan.*

Susana _____ asistir al baile con Juan.

35. *The tourists are interested in traveling to Europe.*

Los turistas _____ viajar a Europa.

36. *The young people enjoy dancing.*

Los jóvenes _____ bailar.

37. *The teacher insists on giving an exam every week.*

La maestra _____ dar un examen todas las semanas.

38. *He pays attention to driving.*

Él _____ conducir.

39. *The students complain about studying so much.*

Los estudiantes _____ estudiar tanto.

40. *The soccer players are thinking about winning the game.*

Los jugadores del fútbol _____ ganar el partido.

Answer Key

1 bajo

2 según

3 tras

4 hasta

5 con

6 en

7 sobre

8 de

9 contra

10 durante

11 X

12 a

13 X

14 a

15 X

16 a

17 a

18 a

19 X

20 a

21 para

22 por

23 por

24 para

25 por

26 por

27 para

28 para

29 por

30 por

31 insisten en

32 nos preocupamos por

33 tratan de

34 consiente en

35 se interesan por

36 gozan de

37 insiste en

38 se fija en

39 se quejan de

40 piensan en

Chapter 14

Acting on Oneself with the Reflexive

• •

In This Chapter

▶ Recognizing reflexive verbs and pronouns

▶ Forming regular, irregular, and stem-changing reflexive verbs

▶ Using reflexive verbs in sentences

• •

Whenever you look at yourself, put yourself to bed, or worry yourself silly, you're taking part in a reflexive action. *You,* the subject, are doing something to *yourself,* the direct object. English has no reflexive verbs; it has only reflexive pronouns, such as *myself, yourself, himself, herself,* and *themselves.* Spanish, on the other hand, delineates reflexive action by using both a reflexive verb and a reflexive pronoun, as in this example:

> **Yo me baño.** (*I bathe myself.*) (*I take a bath.*)

In the Spanish version, you use the reflexive verb **bañarse** (*to bathe oneself*) along with the reflexive pronoun **me** (*myself*). In English, the reflexive pronoun *myself* does all the work because English doesn't have reflexive and nonreflexive verbs.

In this chapter, you get to know reflexive verbs and pronouns, and you figure out how to put them to work in sentences.

Getting to Know Reflexive Verbs and Pronouns

Before you delve into the nitty-gritty of reflexive constructions, take some time to get to know some of the more common reflexive verbs and pronouns that I present in the following sections.

Checking out some common reflexive verbs

The following table lists some of the most commonly used reflexive verbs in Spanish. Note that the infinitive form of a reflexive verb always has **se** (*himself, herself, yourself, themselves, and yourselves*) attached to the end.

Reflexive Verb	*English Translation*
adelantarse	to go forward, to move ahead, to take the lead
afeitarse	to shave oneself
alegrarse	to be glad
alumbrarse	to become tipsy or lively (from liquor)
apoderarse	to take power, to take possession
apresurarse	to hasten, to hurry, to rush
apurarse	to fret, to grieve, to worry
asustarse	to be frightened, to be scared
atreverse	to dare, to venture
bañarse	to bathe oneself
burlarse	to make fun of, to ridicule
callarse	to be silent, to keep quiet
cansarse	to become tired
casarse (con alguien)	to get married, to marry (someone)
cepillarse (el pelo)	to brush (one's hair)
cepillarse (los dientes)	to brush (one's teeth)
cortarse (las uñas)	to cut (one's nails)
cuidarse	to take care of oneself
dedicarse	to devote oneself
desayunarse	to have breakfast
descuidarse	to be negligent or careless
desesperarse	to become desperate, to lose hope
ducharse	to take a shower
enfermarse	to get sick
enojarse	to become angry or mad
lavarse	to wash oneself
levantarse	to stand up, to get up
limarse (las uñas)	to file (one's nails)
limpiarse	to clean oneself
llamarse	to call oneself
maquillarse	to put makeup on
marcharse	to go away, to leave
mirarse	to look at oneself
mojarse	to get wet
pararse	to stop oneself
peinarse	to comb one's hair

Reflexive Verb	English Translation
pintarse (los labios)	*to put on lipstick*
preocuparse (de)	*to worry (about)*
prepararse	*to get ready, to prepare oneself*
quedarse	*to remain, to stay*
quejarse	*to complain*
quitarse (la ropa)	*to take off, to remove (clothing)*
secarse	*to dry oneself*

Many reflexive verbs serve double duty as nonreflexive verbs. For example, you can use the verb **bañarse** (*to bathe oneself*) nonreflexively and reflexively. When you bathe yourself, you use the verb reflexively — that is, with a reflexive pronoun:

> **Yo me baño.** (*I bathe myself.*) (*I take a bath.*)

When you bathe someone other than yourself, you use the verb nonreflexively — that is, without a reflexive pronoun:

> **Yo baño al bebé.** (*I bathe the baby.*)

Introducing the reflexive pronouns

In Spanish, a reflexive pronoun must always accompany a reflexive verb. The following table lists the reflexive pronouns and their English equivalents:

me (*myself*)	**nos** (*ourselves*)
te (*yourself*)	**os** (*yourselves*)
se (*himself, herself, yourself*)	**se** (*themselves, yourselves*)

Note that you use **se** for **usted, ustedes, él, ella, ellos,** and **ellas.**

Another set of pronouns in Spanish translate to mean the same as the reflexive pronouns. These pronouns are

> **mismo/misma** (*myself, yourself, himself, herself*)
>
> **mismos/mismas** (*yourselves, themselves, ourselves*)

In Spanish, you add the **mismo(s)/misma(s)** pronouns for emphasis just as you add the reflexive pronouns for emphasis in English. Specifically, these pronouns emphasize the person who did the action. Here are a couple of examples:

> **Yo mismo limpio la casa.** (*I clean the house myself.*)
>
> **Ellos mismos preparan la cena.** (*They prepare the dinner themselves.*)

Fill in the blank with the reflexive pronoun you'd use for each of the following subjects. Here's an example:

0. mis amigos = _____

A. se

1. ellos = _____

2. nosotros = _____

3. yo = _____

4. Ricardo = _____

5. tú = _____

6. mis padres = _____

7. los estudiantes = _____

8. vosotras = _____

9. usted = _____

10. Ramón y yo = _____

Forming Regular Reflexive Verbs

Forming the reflexive is a three-step process:

1. **Conjugate the verb to match the subject of the sentence in person and number.**

   Fortunately (for your memory's sake), conjugating a regular reflexive verb is exactly the same as conjugating any other verb except that you have to drop the **se** ending from the reflexive verb first. For **-ar** reflexive verbs, just add the endings **-o, -as, -a, -amos, -áis,** and **-an** based on the person and number of the subject. For **-er** verbs, add the endings **-o, -es, -e, -emos, -éis,** and **-en,** and for **-ir** verbs, add the endings **-o, -es, -e, -imos, -ís,** and **-en.** (See Chapter 6 for more details on conjugating verbs in the present tense. For all other tenses, see Part IV.) The table that follows this step list shows how to conjugate the regular reflexive verb **bañarse** (*to bathe oneself*) in the present tense.

2. **Choose a reflexive pronoun that matches the subject of the sentence in person and number.**

   See the earlier section "Introducing the reflexive pronouns" for your pronoun options.

3. **Place the reflexive pronoun before the verb.**

For example, in **Yo me baño** (*I bathe myself*) (*I take a bath*), the subject is **Yo** (first person singular), **baño** is the first person singular of the verb **bañarse,** and **me** is the reflexive pronoun that precedes the verb. Here's what the verb **bañarse** looks like when you conjugate it:

bañarse (to bathe oneself)	
me baño (*[I] bathe myself*)	**nos bañamos** (*[we] bathe ourselves*)
te bañas (*[you] bathe yourself*)	**os bañáis** (*[you] bathe yourselves*)
se baña (*[he] bathes himself, [she] bathes herself, [you] bathe yourself*)	**se bañan** (*[they] bathe themselves, [you] bathe yourselves*)

If a sentence has two verbs (one conjugated verb and one infinitive), you have two options for where to place the reflexive pronoun. You can place the reflexive pronoun in front of the conjugated verb, as in this example:

Yo me necesito bañar. (*I need to take a bath.*) (*I need to bathe myself.*)

Or you can place the reflexive pronoun after and attached to the second verb (which is in the infinitive form), as in this example:

Yo necesito bañarme. (*I need to take a bath.*) (*I need to bathe myself.*)

Translate the following sentences into Spanish, using the reflexive verbs from the list that follows. Use an English-Spanish dictionary for any words you don't know. An example follows the list of verbs.

afeitarse	**levantarse**
bañarse	**limarse**
cepillarse	**maquillarse**
cortarse	**peinarse**
ducharse	**pintarse**
enfermarse	**quitarse**

0. *She gets sick a lot when she travels.*

A. **Ella se enferma mucho cuando viaja.**

11. *They take a bath at night.*

_____

12. *He cuts his nails after bathing.*

_____

13. *We get up late on Saturdays.*

_____

14. *He takes off his clothes before showering.*

_____

15. *You guys shave after showering.*

_____

16. *She puts on lipstick in the morning.*

_____

17. *I put on makeup every day.*

_____

18. *You* (singular, informal) *comb your hair a lot.*

_____

19. *Sometimes she files her nails.*

_____

20. *We brush our teeth after eating.*

_____

Conjugating Stem-Changing and Irregular Reflexive Verbs

The verbs in the following table have stem changes, as indicated in the second column. Keep in mind that these stem changes occur in all the conjugated forms except **nosotros/nosotras** and **vosotros/vosotras**. For details on conjugating stem-changing verbs in the present tense, check out Chapter 6.

Reflexive Verb	Stem Change	English Translation
acordarse	o → ue	to remember, to agree
acostarse	o → ue	to go to bed
despedirse	e → i	to say goodbye
despertarse	e → ie	to wake up
desvestirse	e → i	to undress oneself
divertirse	e → ie	to have a good time, to enjoy oneself
dormirse	o → ue	to go to sleep
negarse	e → ie	to refuse

Reflexive Verb	Stem Change	English Translation
probarse	o → ue	*to try on (clothes)*
reírse	e → i	*to laugh (at)*
sentarse	e → ie	*to sit down*
sentirse	e → ie	*to feel (well, ill)*
vestirse	e → i	*to dress oneself*

The following reflexive verbs have irregular present tense conjugations, as you can see in their conjugation tables:

abstenerse (*to abstain*)	
yo **me abstengo**	nosotros/nosotras **nos abstenemos**
tú **te abstienes**	vosotros/vosotras **os abstenéis**
él/ella/usted **se abstiene**	ellos/ellas/ustedes **se abstienen**

atenerse (*to rely on, to depend on*)	
yo **me atengo**	nosotros/nosotras **nos atenemos**
tú **te atienes**	vosotros/vosotras **os atenéis**
él/ella/usted **se atiene**	ellos/ellas/ustedes **se atienen**

caerse (*to fall [down]*)	
yo **me caigo**	nosotros/nosotras **nos caemos**
tú **te caes**	vosotros/vosotras **os caéis**
él/ella/usted **se cae**	ellos/ellas/ustedes **se caen**

distraerse (*to distract oneself*)	
yo **me distraigo**	nosotros/nosotras **nos distraemos**
tú **te distraes**	vosotros/vosotras **os distraéis**
él/ella/usted **se distrae**	ellos/ellas/ustedes **se distraen**

irse (*to go away*)	
yo **me voy**	nosotros/nosotras **nos vamos**
tú **te vas**	vosotros/vosotras **os vais**
él/ella/usted **se va**	ellos/ellas/ustedes **se van**

ponerse (*to become, to put on [clothes]*)	
yo **me pongo**	nosotros/nosotras **nos ponemos**
tú **te pones**	vosotros/vosotras **os ponéis**
él/ella/usted **se pone**	ellos/ellas/ustedes **se ponen**

reponerse (*to get better*)	
yo **me repongo**	nosotros/nosotras **nos reponemos**
tú **te repones**	vosotros/vosotras **os reponéis**
él/ella/usted **se repone**	ellos/ellas/ustedes **se reponen**

sostenerse (*to support, to sustain oneself*)	
yo **me sostengo**	nosotros/nosotras **nos sostenemos**
tú **te sostienes**	vosotros/vosotras **os sostenéis**
él/ella/usted **se sostiene**	ellos/ellas/ustedes **se sostienen**

verse (*to see oneself*)	
yo **me veo**	nosotros/nosotras **nos vemos**
tú **te ves**	vosotros/vosotras **os veis**
él/ella/usted **se ve**	ellos/ellas/ustedes **se ven**

Choose an irregular or stem-changing reflexive verb to complete each of the following sentences. Here's an example:

Q. Él _____ de sus padres.

A. se atiene

21. Yo _____ de comer chocolate durante la estación de Lent.

22. Nosotros _____ mucho en la fiesta.

23. Cuando yo uso un espejo _____.

24. Ella _____ de su chiste.

25. Yo _____ la ropa antes de comprarla.

26. Él no _____ bien.

27. Roberto _____ muy temprano todos los días para ir a su trabajo.

28. Los estudiantes _____ al maestro para una explicación de la lección.

29. De vez en cuando ellos _____ de comer carne.

30. Ustedes _____ en las sillas cuando entran en la clase.

Understanding the Uses of Reflexive Verbs

Knowing *how* to form reflexive constructions (which I explain in the preceding sections) is only half of what you need to know. You also need to know *when* to use the reflexive. The following sections explain the various uses of the reflexive so you know when to call it into action.

Describing actions of personal care and habitual routines

Reflexive verbs often describe actions of personal care or actions performed as a part of a habitual routine. When you bathe (yourself), shower (yourself), dress (yourself), and shave (yourself), you're doing actions to . . . well . . . yourself. In English, you don't usually use the reflexive pronouns in such expressions unless you want to emphasize that you're the one who performed the action. So instead of saying, *I bathed myself, I showered myself,* or *I dressed myself,* you'd simply say, *I took a bath*, *I took a shower*, or *I got dressed.*

Note: In English, you use possessive adjectives when you talk about what is being washed, combed, or whatever, as in *I comb my hair every morning.* In Spanish, you use the definite articles (**el**, **la**, **los**, or **las**).

First decide whether you should use the reflexive or nonreflexive form of the following verbs to complete these sentences. Then conjugate the verbs appropriately. Here's an example:

Q. Luisa _____ (acostar/acostarse) en la cama.

A. se acuesta

31. Yo _____ (preparar/prepararse) la comida.

32. Ellos _____ (levantar/levantarse) temprano.

33. Tú _____ (llamar/llamarse) Susi.

34. La madre _____ (acostar/acostarse) a los niños a las ocho.

35. Él _____ (ver/verse) en el espejo.

36. Ella _____ (maquillar/maquillarse) al payaso.

37. Luisa _____ (lavar/lavarse) el carro.

38. Ustedes _____ (cortar/cortarse) las uñas.

39. Diego _____ (bañar/bañarse) al perro.

40. Nosotros _____ (probar/probarse) el pastel.

Becoming with the reflexive construction

Several reflexive verbs express becoming. For example, **hacerse, ponerse,** and **volverse** all translate as *to become.* Each of these verbs has a subtle difference in meaning and requires a specific use:

✔ **Hacerse** used with a noun or an adjective expresses attainment of a social status or a profession that requires considerable effort, as in this example:

  Se puede hacerse una juez. (*You can become a judge.*)

✔ **Ponerse** used with an adjective expresses a change in an emotional or physical state, as in the following example:

  Ella se pone nerviosa cuando tiene que hablar enfrente del grupo. (*She becomes nervous when she has to speak in front of the group.*)

✔ **Volverse** used with an adjective expresses an involuntary and sudden change, as in this example:

  Él se vuelve loco cuando no le permiten ver a sus niños. (*He goes crazy when they don't permit him to see his children.*)

Using the reflexive to change a verb's meaning

Many verbs retain their meaning whether you use them reflexively or nonreflexively, as in the following examples:

  Lavo los platos. (*I wash the dishes.*)

  Me lavo las manos. (*I wash my hands.*)

In cases like this, the reflexive use merely points out that the subject and the object are the same.

However, some verbs change their meaning significantly in the reflexive, as in these examples:

  Los estudiantes ponen los libros en los escritorios. (*The students put the books on the desks.*)

  Ella se pone contenta cuando recibe una buena nota. (*She is [becomes] happy when she gets a good grade.*)

The following verbs change their meaning significantly when you use them reflexively:

Nonreflexive	*Reflexive*
acordar (*to agree*)	**acordarse** (*to remember*)
colocar (*to place*)	**colocarse** (*to get a job*)
llevar (*to take, to carry*)	**llevarse con** (*to get along with [someone]*)
negar (*to deny*)	**negarse** (*to refuse*)
poner (*to put*)	**ponerse** (*to become [profession]*)
preparar (*to prepare*)	**prepararse** (*to get ready*)
volver (*to return*)	**volverse** (*to become*)

Acting on each other: Expressing reciprocal actions with the reflexive form

The reflexive enables you to describe reciprocal actions between or among people, animals, and objects. In such cases, use the plural forms of the reflexive conjugations, as in the following examples:

> **Yolanda y yo nos ayudamos.** (*Yolanda and I help each other.*)

> **Mis gatos se pelean de vez en cuando.** (*My cats fight each other once in a while.*)

When the context needs clarification, use the reflexive conjugations with the phrases **el uno con el otro, la una con la otra, los unos con los otros,** and **las unas con las otras** (*with each other*) or **mutuamente** (*mutually*) to indicate reciprocal action, as in the following examples:

> **Nunca se enfadan el uno con el otro.** (*They are never upset with each other.*)

> **Siempre nos peleamos los unos con los otros.** (*We always fight with each other.*)

> **Se ayudan mutuamente.** (*They help each other.*)

Answer Key

1 se

2 nos

3 me

4 se

5 te

6 se

7 se

8 os

9 se

10 nos

11 Ellos se bañan por la noche.

12 Él se corta las uñas después de bañarse.

13 Nosotros nos levantamos tarde los sábados.

14 Él se quita la ropa antes de ducharse.

15 Ustedes se afeitan después de ducharse.

16 Ella se pinta los labios por la mañana.

17 Yo me maquillo todos los días.

18 Tú te peinas mucho.

19 A veces ella se lima las uñas.

20 Nosotros nos cepillamos los dientes después de comer.

21 me abstengo

22 nos divertimos

23 me veo

24 se ríe

25 **me pruebo**

26 **se siente**

27 **se despierta**

28 **se atienen**

29 **se abstienen**

30 **se sientan**

31 **preparo**

32 **se levantan**

33 **te llamas**

34 **acuesta**

35 **se ve**

36 **maquilla**

37 **lava**

38 **se cortan**

39 **baña**

40 **probamos**

Chapter 15

Using the Passive Voice

Grammatically speaking, *voice* indicates the relationship between the subject of the verb and the action that the verb expresses. English and Spanish both have an active voice and a passive voice:

✔ In *active voice,* the subject of the sentence performs the action. Here's an example: **El chico lava el carro.** (*The boy washes the car.*) In this sentence, the subject, **el chico** (*the boy*), does the action, **lava** (*washes*), to the direct object, **el carro** (*the car*).

✔ In *passive voice,* the subject of the sentence receives the action, and the doer of the action typically remains a mystery. Here's an example: **El carro es lavado.** (*The car is washed.*) In this sentence, **el carro** is the subject of the sentence, but you don't know who washed the car. Thus, passive voice draws attention away from the *agent* — the person or thing that's performing the action.

This chapter introduces you to the passive voice in Spanish and explains how and when to use it.

Setting Up Passive Voice with Ser

To use the passive voice in Spanish, you need to know how to form it and how to identify the agent, assuming, of course, that you want to identify the agent. In the following sections, I show you how to form passive constructions with and without a specified agent of action, using the verb **ser** (*to be*). (See the later section "Forming Passive Constructions with **Se**" for details on a slightly different method.)

Forming the passive voice with ser and a past participle

The formula for forming the passive voice with the verb **ser** looks like this:

subject + conjugated form of **ser** + past participle of action verb = passive voice

You start with the conjugated form of the verb **ser** (*to be*) that agrees with the subject in person and number. Here's an example: **Todos los animales son alimentados.** (*All of the animals are fed.*) In this sentence, the subject is **todos los animales**, which is third person plural (*they*), so the correct form of **ser** is **son,** as shown in the following table. (For more about conjugating **ser** in the present tense, see Chapter 7.)

ser (*to be*)	
yo **soy**	nosotros/nosotras **somos**
tú **eres**	vosotros/vosotras **sois**
él/ella/usted **es**	ellos/ellas/ustedes **son**

Note: For simplicity's sake, I focus on the present tense here, but the passive voice is most often expressed in the preterit (past) and future tenses. To find out how to conjugate **ser** in the past tense, see Chapter 18. For information on how to conjugate regular **-er** verbs in the future (which is what **ser** is in the future), see Chapter 20.

After you get the right form of **ser**, you have to add the past participle of the action verb. To form the past participle, follow these guidelines (and see Chapter 21 for details):

- ✔ For regular **-ar** verbs, drop the **-ar** and add **-ado**. For example, **alimentar** (*to feed*) becomes **alimentado** (*fed*).

- ✔ For **-er** and **-ir** verbs, drop the **-er** or **-ir** and add **-ido**. For example, **comer** (*to eat*) becomes **comido** (*eaten*).

The past participle functions as an adjective that describes the subject, so it has to agree with the subject in gender (masculine or feminine) and number (singular or plural). Consider the example we use at the beginning of this section: **Todos los animales son alimentados.** (*All of the animals are fed.*) Because the subject **todos los animales** (*all of the animals*) is masculine plural, **alimentado** must also be masculine plural — **alimentados**. (For more about using past participles as adjectives, check out Chapter 4.)

Here are some more examples of using **ser** and a past participle to form the passive voice:

> **El edificio es construido.** (*The building is built.*)
>
> **El carro es arreglado.** (*The car is repaired.*)
>
> **Las pólizas de seguro son vendidas.** (*The insurance policies are sold.*)

Using the subjects and past participles provided, write sentences in the passive voice to express what is occurring. Here's an example:

Q. el auto/reparar

A. El auto es reparado.

1. los estudiantes/despedir

2. los papeles/entregar

_____

3. el informe/fichar

_____

4. la casa/construir

_____

5. el desayuno/servir

_____

6. los refrescos/beber

_____

7. el cumpleaños/celebrar

_____

8. la computadora/usar

_____

9. el fútbol/jugar

_____

10. la cena/comer

_____

Expressing an agent with por

The passive voice enables you to form a complete sentence when you don't know or don't want to mention the (secret) agent. When you want to add an agent to a sentence in the passive voice, you have to create an *agent phrase* that starts with the preposition **por** (*by*). A passive voice sentence that includes an agent phrase contains the following elements:

subject + conjugated form of **ser** + past participle of action verb + **por** + agent

In the following examples, I've added an agent phrase to the examples from the preceding section:

Todos los animales son alimentados por los visitantes. (*All of the animals are fed by the visitors.*)

El edificio es construido por los obreros. (*The building is built by the workers.*)

El carro es arreglado por el mecánico. (*The car is repaired by the mechanic.*)

Las pólizas de seguro son vendidas por el agente. (*The insurance policies are sold by the agent.*)

Rewrite the following sentences in the passive voice. Use the present tense of the verb **ser.** Be sure to introduce the agent with the preposition **por.** Here's an example:

0. Susana lava el carro.

A. El carro es lavado por Susana.

11. Ellos construyen la casa.

_____

12. La peluquera peina su pelo.

_____

13. La maestra da los exámenes.

_____

14. Los estudiantes entregan la tarea.

_____

15. Carmen da a comer a su gato.

_____

16. Paco camina a su perro.

_____

17. Los mecánicos reparan los camiones.

_____

18. Mi madre prepara la cena.

_____

19. El policía detiene al hombre.

_____

20. El artista dibuja el retrato.

_____

Forming Passive Constructions with Se

In addition to using the verb **ser** (as I explain earlier in this chapter), Spanish has another way to form a passive construction; it uses the reflexive pronoun **se** (*himself, herself, yourself*). You can use **se** to form both passive voice constructions and impersonal voice expressions (which use vague agents like *one*), as I explain in the following sections. (Check out Chapter 14 for an introduction to reflexive pronouns.)

Creating the passive voice with se

To use **se** to create the passive voice, just follow this simple formula:

> reflexive pronoun **se** + third person singular form of verb = passive voice

Here are a couple of examples of the passive construction with **se**. Notice that you just add the *direct object* (the thing or person being acted upon) after the verb.

> **Se repara el carro**. (*The car is being repaired.*)
>
> **Se sirve el almuerzo a las dos**. (*Lunch is being served at 2:00.*)

Whether you use **ser** plus the past participle (as I describe earlier in this chapter) or **se** plus the third person singular form of the verb to form the passive voice is up to you. For example, the following two sentences mean exactly the same thing:

> **La cena es preparada.** (*The dinner is being prepared.*)
>
> **Se prepara la cena.** (*The dinner is being prepared.*)

The only time you have to use one form over the other is when you want to specify an agent. To specify an agent, you must use the **ser** + past participle + **por** + agent construction; check out the earlier section "Expressing an agent with **por**" for details. You can't specify an agent with the **se** passive construction.

Convert the following sentences into the passive construction with **se**. Here's an example:

0. **El carro es lavado.**

A. **Se lava el carro.**

21. **El hotel es construido.**

_____

22. **La película es mirada.**

_____

23. Los libros son leídos.

_____

24. La casa es limpiada.

_____

25. El caballo es montado.

_____

26. El niño es bañado.

_____

27. Los camiones son pintados.

_____

28. El sandwich es preparado.

_____

29. El ladrón es detenido.

_____

30. La música es escuchada.

_____

Forming expressions in the impersonal voice

The _impersonal voice_ is sort of a cross between active voice and passive voice. With the impersonal voice, you specify an agent of action, but the agent is vague. In English, you find the impersonal voice in expressions like the following:

> _One never knows when guests will arrive._
>
> _They say the economy will turn around soon._
>
> _It is said that opening an umbrella inside brings bad luck._

Note: In English, impersonal expressions often contain the expression _one_, such as "_One never knows when they will show up._"

In Spanish, you form the impersonal voice by using the reflexive pronoun **se** and the third person singular conjugation of the verb to say that something is done (or was done or will be done). Here are some examples of impersonal expressions in Spanish:

No se fuma aquí. (*One does not smoke here.*)

Se está mejor aquí. (*One is better off here.*)

Se entra por aquí. (*One goes in this way.*)

In impersonal expressions, the Spanish **se** is equivalent to the English *one*. The impersonal **se** refers to an unidentified human agent. It uses only intransitive verbs and objectless transitive verbs, as in **En Francia se come mucho** (*In France one eats a lot*). The sentence doesn't mention what one eats. Also, the verb is always singular in the impersonal voice.

Considering the Uses of Passive Voice

In Spanish, you generally use active voice for everyday communication. But journalists, doctors, scientists, lawyers, and politicians often use passive voice when they write official documents and articles that appear in magazines, journals, or newspapers.

The most common uses of passive voice are

✔ **To express an action whose subject is unknown:** When you don't know who performed an action, the passive voice comes in very handy. You can simply state that a particular action happened to a specific person or thing. You don't have to worry about stating who or what performed the action. Here are a couple of examples:

  Las ventanas son cerradas. (*The windows are closed.*)

  El paquete es entregado. (*The package is delivered.*)

✔ **To be tactful or act to your advantage:** Sometimes you may know (or suspect) who did an action, but you want to be tactful about the situation and not mention the person by name. In other cases, not mentioning who performed the action that you're talking about may be to your advantage. In situations like these, you can simply use the passive voice without mentioning the agent, as in the following examples:

  Sus primos son invitados. (*His cousins are invited.*)

  Los votos son contados. (*The votes are counted.*)

✔ **To emphasize an action over an actor:** When you know the agent but you want to emphasize the action or whatever has been acted upon, you can use the passive voice to place the recipient of the action and the action first in the sentence. Just remember to use the preposition **por** (*by*) to introduce the agent (see the earlier section "Expressing an agent with **por**" for details). Here are some examples:

  La cuenta es pagada por el jefe. (*The bill is paid by the boss.*)

  Las casas son vendidas por los agentes. (*The houses are sold by the agents.*)

  La comida es donada por la iglesia. (*The food is donated by the church.*)

Answer Key

1. Los estudiantes son despedidos.

2. Los papeles son entregados.

3. El informe es fichado.

4. La casa es construida.

5. El desayuno es servido.

6. Los refrescos son bebidos.

7. El cumpleaños es celebrado.

8. La computadora es usada.

9. El fútbol es jugado.

10. La cena es comida.

11. La casa es construida por ellos.

12. Su pelo es peinado por la peluquera.

13. Los exámenes son dados por la maestra.

14. La tarea es entregada por los estudiantes.

15. Su gato es dado a comer por Carmen.

16. Su perro es caminado por Paco.

17. Los camiones son reparados por los mecánicos.

18. La cena es preparada por mi madre.

19. El hombre es detenido por el policía.

20. El retrato es dibujado por el artista.

21. Se construye el hotel.

22. Se mira la película.

23. Se leen los libros.

24. Se limpia la casa.

25 Se monta el caballo.

26 Se baña al niño.

27 Se pintan los camiones.

28 Se prepara el sandwich.

29 Se detiene al ladrón.

30 Se escucha la música.

Chapter 16

It's All Relative: Making Comparisons

....

In This Chapter

▶ Making comparisons of unequal and equal things

▶ Describing the best and the brightest with superlatives

▶ Using irregular comparatives

....

Rarely are people, places, and things exactly the same. Most of the time one place is more beautiful than another, one person is nicer than another, or a particular restaurant is better than all the rest. To make these distinctions — however significant or insignificant they may seem — you have to make comparisons. You already compare things in English without even thinking about what you're doing, and you can make comparisons in Spanish just as easily because the approach is very similar.

In Chapter 4, I explain how to describe people, places, and things with adjectives. In Chapter 12, I explain how to make comparisons with adverbs, such as **es muy rápido** (*he's fast*), **corre más rápido** (*she runs faster*), and **yo corro el más rápido** (*I run the fastest*). In this chapter, I pull everything together to give you even more ways to describe what you see and do.

Expressing Comparisons of Inequality

When you want to say that one thing or person has more or less of some quality than another, you need to use comparisons of inequality. I explain how to do so in the following sections.

Saying "more than" or "less than"

In English, when things or people are different, you often describe their differences with phrases like *more than* or *less than,* as in the following sentences:

She is more generous than her brother.

That car costs less than this one.

In other cases, English adds *-er* to adjectives to make comparisons of inequality, as in these examples:

He's taller than his father.

I'm shorter than he is.

They're richer than we are.

That house is bigger than ours.

In Spanish, you form comparisons of inequality in two ways:

- **más** + adjective + **que** (*more* + adjective + *than*)

    Ella es más alta que él. (*She is taller than him.*) (Literally: *She is more tall than he.*)

- **menos** + adjective + **que** (*less* + adjective + *than*)

    Él es menos alto que ella. (*He is shorter than her.*) (Literally: *He is less tall than she.*)

When you create comparisons of inequality, make sure that the adjective you use agrees in number and gender with the noun it modifies. See Chapter 4 for the full scoop on making adjectives agree in gender and number with the nouns they modify.

Complete the following sentences by conjugating the verb in parentheses and using a comparative of *more than* with the adjective given, as shown in the following example:

0. Tomás _____ (ser/rico) yo.

A. es más rico que

1. Los hijos _____ (ser/alto) sus padres.

2. Yo _____ (ser/listo) mi hermano.

3. Felipa _____ (ser/rápido) Alicia.

4. Alejandra y Raúl _____ (ser/inteligente) los otros estudiantes.

5. Nosotros _____ (ser/atlético) ustedes.

6. Este vestido _____ (ser/caro) el otro.

7. Los estudiantes en su clase _____ (ser/estudioso) los estudiantes en la otra clase.

8. En Francia las personas _____ (ser/hablador) las personas de los Estados Unidos.

9. Carlos come mucho, y por eso _____ (ser/grande) sus otros hermanos.

10. Vosotros no trabajáis muchas horas, y por eso _____ (ser/pobre) los otros empleados.

Complete the following sentences by conjugating the verb in parentheses and using a comparative of *less than* with the adjective given, as shown in the following example:

0. Carmen _____ (ser/alto) Teresa.

A. es menos alta que

11. Ellas _____ (ser/amable) mis amigas.

12. Rosa _____ (ser/trabajador) su hermano.

13. Esta blusa _____ (ser/caro) la otra.

14. En Miami _____ (ser/peligroso) en Chicago.

15. Sus hermanas _____ (ser/agradable) que ella.

16. Sus padres _____ (ser/divertido) ella.

17. Esa motocicleta _____ (ser/rápido) mi coche.

18. Nosotros _____ (ser/peleador) ellos.

19. Yo _____ (ser/pesimista) ella.

20. Los estudiantes en aquella clase _____ (ser/interesante) que los estudiantes en mi clase.

Including numbers

If you want to follow a comparison of inequality with a number (as in, *more than four*), use **de** rather than **que**. Here are a couple of examples:

> **Hay más de treinta estudiantes en la clase.** (*There are more than thirty students in the class.*)

> **El libro tiene menos de cien páginas.** (*The book has fewer than one hundred pages.*)

However, when a comparison that uses numbers is negative (as in, *no more than four*), use **que**. Here are two examples:

> **No hay más que veinte estudiantes en la clase.** (*There are no more than twenty students in the class.*)

> **No hay menos que cien páginas en el libro.** (*There are no fewer than one hundred pages in the book.*)

Translate the following sentences, which all have comparisons of inequality with numbers, into Spanish, as shown in the example:

Q. *She has more than five children.*

A. **Ella tiene más de cinco hijos.**

21. *There are no more than thirty students in the class.*

_____

22. *She has less than two hours to spend with us.*

_____

23. *He has no more than five dollars for his lunch.*

_____

24. *José speaks more than ten languages.*

_____

25. *Virginia is more than eighty years old.*

_____

26. *We have more than three cars.*

_____

27. *The workers don't have more than two breaks a day.*

_____

28. *They earn more than eight hundred dollars per week.*

_____

29. *The zoo doesn't have more than two elephants.*

_____

30. *Her garden has more than a hundred flowers.*

_____

Making Comparisons of Equality

Sometimes you may want to compare things and people by finding ways in which they're similar to one another. To compare things that have equal characteristics, you use *comparisons of equality,* such as in the following English examples:

> *That movie is as good as the one we saw last weekend.*
>
> *She is as smart as her brother.*

In Spanish, you form comparisons of equality by using the following formula:

> **Tan** + adjective + **como** (*as* + adjective + *as*)

Here are some examples:

> **Él es tan cómico como su padre.** (*He is as funny as his father.*)
>
> **Ella es tan alta como su hermano.** (*She is as tall as her brother.*)
>
> **Ellos son tan astutos como nosotros.** (*They are as astute as us.*)

As in comparisons of inequality (which I describe earlier in this chapter), make sure that the adjectives you use agree in number and gender with the nouns they modify. See Chapter 4 for details.

For each pair of nouns, write a sentence to compare them by using a comparison of equality with the adjective given in parentheses. See the following example:

0. **ella/su hermana (bonito)**

A. **Ella es tan bonita como su hermana.**

31. **Cecilia/Carolina (atlético)**

_____

32. **ellos/Marta (paciente)**

_____

33. **Luisa/Diego (artístico)**

_____

34. **Mateo/su hermano (generoso)**

_____

35. **vosotros/ellos (impaciente)**

_____

36. **mis amigos/yo (divertido)**

_____

37. **los otros estudiantes/tú (popular)**

_____

38. **las chicas/los chicos (cómico)**

_____

39. **él/Sarita (tímido)**

_____

40. **Magda y Sofía/Sergio y Pablo (orgulloso)**

_____

Rising to the Highest Degree with Superlatives

When something is the best or worst in its class, you have to take the adjective to the *superlative,* or extreme, degree. To express the superlative in English, you can do one of three things:

✔ Add *-est* to the adjective, as in the following examples:

> *She's the fastest runner in the school.*
>
> *He's the smartest student in the class.*

✔ Put *most* in front of the adjective, as in the following examples:

> *He's the most popular student in the class.*
>
> *They're the most entertaining comedians in the club.*

✔ Put *least* in front of the adjective, as shown in the following examples:

> *They are the least funny comedians in the club.*
>
> *It is the least expensive ring in the store.*

In Spanish, you generally form the superlative of an adjective by putting **el más**, **la más**, **los más**, or **las más** (*the most*) in front of it. Or if you're describing the least in its class, you use **el menos**, **la menos**, **los menos**, or **las menos** (*the least*) in front of the adjective. You determine which article (**el, la, los,** or **las**) to use in front of **más** or **menos** based on the number and gender of the noun being modified. The following examples show both types of superlative:

> **Él es el más inteligente de todos.** (*He is the most intelligent of all.*)
>
> **Ellos son los más rápidos del grupo.** (*They are the fastest of the group.*)
>
> **Ella es la menos habladora de su familia.** (*She is the least talkative of her family.*)
>
> **Ellas son las menos capaces de la oficina.** (*They are the least capable in the office.*)

You can also form the superlative in Spanish by using the following constructions:

noun + **más** + adjective + **de(l)** + noun

noun + **menos** + adjective + **de(l)** + noun

Here are two examples:

> **Es el día más frío del invierno.** (*It is the coldest day of the winter.*)
>
> **Es la clase menos popular de la escuela.** (*It is the least popular class at the school.*)

Translate the following superlatives into Spanish, as in the following example:

0. *He is the <u>strongest</u> in the country.*

> **Él es el _____ del país.**

A. **más fuerte**

41. *They are the <u>most popular</u> students in the school.*

Ellos son los estudiantes _____ de la escuela.

42. *It is the <u>fastest</u> car in the race.*

Es el carro _____ en la carrera.

43. *Those flowers are the <u>most beautiful</u> in the garden.*

Esas flores son las _____ del jardín.

44. *She is the <u>shyest</u> girl in the class.*

Ella es la chica _____ de la clase.

45. *He is the <u>least interesting</u> boy in the group.*

Él es el chico _____ del grupo.

46. *January is the <u>coldest</u> month in winter.*

Enero es el mes _____ del invierno.

47. *They have the <u>strongest</u> bulls in all of Spain.*

Ellos tienen los toros _____ de España.

48. *It is the <u>biggest</u> mall in North America.*

Es el centro comercial _____ de Norteamérica.

49. *It is the <u>least popular</u> book in the store.*

Es el libro _____ de la tienda.

50. *They have the <u>fiercest</u> dog in the neighborhood.*

Ellos tienen el perro _____ del barrio.

Investigating Irregular Comparatives

Generally speaking, when making comparatives in Spanish, you simply say that something is more or less a certain way than something else. A few adjectives, however, don't follow these rules and have irregular comparative forms, as you find out in the following sections.

Going from good to best and from bad to worst

The following list shows you how to form the comparative and superlative with **bueno** and **malo**:

Adjective	Comparative Form	Superlative Form
bueno (*good*)	**mejor** (*better*)	**el/la mejor** and **los/las mejores** (*the best*)
malo (*bad*)	**peor** (*worse*)	**el/la peor** and **los/las peores** (*the worst*)

Here are some examples:

> **Juan es un buen jugador.** (*Juan is a good player.*)
>
> **Jacinto es mejor que Juan.** (*Jacinto is better than Juan.*)
>
> **Pancho es el mejor.** (*Pancho is the best.*)
>
> **Antonia es una mala estudiante.** (*Antonia is a bad student.*)
>
> **Benjamín es un estudiante peor que Antonia.** (*Benjamín is a worse student than Antonia.*)
>
> **Margarita es la peor estudiante.** (*Margarita is the worst student.*)

Note: When you use **bueno** in front of a masculine singular noun, you drop the **o**, as shown in the first example in the preceding list. The same goes for **malo;** when you use **malo** in front of a masculine singular noun, you drop the **o**. When using **bueno** and **malo** with plural nouns, they must also agree in number and gender with the noun they're modifying, such as in these examples:

> **Ellos son malos estudiantes.** (*They are bad students.*)
>
> **Ellas son buenas cantantes.** (*They are good singers.*)

Describing age

In Spanish, if you want to compare people's ages, you use the adjectives **mayor** (*older*) and **menor** (*younger*) and their superlative forms **el/la mayor** and **los/las mayores** (*oldest*) and **el/la menor** and **los/las menores** (*youngest*). See the following examples:

> **Mi hermano es mayor que mi hermana.** (*My brother is older than my sister.*)
>
> **Yo soy menor que mi hermana.** (*I am younger than my sister.*)
>
> **Mi padre es mayor que mi madre.** (*My father is older than my mother.*)
>
> **Mi madre es mayor que mi tía.** (*My mother is older than my aunt.*)
>
> **Mi abuelo es el mayor.** (*My grandfather is the oldest.*)

Using a special suffix to express "really"

You can turn any adjective into the absolute best in its class by adding the suffix **-ísimo** to the end of the adjective. This suffix adds the idea of *really* to the adjective. Check out the examples in the following list. (Note that if an adjective ends in **o** or **a,** you drop that letter before you add **-ísimo** and you change **c** to **qu**, **g** to **gu**, and **z** to **c**.)

Adjective	*Adjective + Really*
caro (*expensive*)	**carísimo** (*really expensive*)
grande (*big*)	**grandísimo** (*really big*)
popular (*popular*)	**popularísimo** (*really popular*)
rico (*tasty, delicious*)	**riquísimo** (*really tasty, really delicious*)
largo (*long*)	**larguísimo** (*really long*)
feliz (*happy*)	**felicísimo** (*really happy*)

When you add **-ísimo** (*really*) to adjectives to create the superlative form, make sure that the adjectives match the nouns they modify in gender and number, as in the following examples:

Miguel es popularísimo. (*Miguel is really popular.*)

Su madre es hermosísima. (*Their mother is really beautiful.*)

Rosa y Silvia son elegantísimas. (*Rosa and Silvia are really elegant.*)

Answer Key

1 son mas altos que

2 soy más listo que

3 es más rápida que

4 son más inteligentes que

5 somos más atléticos que

6 es más caro que

7 son más estudiosos que

8 son más habladoras que

9 es más grande que

10 sois más pobres que

11 son menos amables que

12 es menos trabajadora que

13 es menos cara que

14 es menos peligroso que

15 son menos agradables que

16 son menos divertidos que

17 es menos rápida que

18 somos menos peleadores que

19 soy menos pesimista que

20 son menos interesantes que

21 No hay más que treinta estudiantes en la clase.

22 Ella tiene menos de dos horas a pasar con nosotros.

23 Él no tiene más que cinco dólares para su almuerzo.

24 José habla más de diez lenguajes.

25 Virginia tiene más de ochenta años.

26 Nosotros tenemos más de tres carros.

27 Los obreros no tienen más que dos pausas al día.

28 Ellos ganan más de ochocientos dólares por semana.

29 El zoológico no tiene más que dos elefantes.

30 Su jardín tiene más de cien flores.

31 Cecilia es tan atlética como Carolina.

32 Ellos son tan pacientes como Marta.

33 Luisa es tan artística como Diego.

34 Mateo es tan generoso como su hermano.

35 Vosotros sois tan impacientes como ellos.

36 Mis amigos son tan divertidos como yo.

37 Los otros estudiantes son tan populares como tú.

38 Las chicas son tan cómicas como los chicos.

39 Él es tan tímido como Sarita.

40 Magda y Sofía son tan orgullosas como Sergio y Pablo.

41 más populares

42 más rápido

43 más hermosas

44 más tímida

45 menos interesante

46 más frío

47 más fuertes

48 más grande

49 menos popular

50 más feroz

Chapter 17

Just Say "No": Negative Words and Expressions

● ●

In This Chapter

▶ Checking out some commonly used negative words and expressions

▶ Recognizing differences in the ways English and Spanish use the negative

● ●

No matter how positive you are, you can't always say **sí** (*yes*). For instance, scheduling conflicts may require that you say **no** (*no*) to certain invitations. Similarly, if you're just wandering around and someone asks you where you're going, you may answer with **a ninguna parte** (*nowhere*). The fact is even if you're a positive person, you still need to use negative words and expressions from time to time. Case in point: What's bothering you? **¡Nada!** (*Nothing!*)

In this chapter, I introduce you to these and other negative words and expressions and reveal the differences between negative usage in English and Spanish.

Introducing Negative Words and Expressions

The best way to begin your exploration of the negative is by warming up with a few commonly used negative words and expressions. In the following sections, I introduce you to numerous negative words and expressions to get you up to speed in a hurry.

Naming the negative words and putting them to use

Like English, Spanish has several negative words that are essentially the opposite of their positive counterparts. Table 17-1 provides a list of commonly used negative words along with their positive counterparts.

Table 17-1	Negative Words and Their Corresponding Affirmatives		
Negative	*English*	**Affirmative**	*English*
no	*no, not*	**sí**	*yes*
nada	*nothing*	**algo**	*something*
nadie	*no one, nobody*	**alguien**	*someone, somebody*
ninguno(s)/ninguna(s)	*no, no one, not any*	**alguno(s)/alguna(s)**	*any, some*
ni . . . ni	*neither . . . nor, not . . . nor*	**o . . . o**	*either . . . or*
nunca, jamás	*never, not ever*	**siempre**	*always*
tampoco	*not either, neither*	**también**	*also*

The easiest and most common way to make a negative declaration is to add **no** before the verb of the positive expression, as in these examples:

> **Juan abre su libro.** (*Juan is opening his book.*)
>
> **Juan no abre su libro.** (*Juan is not opening his book.*)
>
> **El bebé duerme.** (*The baby is sleeping.*)
>
> **El bebé no duerme.** (*The baby is not sleeping.*)

Negative words can also be adjectives, such as **ninguno/ninguna** (*none*), pronouns, such as **nadie** (*no one, nobody*), adverbs, such as **nunca** (*never*), and conjunctions, such as **ni . . . ni** (*neither . . . nor*), as you can see in the following examples:

> **No tengo ninguna moneda.** (*I don't have any change.*)
>
> **No viene nadie.** (*Nobody is coming.*)
>
> **Ella no trabaja nunca.** (*She never works.*)
>
> **No voy a llamar ni ahora ni nunca.** (*I'm not going to call either now or ever.*)

Keep these usage rules in mind when you use negative words:

✔ In Spanish, you can place negative words before or after the verb. If they go after the verb, add **no** before the verb. English considers this a double negative (and strict grammarians will slap you with a ruler for committing such offenses), but Spanish requires it. (Go figure!) See the later section "Pointing Out the Differences between Spanish and English Negatives" for more details.

✔ Don't use the word **no** by itself to negate a noun in Spanish. To negate a noun, you must use a form of the word **ninguno** (*not any*), as in the following examples:

> **Correct: No tengo ningún dinero.** (*I don't have any money.*)
>
> **Incorrect: Tengo no dinero.** (*I have no money.*)

✔ Use **ninguno/ninguna** to say *none, not (a single) one.* You usually use **ninguno/ninguna** in its singular form, and it must match the noun it's describing in gender and number. It can also stand alone or go in front of a noun. When using **ninguno** before a masculine singular noun, you must change it to **ningún**. For example:

> **Ningunos de los estudiantes tiene su libro.** (*Not one of the students have their book.*)

> **Él no tiene ningún dólar.** (*He doesn't have a single dollar.*)

✔ Use the personal **a** in front of **nadie** when **nadie** is a direct object and in front of any form of **ninguno** when it refers to people who are direct objects. For example:

> **Él no invita a nadie al baile.** (*He's not inviting anyone to the dance.*)

> **Ella no llama a ningunos muchachos.** (*She doesn't call any boys.*)

Complete each sentence by using one of the negative words from Table 17-1, as in the following example:

0. _____ **cartas llegaron hoy.**

A. **Ningunas**

1. **No hay _____ problema.**

2. **_____ representa ese país.**

3. **No hay _____ representante de nuestra unión aquí.**

4. **Ella no tiene _____ vacaciones _____ permiso por enfermedad.**

5. **No hay _____ quien puede ayudar.**

6. **No hacen _____ los domingos.**

7. **Vosotros no usáis salsa picante para _____.**

8. **No hay _____ trenes a esta hora de la noche.**

9. **No me permiten comentario acerca de _____.**

10. **Los estudiantes no tienen _____ proyectos _____ presentaciones este semestre.**

Identifying some common negative expressions

In addition to its robust collection of negative words (see the preceding section), Spanish features a host of negative idiomatic expressions, made up of two or more words (one of which is a negative word). Table 17-2 lists some of the most common negative expressions.

Table 17-2	Negative Expressions
Spanish	*English*
ahora no	*not now*
apenas	*scarcely, hardly*
de ninguna manera	*no way, by no means*
de ningún modo	*no way, by no means*
en ninguna parte	*nowhere*
en/por ningún lado/sitio/lugar	*nowhere*
ni hablar	*no way*
ni (él/ella) tampoco	*nor (he/she) either*
ni siquiera	*not even*
no en absoluto	*absolutely not*
no más de (followed by a number)	*no more than (followed by a number)*
no más que (followed by a verb infinitive)	*only (followed by a verb infinitive)*
no sólo . . . sino también . . .	*not only . . . but also . . .*
nunca, no en mi vida	*never in my life*
nunca jamás	*never ever (emphatic!)*
nunca más	*never again*
todavía no	*still not, not yet*
sin novedad	*nothing new*
ya no	*no longer*

Use the negative expressions in Table 17-2 exactly as shown. After all, they're *idiomatic*, which means each phrase conveys a meaning that differs from the collection of words that makes it up. Here are some examples of these negative expressions in action:

> **Nunca en mi vida esperaba ver tal cosa.** (*I never in my life expected to see such a thing.*)
>
> **Nunca más hablaré con él.** (*I will never again speak to him.*)
>
> **Ya no vamos a ir.** (*We're no longer going to go.*)
>
> **Todavía no han llegado.** (*They still have not arrived.*)
>
> **No más que veinte personas vinieron.** (*No more than twenty people came.*)

With the help of an English-Spanish dictionary if needed, translate the following negative statements into Spanish. Here's an example:

Q. *She no longer works for him.*

A. **Ella ya no trabaja para él.**

11. *They are never again going to eat in that restaurant.*

_____

12. *No more than three books can be checked out from the library at a time.*

_____

13. *I am never ever going to talk with them again.*

_____

14. *They still don't have his present.*

_____

15. *Not only does she sing, but she also dances.*

_____

16. *Not even one answer is wrong.*

_____

17. *Not only is he stingy, but he's also rude.*

_____

18. *Susana is not going either.*

_____

19. *They can't find the keys anywhere (nowhere).*

_____

20. *I don't have enough money, not even to buy a hamburger.*

_____

Piecing together your sentences with pero and sino

Both **pero** and **sino** are coordinating conjunctions that connect two words or phrases with similar grammatical functions. They both essentially mean *but* and can be used to contrast two words, sentences, or phrases. However, **sino** means something more like *rather, but rather,* or *instead,* and they differ subtly in usage:

✔ Use **pero** to follow a positive statement with a statement that undermines the positive statement, as in the following examples:

> **Me gustaría hacer la tarea ahora, pero tengo que esperar hasta más tarde.** (*I would prefer to do the assignment now, but I have to wait until later.*)

> **Alejandro es simpático, pero a veces es tacaño.** (*Alejandro is nice, but sometimes he is stingy.*)

> **Nosotros queremos salir hoy, pero ella dice que no puede salir hasta mañana.** (*We want to leave today, but she says that she can't leave until tomorrow.*)

✔ Use **sino** to open with a negative statement and follow up with a positive statement that clarifies the opening statement in the positive, as in the following examples:

> **No vengo a comer, sino visitar.** (*I'm not coming to eat, but rather to visit.*)

> **Ella no es baja, sino alta.** (*She is not short, but rather she is tall.*)

> **Él no es el presidente del club, sino el vicepresidente.** (*He is not the president of the club, but rather the vice president.*)

✔ Use **sino que** to contrast two conjugated verbs in your sentence, as in the following examples:

> **Ella no escribió la carta, sino que escribió la carta a máquina.** (*She didn't [hand] write the letter, but instead typed the letter.*)

> **Nosotros no vamos a llamar, sino que vamos a escribir.** (*We are not going to call, but rather write.*)

> **No viajarán en avión, sino que viajarán por tren.** (*They won't travel by airplane, but instead will travel by train.*)

Complete the following sentences by filling in the blanks with **pero**, **sino**, or **sino que**. Here's an example:

0. Les gustaría ir, _____ no tienen bastante dinero.

A. pero

21. Él no corre, _____ hace muchos ejercicios.

22. Ella nunca nos llama por teléfono, _____ viene a visitar mucho.

23. Sandra prefiere comer en este restaurante, _____ nosotros queremos ir al otro.

24. El sol no es un planeta, _____ una estrella.

25. Nuestro perro piensa que es una persona, _____ solamente es un animal.

26. Ellos no comen carne, _____ comen huevos, queso, y legumbres.

27. No compró las rosas, _____ las vendió.

28. La astronomía no es un juego, _____ una ciencia.

29. No queremos ir, _____ es necesario.

30. Ramón no viene, _____ sale.

Pointing Out the Differences between Spanish and English Negatives

The big similarity between forming negative expressions in English and forming them in Spanish is that **no** means *no*. Yes, Spanish and English have the same word for **no**. But the similarities pretty much end there. Negative words and expressions in the two languages are quite different, as you can see in the previous sections. In addition, Spanish and English differ in where you place the negative word in the sentence and which rules you follow for double negatives.

The main difference between using negative words and expressions in Spanish and using them in English is their placement in the sentence:

- English usually places the negative word or expression in front of the verb.
- Spanish allows negative words and expressions to float. If you place the negative word or expression after the verb in Spanish, all you have to do is add **no** before the verb.

Here are a few examples of the different ways you can use negative words and expressions in Spanish. Note the difference between the Spanish and English translations.

Ellos nunca comen en este restaurante. (*They never eat in this restaurant.*)

Ellos no comen en este restaurante nunca. (*They never eat in this restaurant.*)

Nadie viene a nuestras fiestas. (*Nobody comes to our parties.*)

No viene nadie a nuestras fiestas. (*Nobody comes to our parties.*)

Nada hay más importante que la felicidad. (*Nothing is more important than happiness.*)

No hay nada más importante que la felicidad. (*Nothing is more important than happiness.*)

As you can see from the preceding examples, Spanish allows double negatives. Every time the negative word comes after the verb and you have to add a **no** in front of the verb, you create a double negative, such as the one in the following example:

No vamos a ir nunca. (*We're not going to go ever.*) (Literally: *We're not going to go never.*)

When you translate this sentence into English, *ever* replaces *never* to avoid the double negative, which is a big no-no in English grammar, as I'm sure you've been told . . . maybe more than once. Here's another example that really grates on the ears of most English grammarians:

No tienen nada. (*They don't have anything.*) (Literally: *They don't have nothing.*)

When you translate this sentence into English, *anything* replaces *nothing* to avoid the double negative.

Translate the following negative sentences into their Spanish equivalents, as in the following example. Use an English-Spanish dictionary for any words you don't know.

0. *No one is home.*

A. **No está nadie en casa.**

   Nadie está en casa.

31. *Nothing is more important than having good friends.*

_____

32. *No one calls at night.*

_____

33. *We never go to her house during the week.*

_____

34. *I never want to do the homework.*

_____

35. *None of them has the money that I'm looking for.*

_____

36. *Nothing is happening.*

_____

37. *No one thinks he is right.*

_____

38. *I never plan to go to Europe.*

_____

39. *Nothing comes in the mail on Saturdays.*

_____

40. *No other place is so beautiful.*

_____

Answer Key

1 ningún

2 Nadie

3 ningún

4 ni, ni

5 nadie

6 nada

7 nada

8 ningunos

9 nada or nadie

10 ni, ni

11 Ellos nunca más van a comer en aquel restaurante.

12 No se puede sacar no más que tres libros de la biblioteca a la vez.

13 Nunca jamás voy a hablar con ellos.

14 Todavía no tienen su regalo.

15 Ella no sólo canta sino también baila.

16 Ni siquiera una respuesta es incorrecta.

17 Él no sólo es tacaño sino también maleducado.

18 Ni Susana tampoco va.

19 Ellos no pueden encontrar las llaves en ninguna parte.

Ellos no pueden encontrar las llaves en/por ningún lado/sitio/lugar.

20 No tengo bastante dinero ni siquiera comprar una hamburguesa.

21 sino que

22 sino que

23 pero

24 sino

25 pero

26 sino que

27 sino que

28 sino

29 pero

30 sino que

31 No hay nada más importante que tener buenos amigos.

   Nada es más importante que tener buenos amigos.

32 No llama nadie por la noche.

   Nadie llama por la noche.

33 No vamos nunca a su casa durante la semana.

   Nunca vamos a su casa durante la semana.

34 No quiero hacer la tarea nunca.

   Nunca quiero hacer la tarea.

35 No tiene ninguno de ellos la moneda que busco.

   Ninguno de ellos tiene la moneda que busco.

36 No pasa nada.

   Nada pasa.

37 No piensa nadie que él tiene razón.

   Nadie piensa que él tiene razón.

38　No pienso ir a Europa nunca.

Nunca pienso ir a Europa.

39　No llega nada por correo los sábados.

Nada llega por correo los sábados.

40　No es tan hermoso ningún otro lugar.

Ningún otro lugar es tan hermoso.

Part IV
Talking about the Past or Future

The 5th Wave
By Rich Tennant

"Here's an idea; let's practice conjugating verbs in Spanish. Last night, you were 'viviste la vida loca'. But this morning, you are 'viviendo la vida Pepto Bismol'."

In this part . . .

You may want to live in the present, but you still need to talk about events that happened in the past or that you expect to happen sometime in the future. This part adds another dimension to Spanish grammar — actually three more dimensions — with the preterit (past), imperfect (past but ongoing or repeated), and future tenses.

As a bonus, I explain how to use the helping verb **haber** to transform the simple tenses into compound tenses — doubling the number of verb tenses you have at your disposal!

Chapter 18

Looking Back with the Preterit

. . . .

In This Chapter

▶ Conjugating regular, stem-changing, spelling-changing, and irregular verbs in the preterit

▶ Putting the preterit to use

▶ Exploring verbs whose meanings can change in the preterit

. . . .

*P*reterit (sometimes spelled *preterite*) is a fancy word for *past*, as in *past tense*. When you're describing events using the preterit, you're talking about actions that happened in the past — actions that are done, over, complete. The actions may have occurred twenty years ago, last week, last night, or three minutes ago. They may have occurred a specific number of times or within an enclosed period of time, but either way, they're done.

In this chapter, I explain how to conjugate regular, stem-changing, spelling-changing, and irregular verbs in the preterit. I also explain when and how to use the preterit and introduce you to words, such as **ayer** (*yesterday*) and **anoche** (*last night*), to describe more specifically when past actions occurred. In addition, I give you the lowdown on some verbs that can change meaning in the preterit, including **conocer,** which usually means *to know* or *to be acquainted with* but in the preterit means *to meet*.

Forming the Preterit Tense of Regular Verbs

To conjugate regular verbs in the preterit, you drop the **-ar**, **-er**, or **-ir** and add the preterit endings. Fortunately, you have to remember only two sets of regular preterit endings — one for **-ar** verbs and another for **-er** and **-ir** verbs, as I explain in the following sections.

Forming the preterit of -ar verbs

To conjugate regular **-ar** verbs in the preterit, drop the **-ar** and add the following endings:

-é	-amos
-aste	-asteis
-ó	-aron

Want to see an example of these endings with a regular **-ar** verb? Here's what **hablar** (*to speak*) looks like in the preterit tense:

hablar (*to speak*)	
yo **hablé**	nosotros/nosotras **hablamos**
tú **hablaste**	vosotros/vosotras **hablasteis**
él/ella/usted **habló**	ellos/ellas/ustedes **hablaron**

Following are some examples of regular **-ar** verbs in action in the preterit tense:

> **Llevé a mi sobrino al circo.** (*I took my nephew to the circus.*)
>
> **Enrico gastó todo su dinero.** (*Enrico spent all of his money.*)
>
> **Pensamos en ir al concierto.** (*We thought about going to the concert.*)

You actually need to memorize only five new verb endings rather than six: The **nosotros** (*we*) form of regular **-ar** verbs stays the same in the present and preterit tenses, as you can see in the following example:

> **Nosotros hablamos.** (*We speak.*) (*We spoke.*)

Forming the preterit of -er and -ir verbs

To conjugate regular **-er** and **-ir** verbs in the preterit, drop the **-er** or **-ir** and add the following endings:

-í	-imos
-iste	-isteis
-ió	-ieron

Here's what one regular **-er** verb, **comer** (*to eat*), looks like in the preterit tense:

comer (*to eat*)	
yo **comí**	nosotros/nosotras **comimos**
tú **comiste**	vosotros/vosotras **comisteis**
él/ella/usted **comió**	ellos/ellas/ustedes **comieron**

Here's what one regular **-ir** verb, **vivir** (*to live*), looks like in the preterit tense:

vivir (*to live*)	
yo **viví**	nosotros/nosotras **vivimos**
tú **viviste**	vosotros/vosotras **vivisteis**
él/ella/usted **vivió**	ellos/ellas/ustedes **vivieron**

Following are some examples of regular **-er** and **-ir** verbs in action in the preterit tense:

> **Me advertiste.** (*You warned me.*)
>
> **El orador encendió a la multitud.** (*The speaker inflamed the crowd.*)
>
> **Isabel y yo partimos para España.** (*Isabel and I departed for Spain.*)

As with regular **-ar** verbs (see the preceding section), the **nosotros** (*we*) forms of **-ir** verbs stay the same in the present and preterit tenses, as you can see in the following example:

> **Recibimos un paquete.** (*We receive a package.*) (*We received a package.*)

Complete the following sentences by filling in the proper preterit tense form of the specified verb, as in the following example:

0. Los jugadores _____ su victoria. (celebrar)

A. celebraron

1. Yo _____ la cena. (preparar)

2. Ella _____ la música. (escuchar)

3. Mi madre _____ la estufa. (encender)

4. Nosotros _____ a los actores. (aplaudir)

5. Ellos _____ paella. (comer)

6. Sofía _____ en la clase. (aburrirse)

7. Lidia y María _____ en la fiesta. (bailar)

8. Tú _____ a hablar ruso. (aprender)

9. Los insurgentes _____ al gobierno. (abatir)

10. Vosotros _____ vuestra casa por un buen precio. (vender)

Dealing with Stem-Changing, Spelling-Changing, and Irregular Verbs

Some verbs don't follow the patterns for conjugating regular **-ar**, **-er**, and **-ir** verbs that I describe earlier in this chapter. To make these verbs more manageable, you can group them according to their differences — that is, whether the verbs have stem changes, have spelling changes, or are irregular in the preterit tense. The following sections deal with each of these groups of verbs and, when possible, classify the verbs into smaller subgroups to make them easier to manage.

Stem-changing verbs

In the preterit tense, none of the **-ar** and **-er** verbs have stem changes. The only verbs that have stem changes in the preterit are **-ir** verbs. Perhaps not surprisingly, the same **-ir** verbs that have stem changes in the present tense (see Chapter 6) also have stem changes in the preterit tense, although (also not surprisingly) the stem changes in the preterit are a little different. They change only in their singular and plural third person preterit forms. The endings for these verbs follow the regular pattern that I describe earlier in this chapter.

For example, the verb **pedir** (*to ask*) is an **e** to **i** stem-changing verb in the present, but its stem changes from **e** to **i** only in the third person preterit:

pedir (*to ask*)	
yo **pedí**	nosotros/nosotras **pedimos**
tú **pediste**	vosotros/vosotras **pedisteis**
él/ella/usted **pidió**	ellos/ellas/ustedes **pidieron**

The verb **preferir** (*to prefer*) is an **e** to **ie** stem-changing verb in the present, but its stem changes from **e** to **i** (*not* **e** to **ie**) in the third person preterit:

preferir (*to destroy*)	
yo **preferí**	nosotros/nosotras **preferimos**
tú **preferiste**	vosotros/vosotras **preferisteis**
él/ella/usted **prefirió**	ellos/ellas/ustedes **prefirieron**

The verb **dormir** (*to sleep*) is an **o** to **ue** stem-changing verb in the present tense, but its stem changes from **o** to **u** (*not* **o** to **ue**) in the third person preterit:

dormir (*to sleep*)	
yo **dormí**	nosotros/nosotras **dormimos**
tú **dormiste**	vosotros/vosotras **dormisteis**
él/ella/usted **durmió**	ellos/ellas/ustedes **durmieron**

When you drop the **-ír** ending from **reír** (*to laugh*) and **sonreír** (*to smile*), the verb stem ends in a vowel, so you have to add an accent to the **i** in the first and second person preterit endings. Here's the preterit tense conjugation chart for **reír** (the same endings apply for **sonreír**):

reír *(to laugh)*	
yo **reí**	nosotros/nosotras **reímos**
tú **reíste**	vosotros/vosotras **reísteis**
él/ella/usted **rió**	ellos/ellas/ustedes **rieron**

Complete the following sentences by filling in the proper preterit tense form of the specified stem-changing verb, as in the following example. (Check out Chapter 6 if you need help remembering these verbs' stem changes.)

Q. Jorge _____ la cuenta. (pedir)

A. pidió

11. Ella _____ cuando vio a su esposo. (sonreír)

12. Los niños _____ mucho ayer. (dormir)

13. Tú _____ tomar el tren. (preferir)

14. Los invitados _____ más vino. (pedir)

15. Yo _____ anoche en la fiesta. (divertirse)

16. Raquel _____ a las seis. (vestirse)

17. Nosotros _____ mucho de sus bromas. (reír)

18. Vosotros _____ una comida especial anoche. (servir)

19. En la clase los estudiantes _____ las palabras nuevas. (repetir)

20. Su mejor amigo _____ en la guerra. (morir)

Spelling-changing verbs

Verbs that change spelling in the preterit fall into two categories:

- One for **-ar** verbs that end in **-car**, **-gar**, or **-zar**
- One for **-er** and **-ir** verbs that have a vowel before the **-er** or **-ir**

In the following sections, I explain these spelling changes and present examples so you can see these aberrations in action.

The verbs that have spelling changes in the present tense aren't necessarily the same verbs that have spelling changes in the preterit. So make sure you pay attention to which verbs I mention in the following sections because they don't follow the same pattern as the present tense verbs I mention in Chapter 6.

Verbs that end in -car, -gar, or -zar

Verbs that end in **-car**, **-gar**, or **-zar** change spelling only in the **yo** (*I*) form of the preterit to preserve the original sound of the verb. For verbs ending in **-car**, the **c** changes to **qu**, for verbs ending in **-gar**, the **g** changes to **gu**, and for verbs ending in **-zar**, the **z** changes to **c**, as in the following examples:

Spelling Change	Example of Verb That Follows It	Yo Form of the Preterit
c → qu	tocar	yo toqué (*I touched*)
g → gu	jugar	yo jugué (*I played*)
z → c	empezar	yo empecé (*I began*)

Otherwise, these verbs follow the regular conjugation pattern that I describe in the earlier section "Forming the preterit of **-ar** verbs." The following table shows what the verb **tocar** looks like in the preterit:

tocar (*to touch, to play [an instrument]*)	
yo **toqué**	nosotros/nosotras **tocamos**
tú **tocaste**	vosotros/vosotras **tocasteis**
él/ella/usted **tocó**	ellos/ellas/ustedes **tocaron**

Verbs that end in -aer, -eer, -oír, and -oer

Some **-er** and **-ir** verbs have a vowel directly preceding the **-er** or **-ir** ending. If you were to just drop the ending and add the preterit endings, you'd end up with a long string of vowels that would be difficult to pronounce. To help with pronunciation in these cases, use the following endings to form the preterit:

-í	-ímos
-íste	-ísteis
-yó	-yeron

Here are the preterit tense conjugation charts for two common verbs (one **-er** verb and one **-ir** verb) that have verb stems ending in a vowel:

leer (*to read*)	
yo **leí**	nosotros/nosotras **leímos**
tú **leíste**	vosotros/vosotras **leísteis**
él/ella/usted **leyó**	ellos/ellas/ustedes **leyeron**

oír *(to hear)*	
yo **oí**	nosotros/nosotras **oímos**
tú **oíste**	vosotros/vosotras **oísteis**
él/ella/usted **oyó**	ellos/ellas/ustedes **oyeron**

Of course, every rule has its exceptions. In this case, you need to be aware of the following exceptions:

✔ **Traer** *(to bring)* is an irregular verb. Its preterit stem is **traj-,** which doesn't end in a vowel. For more about conjugating irregular verbs, including **traer**, in the preterit, see the next section.

✔ With verbs that end in **-uir,** such as **concluir** *(to conclude)*, **destruir** *(to destroy)*, and **sustituir** *(to substitute)*, you don't accent the **i** in the **tú, nosotros,** or **vosotros** forms. For an example, check out the preterit conjugation chart for **destruir:**

destruir *(to destroy)*	
yo **destruí**	nosotros/nosotras **destruimos**
tú **destruiste**	vosotros/vosotras **destruisteis**
él/ella/usted **destruyó**	ellos/ellas/ustedes **destruyeron**

Complete the following sentences by filling in the proper preterit tense form of the specified verb, as in the following example:

Q. **Ayer por la noche yo _____ un juego electrónico. (jugar)**

A. **jugué**

21. **Anoche yo _____ un buen libro. (leer)**

22. **Los obreros _____ el edificio rápidamente. (destruir)**

23. **Yo _____ antes de acostarme. (rezar)**

24. **El partido de fútbol _____ tarde. (empezar)**

25. **Los estudiantes _____ el timbre. (oír)**

26. **Anoche vosotros _____ los platos. (secar)**

27. **Nosotros _____ que él vino de Grecia. (concluir)**

28. Tú _____ el pescado por el pollo en el plato. (sustituir)

29. Yo _____ el problema matemático a los otros estudiantes. (explicar)

30. Nuestros vecinos _____ una casa nueva. (construir)

Irregular verbs

Several verbs are more or less irregular in the preterit. The less irregular verbs fall into categories, which make them easier to remember. The irregular verbs that fall into categories use the following endings in the preterit:

-e	-imos
-iste	-isteis
-o	-ieron (or -eron if the stem ends in **j**)

The more irregular verbs, such as **ser** (*to be*) and **ir** (*to go*), are so irregular that you just have to memorize their preterit forms.

In the following sections, I present a number of irregular verbs and provide conjugation charts for the preterit tense so you know how to conjugate each type.

Verbs whose stems change from a or e to i

A few Spanish verbs that have **a** or **e** in their stems change the **a** or **e** to **i** in the preterit. The verb **decir** (*to say*) is one example, as you can see in the following table. Also note that the **c** in the stem changes to a **j**; for more examples of verbs with this particular change, see the later section "Verbs whose stems use **j** in the preterit."

decir (*to say*)	
yo **dije**	nosotros/nosotras **dijimos**
tú **dijiste**	vosotros/vosotras **dijisteis**
él/ella/usted **dijo**	ellos/ellas/ustedes **dijeron**

Several other verbs contain **decir** and follow the same conjugation pattern in the preterit. These verbs include **bendecir** (*to bless*), **contradecir** (*to contradict*), and **maldecir** (*to curse*).

The verb **hacer** (*to make, to do*) is another example. Note that in the third person singular, **hacer**'s **c** changes to **z** to help with the pronunciation.

hacer (*to make, to do*)	
yo **hice**	nosotros/nosotras **hicimos**
tú **hiciste**	vosotros/vosotras **hicisteis**
él/ella/usted **hizo**	ellos/ellas/ustedes **hicieron**

Two other examples are **querer** (*to want*) and **venir** (*to come*). With the verb **querer,** not only does the **e** in the stem change to an **i,** but the **r** changes to an **s.**

querer (*to want*)	
yo **quise**	nosotros/nosotras **quisimos**
tú **quisiste**	vosotros/vosotras **quisisteis**
él/ella/usted **quiso**	ellos/ellas/ustedes **quisieron**

venir (*to come*)	
yo **vine**	nosotros/nosotras **vinimos**
tú **viniste**	vosotros/vosotras **vinisteis**
él/ella/usted **vino**	ellos/ellas/ustedes **vinieron**

Several other verbs contain **venir** and follow the same conjugation pattern in the preterit. These verbs include **convenir** (*to agree*), **intravenir** (*to take part*), and **prevenir** (*to prevent*).

Verbs whose stems change from a or o to u

For some irregular verbs that have an **a** or **o** in their stems, the **a** or **o** changes to **u,** as in the following examples:

caber (*to fit*)	
yo **cupe**	nosotros/nosotras **cupimos**
tú **cupiste**	vosotros/vosotras **cupisteis**
él/ella/usted **cupo**	ellos/ellas/ustedes **cupieron**

poder (*to be able*)	
yo **pude**	nosotros/nosotras **pudimos**
tú **pudiste**	vosotros/vosotras **pudisteis**
él/ella/usted **pudo**	ellos/ellas/ustedes **pudieron**

poner (*to put*)	
yo **puse**	nosotros/nosotras **pusimos**
tú **pusiste**	vosotros/vosotras **pusisteis**
él/ella/usted **puso**	ellos/ellas/ustedes **pusieron**

saber (to know)	
yo **supe**	nosotros/nosotras **supimos**
tú **supiste**	vosotros/vosotras **supisteis**
él/ella/usted **supo**	ellos/ellas/ustedes **supieron**

Notice how the **b** in the verbs **caber** and **saber** changes to a **p** and the **d** in the verb **poder** changes to an **s**.

Verbs whose stems use j in the preterit

In **traer** (to bring), the stem adds **j** in the preterit, and in all verbs that end in **-ducir** along with the verb **decir** (to say), the **c** changes to **j**. Here are the preterit conjugation charts for **traer** and **inducir** (to induce). (I show you how to conjugate **decir** earlier in this chapter.)

traer (to bring)	
yo **traje**	nosotros/nosotras **trajimos**
tú **trajiste**	vosotros/vosotras **trajisteis**
él/ella/usted **trajo**	ellos/ellas/ustedes **trajeron**

Several other verbs contain **traer** and follow the same conjugation pattern in the preterit. These verbs include **atraer** (to attract), **contraer** (to contract), and **extraer** (to extract).

inducir (to induce)	
yo **induje**	nosotros/nosotras **indujimos**
tú **indujiste**	vosotros/vosotras **indujisteis**
él/ella/usted **indujo**	ellos/ellas/ustedes **indujeron**

For verbs like these, the third person plural ending is **-eron**. No **i** precedes it because the **j** essentially replaces the **i**.

Verbs whose stems use uv in the preterit

Three verbs use **uv** in their preterit conjugations. Following are the preterit conjugation charts for these verbs:

andar (to walk)	
yo **anduve**	nosotros/nosotras **anduvimos**
tú **anduviste**	vosotros/vosotras **anduvisteis**
él/ella/usted **anduvo**	ellos/ellas/ustedes **anduvieron**

estar (*to be*)	
yo **estuve**	nosotros/nosotras **estuvimos**
tú **estuviste**	vosotros/vosotras **estuvisteis**
él/ella/usted **estuvo**	ellos/ellas/ustedes **estuvieron**

tener (*to have*)	
yo **tuve**	nosotros/nosotras **tuvimos**
tú **tuviste**	vosotros/vosotras **tuvisteis**
él/ella/usted **tuvo**	ellos/ellas/ustedes **tuvieron**

The verbs dar and ver

When you drop the endings of the verbs **dar** (*to give*) and **ver** (*to see*), you don't have much to work with. In addition, in the preterit tense, the endings for these verbs are irregular. Both **dar** and **ver** use the regular **-er** and **-ir** preterit verb endings, but they don't use any accents. Here's what **dar** and **ver** look like in the preterit:

dar (*to give*)	
yo **di**	nosotros/nosotras **dimos**
tú **diste**	vosotros/vosotras **disteis**
él/ella/usted **dio**	ellos/ellas/ustedes **dieron**

ver (*to see*)	
yo **vi**	nosotros/nosotras **vimos**
tú **viste**	vosotros/vosotras **visteis**
él/ella/usted **vio**	ellos/ellas/ustedes **vieron**

The verbs ser and ir

The verbs **ser** (*to be*) and **ir** (*to go*) are the most unusual of the irregular verbs in the preterit tense, but the good thing (or bad, depending on how you look at it) is that they're identical to each other. That's right, in the preterit tense, you use the same verb conjugation to mean *to be* that you use to mean *to go*. You clarify the intended meaning in the context of the sentence. Here's the preterit conjugation chart for **ser** and **ir**:

ser (*to be*), ir (*to go*)	
yo **fui**	nosotros/nosotras **fuimos**
tú **fuiste**	vosotros/vosotras **fuisteis**
él/ella/usted **fue**	ellos/ellas/ustedes **fueron**

Complete the following sentences by filling in the preterit tense form of the specified irregular verb, as in the following example:

0. El público _____ al dramaturgo por la falta de imaginación. (maldecir)

A. maldijo

31. Anoche nosotros _____ el postre. (traer)

32. Ella _____ al supermercado ayer. (andar)

33. Timoteo _____ la verdad. (decir)

34. Ayer mi madre _____ al supermercado. (ir)

35. Yo _____ mucho dinero al orfanato. (dar)

36. La fábrica _____ arte del siglo de oro. (reproducir)

37. Los jóvenes _____ sus libros en la mesa. (poner)

38. Tú _____ la verdad. (saber)

39. Él _____ que nuestro equipo perdería. (predecir)

40. Vosotros _____ la puesta del sol. (ver)

Using the Preterit Tense

Knowing how to conjugate verbs in the preterit tense is one thing. Knowing when to use the preterit is something else entirely. Fortunately, knowing when to use it is the easy part. The general rule is that you use the preterit to describe an action that happened and was completed in the past. In the following sections, I explain when to use the preterit tense in a little more detail and provide some time-related words that can help you be more specific about when in the past an action occurred.

Completing an action or a series of actions in the past

The standard use of the preterit is to describe one or more actions that were completed in the past, as in the following examples:

Ellos fueron a Madrid. (*They went to Madrid.*)

Abrí el paquete y me sorprendí al encontrarlo vacío. (*I opened the package and was surprised to find it empty.*)

Ella lavó, secó y peinó el pelo de Rosario. (*She shampooed, dried, and styled Rosario's hair.*)

Compramos un Ferrari. (*We bought a Ferrari.*)

Being specific about a past action

The preterit tense often describes an action that occurred at a specific time in the past, such as last month, last week, two days ago, or yesterday. When you want to use the preterit to describe an action that happened at a specific time in the past, having a few preterit-specific adverbs at your disposal sure comes in handy. Table 18-1 presents several adverbs that are commonly used to describe actions completed in the past. (See Chapter 5 for more information on dates and times and Chapter 12 for more about adverbs.)

Table 18-1	Adverbs That Describe Completed Actions
Adverb	*English Translation*
anoche	*last night*
anteayer	*day before yesterday*
ayer	*yesterday*
ayer por la mañana	*yesterday morning*
ayer por la tarde	*yesterday afternoon*
el año pasado	*last year*
el mes pasado	*last month*
el otro día	*the other day*
en ese momento	*at that moment*
entonces	*then*
esta mañana	*this morning*
esta tarde	*this afternoon*
hace dos días	*two days ago (substitute any word or number with **hace**, as in **hace cinco semanas** [five weeks ago])*
la semana pasada	*last week*

Following are a few sample sentences that describe actions that occurred at a specific time in the past:

Vi a tu madre en la tienda ayer. (*I saw your mother at the store yesterday.*)

El tren partió de la estación a las cuatro y media de la tarde. (*The train left the station at 4:30 p.m.*)

Anoche fuimos al cine. (*Last night we went to the movies.*)

Translate the following expressions from English to Spanish; you can use an English-Spanish dictionary if necessary. Here's an example:

Q. *They sailed across the Gulf of Mexico.*

A. **Navegaron a través del Golfo de México.**

41. *My friends went to the party last night.*

_____

42. *We put the kids to bed at 8:30.*

_____

43. *They left two weeks ago.*

_____

44. *My sister arrived yesterday afternoon.*

_____

45. *Alberto played on the school team last year.*

_____

46. *I attended their church last Sunday.*

_____

47. *Guillermo invited his girlfriend to the dance.*

_____

48. *My mother received the package last week.*

_____

49. *You played the trumpet in the band last week.*

_____

50. *You guys moved to Europe last year.*

_____

Changing Verb Meanings in the Preterit

A handful of verbs change meaning in the preterit. The following list introduces these flip-floppers and presents an example to illustrate the change in meaning for each one:

✔ **Conocer** (*to know*) means *to meet* in the preterit:

Nos conocimos cuando éramos jóvenes. (*We met when we were young.*)

✔ **Poder** (*to be able*) means *to manage (to do something)* in the preterit:

Él pudo hacer el trabajo anoche. (*He managed to do the work last night.*)

✔ **No poder** (*to be unable*) means *to fail (to do something)* in the preterit:

Ella no pudo terminar la tarea anoche. (*She failed to finish the assignment last night.*)

✔ **Querer** (*to want*) means *to try* in the preterit:

Quisimos aprender el francés pero no pudimos. (*We tried to learn French but we failed.*)

✔ **No querer** (*to not want*) means *to refuse* in the preterit:

Ellos no quisieron ir al concierto. (*They refused to go to the concert.*)

✔ **Saber** (*to know*) means *to find out* in the preterit:

Supimos que ellos vivían muy cerca. (*We found out that they lived very near.*)

✔ **Sentir** (*to feel sorry*) means *to regret* in the preterit:

Nosotros nos sentimos la pérdida. (*We regretted the loss.*)

✔ **Tener** (*to have*) means *to receive* in the preterit:

Tú tuviste el paquete anoche. (*You received the package last night.*)

Answer Key

1	preparé
2	escuchó
3	encendió
4	aplaudimos
5	comieron
6	se aburrió
7	bailaron
8	aprendiste
9	abatieron
10	vendisteis
11	sonrió
12	durmieron
13	preferiste
14	pidieron
15	me divertí
16	se vistió
17	reímos
18	servisteis
19	repitieron
20	murió
21	leí
22	destruyeron
23	recé

24 empezó

25 oyeron

26 secasteis

27 concluimos

28 sustituiste

29 expliqué

30 construyeron

31 trajimos

32 anduvo

33 dijo

34 fue

35 di

36 reprodujo

37 pusieron

38 supiste

39 predijo

40 visteis

41 Mis amigos fueron a la fiesta anoche.

42 Nosotros acostamos a los niños a las ocho y media.

43 Ellos salieron hace dos semanas.

44 Mi hermana llegó ayer por la tarde.

45 Alberto jugó en el equipo de la escuela el año pasado.

46 Yo asistí a su iglesia el domingo pasado.

47 Guillermo invitó a su novia al baile.

48 Mi madre recibió el paquete la semana pasada.

49 Tú tocaste la trompeta en la banda la semana pasada.

50 Vosotros os mudasteis a Europa el año pasado.

Chapter 19

Describing Ongoing Past Action with the Imperfect

The *imperfect tense,* an imprecise version of the preterit (past) tense that I talk about in Chapter 18, enables you to describe events that were happening or used to happen at no specific time in the past. In English, you typically use the phrases *used to* or *always* to express action in the imperfect tense, as in the following examples:

> *My family always went to the movies on holidays.*

> *I used to go to Cancun for spring break.*

> *Woolly mammoths used to roam the Earth.*

In this chapter, I explain how to conjugate regular and irregular Spanish verbs in the imperfect tense. (The good news is that you don't have to deal with spelling- or stem-changing verbs in the imperfect because they don't exist.) I also explain when to use the imperfect rather than the preterit tense and provide plenty of practice exercises to help you choose the correct past tense even when the choice seems unclear.

Forming the Regular Imperfect Tense

Forming the imperfect tense for regular verbs follows the standard operating procedure for conjugating verbs:

1. **Drop the -ar, -er, or -ir ending.**

2. **Add the endings for the tense, in this case the imperfect endings.**

As in most cases, you have two sets of endings to choose from: one for **-ar** verbs and one for **-er** and **-ir** verbs. The following sections give you the full scoop. (Flip to Chapter 6 for an introduction to regular Spanish verbs.)

Forming the imperfect of regular -ar verbs

To conjugate regular **-ar** verbs in the imperfect, drop the **-ar** ending and add the following imperfect endings:

-aba	**-ábamos**
-abas	**-abais**
-aba	**-aban**

A regular **-ar** verb conjugated in the imperfect tense looks like this:

entrar (*to enter*)	
yo **entraba**	nosotros/nosotras **entrábamos**
tú **entrabas**	vosotros/vosotras **entrabais**
él/ella/usted **entraba**	ellos/ellas/ustedes **entraban**

Here are a few examples of regular **-ar** verbs in action in the imperfect:

Me bañaba cuando sonó el teléfono. (*I was taking a bath when the telephone rang.*)

Ricardo siempre se afeitaba antes de ir a trabajar. (*Ricardo always shaved before going to work.*)

Los niños jugaban todos los días. (*The children played every day.*)

Forming the imperfect of regular -er and -ir verbs

To conjugate regular **-er** and **-ir** verbs in the imperfect, drop the **-er** or **-ir** ending and add the following imperfect endings:

-ía	**-íamos**
-ías	**-íais**
-ía	**-ían**

Following are a couple of examples of conjugation charts for regular **-er** and **-ir** verbs in the imperfect:

embeber (*to soak in*)	
yo **embebía**	nosotros/nosotras **embebíamos**
tú **embebías**	vosotros/vosotras **embebíais**
él/ella/usted **embebía**	ellos/ellas/ustedes **embebían**

unir (*to connect*)	
yo **unía**	nosotros/nosotras **uníamos**
tú **unías**	vosotros/vosotras **uníais**
él/ella/usted **unía**	ellos/ellas/ustedes **unían**

Here's what regular **-er** and **-ir** verbs look like in action in the imperfect:

> **Él bebía café.** (*He used to drink coffee.*)

> **Siempre salíamos de la playa antes del atardecer.** (*We always left the beach before sunset.*)

Conjugate the following verbs into their correct imperfect forms based on the subjects provided, as in the following example:

0. **tú/celebrar** = _____

A. **celebrabas**

1. **ellos/empezar** = _____

2. **yo/comprar** = _____

3. **ella/comprender** = _____

4. **nosotros/repetir** = _____

5. **mi padre/ganar** = _____

6. **los estudiantes/estudiar** = _____

7. **el paciente/sufrir** = _____

8. **tú/esperar** = _____

9. **el conductor/conducir** = _____

10. **vosotros/poner** = _____

Recognizing Some Irregular Imperfect Verbs

The good news is that you don't have to wrestle with spelling- or stem-changing verbs in the imperfect because none exist. More good news is that only three verbs are irregular in the imperfect: **ir, ser,** and **ver.** The bad news is that for these verbs, you have to memorize their imperfect conjugations, but doing so shouldn't be too hard because you'll probably use them fairly frequently. The following tables show what these three verbs look like in the imperfect:

ir (*to go*)	
yo **iba**	nosotros/nosotras **íbamos**
tú **ibas**	vosotros/vosotras **ibais**
él/ella/usted **iba**	ellos/ellas/ustedes **iban**

ser (*to be*)	
yo **era**	nosotros/nosotras **éramos**
tú **eras**	vosotros/vosotras **erais**
él/ella/usted **era**	ellos/ellas/ustedes **eran**

ver (*to see*)	
yo **veía**	nosotros/nosotras **veíamos**
tú **veías**	vosotros/vosotras **veíais**
él/ella/usted **veía**	ellos/ellas/ustedes **veían**

Conjugate the following irregular verbs into their correct imperfect forms based on the subjects provided, as in the following example:

0. **nosotros/ir** = _____

A. **íbamos**

11. **yo/ser** = _____

12. **el gato/ir** = _____

13. **vosotros/ver** = _____

14. **ellos/ir** = _____

15. **tú/ser** = _____

16. **Carlos y Ana/ver** = _____

17. **mi familia/ir** = _____

18. **nosotros/ser** = _____

19. **Pepe y yo/ver** = _____

20. **ustedes/ser** = _____

Using the Imperfect Tense in Certain Ways

The imperfect tense is often the perfect choice for describing certain types of past actions and events. In the following sections, I describe specific uses for the imperfect tense and provide plenty of practice along the way.

Describing past conditions or states of mind

Use the imperfect to describe the past conditions of people, places, things, states of mind, time, or weather. Here are some examples:

> **Deseaba ganar la lotería.** (*He wanted to win the lottery.*)
>
> **La sesión de la tarde era a las 2:00.** (*The matinee was at 2:00.*)
>
> **Nevaba.** (*It was snowing.*)
>
> **¡Nuestras vacaciones eran fantásticas!** (*Our vacation was fantastic!*)
>
> **¿Estaban contentos?** (*Were they happy?*)

Note: You always express time (as in the second example in the preceding list) with the imperfect in the past.

Translate the following sentences into Spanish by using the imperfect tense to describe past conditions or states of mind. Use an English-Spanish dictionary for words you don't know. Here's an example:

0. *They were happily married.*

A. **Ellos estaban casados felizmente.**

21. *It was raining.*

_____

22. *I was very sad.*

_____

23. *You (plural, informal)* *wanted to go to the beach.*

_____

24. *The party was at 8:00 p.m.*

_____

25. *It was very hot and sunny.*

_____

26. *My father wanted a new car.*

_____

27. *Their house was enormous.*

_____

28. *You* (singular, informal) *were always very careful.*

_____

29. *Carlos was a lawyer.*

_____

30. *We were very hungry.*

_____

Describing continuing or ongoing past actions

When an action occurred in the past but has no clear beginning or ending, use the imperfect tense to describe it, as in the following examples:

> **Leía sobre eso.** (*I was reading about that.*)
>
> **¿Cuándo planeabas visitar?** (*When were you planning to visit?*)
>
> **El presidente analizaba sus opciones.** (*The president was analyzing her options.*)

Describing repeated or habitual past actions

When past actions are repeated or habitual, use the imperfect to describe them. For example, if your mother always took you shopping the day after Thanksgiving, you'd use the imperfect to tell someone about it:

> **Mi madre siempre me llevaba de compras el día después de la Acción de Gracias.** (*My mother always took me shopping the day after Thanksgiving.*)

Here's an example of using the imperfect to describe habitual action from the past:

> **Yo jugaba al fútbol en la escuela secundaria.** (*I played soccer in high school.*)

Note: You could make a case that the preterit is more appropriate for the preceding example because you're describing an action that's been over since high school. However, playing soccer was an activity that you performed regularly in the past, so you use the imperfect.

Expressing "would"

In certain cases, you may use the imperfect to describe habitual actions that somebody *would* do in the past, as in the following examples:

> **Mi abuelo pasaba mucho tiempo en su garaje.** (*My grandfather would spend a lot of time in his garage.*)
>
> **Nadie la visitaba los fines de semanas.** (*Nobody would visit her on the weekends.*)
>
> **Mis padres siempre venían a mis competiciones de natación.** (*My parents would always come to my swim meets.*)

Don't confuse this use of the word *would* with its use in the context of being able to do something under certain conditions, as in *I would repair my own car if I were a mechanic.* Use the imperfect only when using *would* to describe habitual or repeated actions in the past. (See Chapter 22 for details on how to handle a conditional *would* situation.)

Describing simultaneous activities in the past

When actions occur simultaneously in the past, use the imperfect to describe them, as in the following examples:

> **Mientras usted trabajaba, yo jugaba en la computadora.** (*While you were working, I was playing on the computer.*)
>
> **Tomás tocaba el piano mientras Charo cantaba.** (*Tomás was playing the piano while Charo was singing.*)
>
> **Mientras que la banda estaba tocando, todo el mundo estaba bailando.** (*While the band was playing, everyone was dancing.*)

Describing actions that were occurring when something else happened

Use the imperfect to describe background actions or actions that were happening when they were suddenly interrupted by a preterit tense action, as in the following examples:

> **¿Qué hacías cuando caíste de la escalera?** (*What were you doing when you fell off the ladder?*)
>
> **Esperanza pescaba cuando se cayó en el agua.** (*Esperanza was fishing when she fell into the water.*)
>
> **Buscábamos a Mateo cuando le oímos reír en el armario.** (*We were searching for Mateo when we heard him laughing in the closet.*)

Translate the following sentences into Spanish by using the imperfect tense; use an English-Spanish dictionary for any words you don't know. Here's an example:

0. *We were preparing for our trip when we heard the news.*

A. **Nos preparábamos para el viaje cuando nos enteramos de la noticia.**

31. *My mother was preparing dinner while we were watching TV.*

_____

32. *He was working when the phone rang.*

_____

33. *She would go to the supermarket every Saturday.*

_____

34. *They would play chess every afternoon.*

_____

35. *The students were taking a test when the bell rang.*

_____

36. *My friends and I were talking on the phone when he interrupted us.*

_____

37. *We would frequently meet at their house.*

_____

38. *The mechanic would usually work on Saturdays.*

_____

39. *The boss was talking while the secretary was typing.*

_____

40. *The family was eating when the guests arrived.*

_____

Comparing the Preterit and Imperfect Tenses

Many people have a hard time distinguishing between the preterit and imperfect tenses because they're both past tenses. To help you tell the difference, think about the preterit tense as a period and the imperfect as ellipses:

- In the preterit tense, the action was completed at a specific point in time, period.
- In the imperfect tense, the action happened (or was happening) sometime . . . , but you really can't pin down when, in the past, it happened, was happening, or finished.

For example, to describe an action that's been completed, you use the preterit, like so:

Cenamos. (*We ate dinner.*)

In other words, we ate dinner. It's over, and it's time for dessert.

Now suppose you want to describe a past action that hasn't necessarily been completed. In this case, you use the imperfect, as in the following example:

Cenábamos. (*We were eating dinner.*)

In the imperfect, the action was clearly being performed in the past, but the description of the action doesn't mention the completion of the action, so you don't know whether we finished eating or whether we could start planning for dessert.

In the following sections, I provide some additional clues to look for in determining whether the preterit or imperfect is the more appropriate of the two past tenses to use.

Knowing when to use the preterit

If you find yourself describing past action in terms of a specific day, week, month, year, or time, use the preterit. Here are a few examples:

Anoche miramos las noticias. (*Last night we watched the news.*)

El semestre pasado, viajamos a Barcelona. (*Last semester, we traveled to Barcelona.*)

¿Me llamaste ayer? (*Did you call me yesterday?*)

Chapter 18 lists some preterit-specific words and phrases that often accompany the preterit tense, including **ayer** (*yesterday*) and **el año pasado** (*last year*).

Knowing when to use the imperfect

When you're describing past actions that are habitual, ongoing, or repetitive in the past, use the imperfect tense. Table 19-1 provides a list of words and phrases that commonly clue you into the fact that you need to use the imperfect.

Table 19-1	Adverbs That Describe Habitual or Repetitive Action
Adverb	*Translation*
a menudo	often
a veces	sometimes
cada día	each day, every day
con frecuencia	frequently
de vez en cuando	from time to time
en general	generally
frecuentemente	frequently
generalmente	generally
habitualmente	habitually
los lunes	on Mondays
los martes	on Tuesdays
los miércoles	on Wednesdays
los jueves	on Thursdays
los viernes	on Fridays
los sábados	on Saturdays
los domingos	on Sundays
normalmente	normally
siempre	always
todo el tiempo	all the time
todos los días	every day
todos los fines de semana	every weekend
usualmente	usually

Following are some examples that use the imperfect tense with imperfect-specific adverbs:

En general él bebía refrescos. (*He usually drank soft drinks.*)

Frecuentemente él caminaba a su perro en el parque. (*He frequently walked his dog at the park.*)

Lala siempre llevaba zapatos rojos. (*Lala always wore red shoes.*)

Complete the following sentences by using the most appropriate tense — preterit or imperfect — for the verb that's provided. For more about forming the past tense, see Chapter 18. Here's an example:

0. La escuela _____ (comprar) los libros la semana pasada.

A. compró

41. Nosotros _____ (comer) en su restaurante todos los domingos.

42. Mi madre _____ (ir) al supermercado el sábado pasado.

43. Ellos _____ (trabajar) hasta las seis y media ayer.

44. Nosotros siempre _____ (ayudar) con los niños.

45. Él _____ (ver) a su padre todos los domingos.

46. Frecuentemente vosotros _____ (ir) al parque.

47. Yo _____ (mirar) la televisión anoche.

48. Tú _____ (visitar) a tus abuelos habitualmente.

49. Mis amigos _____ (salir) a las dos ayer por la tarde.

50. Ella siempre _____ (poner) el azúcar en su café.

Answer Key

1. empezaban

2. compraba

3. comprendía

4. repetíamos

5. ganaba

6. estudiaban

7. sufría

8. esperabas

9. conducía

10. poníais

11. era

12. iba

13. veíais

14. iban

15. eras

16. veían

17. iba

18. éramos

19. veíamos

20. eran

21. Llovía.

22. Yo estaba muy triste.

23. Vosotros queríais ir a la playa.

24 La fiesta era a las ocho de la noche.

25 Hacía mucho calor y mucho sol.

26 Mi padre quería un coche nuevo.

27 Su casa era enorme.

28 Tú siempre eras muy cuidadoso.

29 Carlos era un abogado.

30 Nosotros teníamos mucha hambre.

31 Mi madre preparaba la cena mientras nosotros mirábamos la televisión.

32 Él trabajaba cuando el teléfono sonó.

33 Ella iba al supermercado todos los sábados.

34 Ellos jugaban al ajedrez todas las tardes.

35 Los estudiantes tomaban un examen cuando el timbre sonó.

36 Mis amigos y yo hablábamos por teléfono cuando él nos interrumpió.

37 Frecuentemente nos reuníamos en su casa.

38 El mecánico normalmente trabajaba los sábados.

39 El jefe hablaba mientras la secretaria escribía por máquina.

40 La familia comía cuando los invitados llegaron.

41 comíamos

42 fue

43 trabajaron

44 ayudábamos

45 veía

46 ibais

47 miré

48 visitabas

49 salieron

50 ponía

Chapter 20

Projecting Forward with the Future Tense

▶ Conjugating regular future tense verbs

▶ Dealing with verbs that are irregular in the future tense

▶ Employing futuristic adverbs and other methods for talking about the future

▶ Putting the future tense to good use

You may get tense thinking about the future, but you don't need to fret about forming the future tense in Spanish because it's one of the easier verb tenses to master. In this chapter, I explain how to form the future tense with both regular and irregular verbs, and I show you how to use the future tense to describe events that *will* happen (or are likely to happen) and talk about the possibility of future events. I also go over a few other methods (besides the future tense) to talk about the future.

Forming the Regular Future Tense

To form the future tense for regular **-ar, -er,** and **-ir** verbs, follow these two simple steps:

1. **Start with the entire verb in its infinitive form.**

   Don't drop the ending.

2. **Add the future ending that's appropriate for the subject in person and number.**

The following list shows the future tense endings:

-é	-emos
-ás	-éis
-á	-án

To help you see how these endings combine with the three different types of regular verbs to form the future tense, consider the following three tables. Here's an example of a regular **-ar** verb in the future tense:

cantar (*to sing*)	
yo **cantaré**	nosotros/nosotras **cantaremos**
tú **cantarás**	vosotros/vosotras **cantaréis**
él/ella/usted **cantará**	ellos/ellas/ustedes **cantarán**

Here's an example of a regular **-er** verb in the future tense:

correr (*to run*)	
yo **correré**	nosotros/nosotras **correremos**
tú **correrás**	vosotros/vosotras **correréis**
él/ella/usted **correrá**	ellos/ellas/ustedes **correrán**

Last but not least, here's an example of a regular **-ir** verb in the future tense:

gruñir (*to grumble*)	
yo **gruñiré**	nosotros/nosotras **gruñiremos**
tú **gruñirás**	vosotros/vosotras **gruñiréis**
él/ella/usted **gruñirá**	ellos/ellas/ustedes **gruñirán**

The following sentences describe present tense action. Identify the regular **-ar, -er,** or **-ir** verb in each sentence and write its future tense equivalent in the space provided, as in the following example:

0. Vendo las manzanas a los estudiantes. _____

A. Venderé

1. Paco viaja a la luna. _____

2. Tomamos la prueba. _____

3. Le gustan las pinturas de la artista. _____

4. El terremoto sacude la ciudad. _____

5. Pisas la alfombra. _____

6. Le felicitamos por sus logros. _____

7. Vosotros habláis mucho. _____

8. Adelita sufre de una crisis de migraña. _____

9. Los niños dependen de sus padres. _____

10. Cambio el video en la tienda. _____

Meeting Some Irregular Future Verbs

A handful of commonly used Spanish verbs are irregular in the future tense. What makes these verbs irregular is the fact that you don't form the future stem simply by using the infinitive form of the verbs. Instead, you have to use (and memorize) the verbs' irregular stems. After you know which stem to use, the rest is easy; you simply add the standard future tense endings that I provide in the preceding section.

To simplify the process of memorizing the rebellious future tense verbs, group them into the following three categories:

Verbs That Drop the Final -e

Infinitive	Meaning	Future Stem
caber	to fit	cabr-
poder	to be able	podr-
querer	to want	querr-
saber	to know	sabr-

Verbs That Replace the Final -e or -i with -d

Infinitive	Meaning	Future Stem
poner	to put	pondr-
salir	to leave	saldr-
tener	to have	tendr-
valer	to be worth	valdr-
venir	to come	vendr-

Verbs You Just Have to Memorize

Infinitive	Meaning	Future Stem
decir	to say	dir-
hacer	to make, to do	har-

To conjugate these irregular verbs, you simply take the irregular stem and add the regular future tense endings. In the case of **saber,** for example, you conjugate the future tense like this:

saber (to know)	
yo **sabré**	nosotros/nosotras **sabremos**
tú **sabrás**	vosotros/vosotras **sabréis**
él/ella/usted **sabrá**	ellos/ellas/ustedes **sabrán**

Note: Fortunately for your memory, the future verbs listed in the previous tables use the same irregular stems they use in the future tense to form the conditional mood. See Chapter 22 for details.

Complete the following sentences by adding the correct future tense conjugation for the verb in parentheses. Here's an example:

0. Ustedes _____ a nuestra casa para celebrar el Cinco de Mayo. (venir)

A. vendrán

11. ¿_____ este sofá en nuestra sala? (caber)

12. Yo _____ esta noche. (salir)

13. Mis amigos _____ las respuestas después de leer el texto. (saber)

14. Esmeralda _____ cualquier cosa. (decir)

15. Ellos _____ bastante dinero mañana. (tener)

16. Tú _____ canastas para vender. (hacer)

17. ¿_____ vosotros ganar el partido esta noche? (poder)

18. Nosotros _____ el hermoso jarrón en un sitio especial en nuestro gabinete. (poner)

19. Esta antigua moneda de oro _____ mucho en el mercado. (valer)

20. Yo _____ palomitas y un refresco en el cine. (querer)

Getting More Specific with Futuristic Adverbs

The future is a mighty long time. To be more specific when you're describing future events, you can use time-relevant adverbs to say when certain events will happen. Table 20-1 provides a list of time-relevant adverbs and adverbial phrases that you may want to use when you write or speak in the future tense.

Table 20-1	Adverbs That Describe Future Action
Spanish	*English*
después	*after*
inmediatamente	*immediately*
más tarde	*later*
el próximo mes	*next month*
el [day of the week] que viene	*next [day of the week]*
la próxima semana	*next week*

Spanish	English
el año que viene	next year
pronto	soon
esta tarde	this afternoon
esta mañana	this morning
este [day of the week]	this [day of the week]
mañana	tomorrow
mañana por la tarde	tomorrow afternoon
mañana por la noche	tomorrow evening
mañana por la mañana	tomorrow morning
esta noche	tonight

For more about adverbs, check out Chapter 12. Chapter 5's coverage of dates and times may also come in handy when you're talking about the future.

Translate the following sentences from English to Spanish by using the future tense and the appropriate adverb or adverbial phrase. I've provided the subjects and verbs in parentheses after the sentence. The time words are from Table 20-1. Use an English-Spanish dictionary to look up any unfamiliar vocabulary. Here's an example:

0. *I will swim this afternoon.* **(yo/nadar)**

A. **Yo nadaré esta tarde.**

21. *The children will clean their rooms tomorrow.* **(los niños/limpiar)**

_____

22. *Armando and I will travel to Oaxaca next month.* **(Armando y yo/viajar)**

_____

23. *I will wash the dishes after dinner.* **(yo/lavar)**

_____

24. *You (plural, informal) will soon discover the truth.* **(vosotros/descubrir)**

_____

25. *We will meet for dinner tonight.* **(nosotros/reunir)**

_____

26. *Evita and Silvio will study together tomorrow.* **(Evita y Silvio/estudiar)**

_____

27. *You* (singular, informal) *will deliver the burritos immediately.* **(tú/entregar)**

_____

28. *They will fix my car this Saturday.* **(ellos/arreglar)**

_____

29. *She will call tomorrow afternoon.* **(ella/llamar)**

_____

30. *The contractors will not start until next year.* **(los contratistas/empezar)**

_____

Exploring Additional Simple Ways to Talk about the Future

You don't necessarily have to form the future tense to talk about the future. Spanish offers a couple of easier alternatives that you can use to talk about events that you expect will happen in the near future. In the following sections, I explain how to use these alternatives.

Using the present tense

When you're asking for directions, expressing a wish or desire, or talking about an event that's going to happen in the near future, you can often get away with using the present tense, as in the following examples:

- **Ellos se quedan en nuestra casa.** (*They'll be staying at our house.*)
- **Espero pasar el próximo verano en Puerto Angel.** (*I hope to spend next summer in Puerto Angel.*)
- **¿Cómo llegamos al teatro?** (*How will we get to the theater?*)
- **Estoy listo en un minuto.** (*I'll be ready in a minute.*)
- **Ella quiere la langosta.** (*She'll have the lobster.*)

Flip to Chapter 6 for an introduction to using the present tense.

Using ir + a + an infinitive

As in English, you can use the verb **ir** (*to go*) to say that a future event "is going to occur." In Spanish, you conjugate the present tense form of the verb **ir** to agree with the subject, add the preposition **a** (which has no translation in this instance), and then add the infinitive of the action verb. The formula looks like this:

ir + **a** + an infinitive

The verb **ir** is irregular in the present tense, so you have to memorize how to conjugate it:

ir (*to go*)	
yo **voy**	nosotros/nosotras **vamos**
tú **vas**	vosotros/vosotras **vais**
él/ella/usted **va**	ellos/ellas/ustedes **van**

Here are some examples of **ir** + **a** + an infinitive in action:

✔ **Voy a tomar un aperitivo.** (*I'm going to have a snack.*)

✔ **¡Te va a encantar esta banda!** (*You're going to love this band!*)

✔ **Nos vamos a disfrutar de nuestro tiempo juntos.** (*We're going to enjoy our time together.*)

✔ **Ellos van a lamentar su decisión.** (*They're going to regret their decision.*)

Using the formula **ir** + **a** + an infinitive to talk about the future, translate the following sentences into Spanish, as shown in the example that follows. Use an English-Spanish dictionary for any words you don't know.

0. *We are going to talk on the phone tomorrow.*

A. **Nosotros vamos a hablar por teléfono mañana.**

31. *I am going to study tonight.*

32. *Roberto is going to visit this weekend.*

33. *You (plural, informal) are going to see our new house soon.*

34. *Juana and Laura are going to travel to Europe this month.*

35. *We are going to learn French this year.*

36. *They are going to eat pizza after studying.*

37. *You (singular, informal) are going to work eight hours this Saturday.*

38. *The team is going to practice all day.*

39. *The students are going to study together at the library this afternoon.*

40. *I am going to read fifty pages every day.*

Putting the Future Tense to Use

Obviously, you use the future tense to describe future action, but Spanish has a few more subtle uses for the future tense. The following sections explain the various uses of the future tense and provide examples for each use.

Describing an action that will happen or is likely to happen

The most obvious use of the future tense is to describe an action that *will* happen or *is likely to* happen, as in the following examples:

El sol saldrá mañana por la mañana. (*The sun will rise tomorrow morning.*)

Te encontraré para almorzar mañana por la tarde. (*I will meet you for lunch tomorrow afternoon.*)

Expressing conjecture, supposition, or probability in the present

In English, people often discuss the possibility that something will happen in the future by using words and phrases such as *probably*, *suppose*, *might*, *I wonder*, and *must be*. In Spanish, you can make a similar type of conjecture with the future tense even when it's about something in the present, as in the following examples:

¿Cuánto costará volar a Mallorca? (*I wonder how much it costs to fly to Majorca?*)

La conferencia durará todo el día. (*The conference might last all day.*)

Tendrán cinco hijos. (*They probably have five children.*)

El avión llegará con una hora de retraso. (*I suppose the flight will arrive an hour late.*)

Describing a future cause-effect relationship

If you expect something to happen as a result of a present action, you use the future tense to describe the resulting action. Here are a few examples:

Si sigues trabajando con diligencia, ganarás más dinero. (*If you continue to work diligently, you will earn a raise.*)

Si siembras bulbos de tulipán en el otoño, tendrás tulipanes en la primavera. (*If you plant tulip bulbs in the fall, you'll have tulips in the spring.*)

Cuando eres una persona amable, generalmente otras personas se comportarán de forma similar. (*When you show others kindness, they will usually return the kindness.*)

Answer Key

1 viajará

2 Tomaremos

3 Le gustarán

4 sacudirá

5 pisarás

6 felicitaremos

7 hablaréis

8 sufrirá

9 dependerán

10 cambiaré

11 Cabrá

12 saldré

13 sabrán

14 dirá

15 tendrán

16 harás

17 Podréis

18 pondremos

19 valdrá

20 querré

21 Los niños limpiarán sus habitaciones mañana.

22 Armando y yo viajaremos a Oaxaca el próximo mes.

23 Lavaré los platos después de la cena.

24 Pronto descubriréis la verdad.

25 Nos reuniremos para cenar esta noche.

26 Evita y Silvio estudiarán juntos mañana.

27 Entregarás los burritos inmediatamente.

28 Ellos arreglarán mi carro este sábado.

29 Ella llamará mañana por la tarde.

30 Los contratistas no empezarán hasta el próximo año.

31 Yo voy a estudiar esta noche.

32 Roberto va a visitar este fin de semana.

33 Vosotros vais a ver nuestra casa nueva pronto.

34 Juana y Laura van a viajar a Europa este mes.

35 Nosotros vamos a aprender francés este año.

36 Ellos van a comer pizza después de estudiar.

37 Tú vas a trabajar por ocho horas este sábado.

38 El equipo va a practicar todo el día.

39 Los estudiantes van a estudiar juntos en la biblioteca esta tarde.

40 Yo voy a leer cincuenta páginas todos los días.

Chapter 21

Forming Compound Tenses with the Helping Verb Haber

In This Chapter

▶ Turning a verb into its past participle

▶ Conjugating verbs in the present perfect, pluperfect, and future perfect

A *compound tense*, as the name indicates, consists of more than one component — an *auxiliary* (helping) *verb* and a *past participle*. In English, a compound tense looks something like *have walked*. The word *have* is the helping verb, and *walked* is the past participle of the action verb *to walk*. Together, they create the present perfect tense — one of several compound tenses.

The great thing about Spanish compound tenses is that conjugating them is a snap: All you have to do is conjugate one helping verb, **haber** (*to have*), and then slap it together with the past participle of the action verb, and you're good to go.

In Spanish, every simple tense has a corresponding compound tense, so you end up with fourteen verb tenses altogether — seven simple and seven compound. For example, **camino** (*I walk*) is a simple present tense statement. **He caminado** (*I have walked*) is its compound equivalent in the present perfect tense. (In case you're wondering, the simple tenses are the present indicative, the imperfect indicative, the preterit, the future, the conditional, the present subjunctive, and the imperfect or past subjunctive; the compound tenses are the present perfect indicative, the pluperfect or past perfect indicative, the preterit perfect, the future perfect, the conditional perfect, the present perfect or past subjunctive, and the pluperfect or past perfect subjunctive.)

In this chapter, you find out how to form past participles; how to conjugate **haber** in the present, imperfect, and future tenses; and how to combine the conjugated **haber** with past participles to form the present perfect, pluperfect, and future perfect — three of the most commonly used compound tenses. In addition, I show you when and how to use these three compound tenses and provide exercises to help you hone your skills.

Forming Past Participles

No matter which of the seven compound tenses you need to form, you use the past participle of the action verb. For regular **-ar, -er,** and **-ir** verbs, forming the past participle is easy, as long as you know the following two rules:

✔ For **-ar** verbs, drop the **-ar** ending from the infinitive and add **-ado.**

✔ For **-er** and **-ir** verbs, drop the **-er** or **-ir** ending from the infinitive and add **-ido.**

Here are some examples:

Infinitive	*Past Participle*
bailar (*to dance*)	**bailado** (*danced*)
aprender (*to learn*)	**aprendido** (*learned*)
pedir (*to ask for*)	**pedido** (*asked for*)

As you can see, forming regular past participles is a cinch. However, the flip side is that quite a few verbs don't form their past participle according to those nice and easy guidelines. To try to keep these verbs from becoming too overwhelming or unwieldy, I've broken them down into the following two groups: Group 1 (**-er** and **-ir** verbs in which a vowel precedes the infinitive ending) and Group 2 (verbs with past participles that follow no pattern).

When used in a compound tense, a past participle doesn't change to agree with the subject in gender or number. Only the conjugated form of **haber** (no matter the tense) must agree with the subject. I show you how to conjugate **haber** in the present, imperfect, and future tenses later in this chapter.

Irregular past participles: Group 1

The first group of irregular past participles consists of **-er** and **-ir** verbs in which a vowel immediately precedes the infinitive ending. These verbs form their past participles regularly, but you have to add an accent mark over the **i** in the **-ido** ending. Table 21-1 lists some common Group 1 verbs and their irregular past participles.

Like most other rules in Spanish (and English, for that matter), this one has an exception. Notice that Table 21-1 doesn't include any verbs that end in **-uir.** No accent mark is necessary when a verb such as **destruir** (*to destroy*) is put into the past participle form; for example, the past participle of **destruir** is **destruido.**

Table 21-1	Group 1 -er and -ir Verbs That Require an Accent in the Past Participle
Verb	*Past Participle*
atraer (*to attract*)	**atraído** (*attracted*)
caer (*to fall*)	**caído** (*fallen*)
creer (*to believe*)	**creído** (*believed*)
leer (*to read*)	**leído** (*read*)
oír (*to hear*)	**oído** (*heard*)
poseer (*to possess*)	**poseído** (*possessed*)
sonreír (*to smile*)	**sonreído** (*smiled*)
traer (*to bring*)	**traído** (*brought*)

Irregular past participles: Group 2

The second group of verbs that have irregular past participles follow no particular pattern, so you just have to memorize them. Table 21-2 lists some common Group 2 verbs and their irregular past participles.

Table 21-2	Group 2 Irregular Past Participles with No Pattern
Verb	*Past Participle*
abrir (*to open*)	**abierto** (*opened*)
cubrir (*to cover*)	**cubierto** (*covered*)
decir (*to say, to tell*)	**dicho** (*said, told*)
describir (*to describe*)	**descrito** (*described*)
descubrir (*to discover*)	**descubierto** (*discovered*)
devolver (*to return [something]*)	**devuelto** (*returned*)
dissolver (*to dissolve*)	**disuelto** (*dissolved*)
envolver (*to wrap [up]*)	**envuelto** (*wrapped [up]*)
escribir (*to write*)	**escrito** (*written*)
freír (*to fry*)	**frito** (*fried*)
hacer (*to do, to make*)	**hecho** (*done, made*)
morir (*to die*)	**muerto** (*died*)
oponer (*to oppose*)	**opuesto** (*opposed*)
poner (*to put*)	**puesto** (*put*)
proveer (*to provide*)	**provisto** (*provided*)
resolver (*to resolve*)	**resuelto** (*resolved*)
romper (*to break*)	**roto** (*broken*)
ver (*to see*)	**visto** (*seen*)
volver (*to return [to a place]*)	**vuelto** (*returned*)

Put the following verbs into their past participle forms and then give their English equivalents (you can use a Spanish-English dictionary if necessary). *Note:* These verbs are a mix of regular and irregular past participles. Here's an example:

Q. crecer = _____ = _____

A. crecer = **crecido** = *grown*

1. servir = _____ = _____

2. poseer = _____ = _____

3. señalar = _____ = _____

4. cortar = _____ = _____

5. oír = _____ = _____

6. encender = _____ = _____

7. decir = _____ = _____

8. insistir = _____ = _____

9. resolver = _____ = _____

10. poner = _____ = _____

Constructing and Using the Present Perfect

To talk about an action that began in the past and ended in the past, as in *I have walked two miles before,* you use the present perfect tense. Forming the present perfect tense in Spanish is essentially a two-step process:

1. **Put the helping verb haber (which translates as *to have*) into the present tense.**

2. **Add the past participle of the action verb (see the preceding section).**

The following sections walk you through the process of building the present perfect tense and then give you the opportunity to put it into action.

Discovering the present tense forms of the verb haber

To form the present perfect, you first need to know how to conjugate the helping verb **haber** (*to have*) in the present tense. **Haber** is an irregular verb, so you need to memorize its present tense forms:

haber (*to have*)	
yo **he**	nosotros/nosotras **hemos**
tú **has**	vosotros/vosotras **habéis**
él/ella/usted **ha**	ellos/ellas/ustedes **han**

Even though **haber** means *to have,* it doesn't have the same meaning as **tener** (*to have*). When you want to talk about what you possess, use **tener**. When you need a helping verb to form a perfect or compound tense, use **haber**.

Forming the present perfect

After you know how to form past participles and how to conjugate **haber** in the present tense, you're ready to form the present perfect. Simply combine the conjugated form of

haber in the present with the past participle of the action verb. For example: **Tomás ha llegado.** (*Tomás has arrived.*)

When you use the present perfect in a sentence, *never* separate the verb **haber** and the past participle with any other words.

Here are two examples of the present perfect tense with action verbs that have regular past participles:

> **Nosotros hemos visitado este museo muchas veces.** (*We have visited this museum many times.*)
>
> **Ellos han hablado por teléfono antes.** (*They have spoken on the phone before.*)

Here are a couple of examples of Group 1 irregular verbs that require an accent in the present perfect:

> **Yo he leído todos sus libros.** (*I have read all of his books.*)
>
> **La miel ha atraído las moscas.** (*The honey has attracted flies.*)

Here are a couple of examples of Group 2 no-pattern irregular verbs in the present perfect:

> **La camarera ha puesto las bebidas en la mesa.** (*The waitress has placed the drinks on the table.*)
>
> **Los estudiantes han devuelto sus libros a la biblioteca.** (*The students have returned their books to the library.*)

When you use an object pronoun with the present perfect, the pronoun must precede the conjugated form of the verb **haber,** such as in this sentence: **Me he lavado el pelo todos los días esta semana** (*I have washed my hair every day this week*). Flip to Chapter 9 for full details on using object pronouns, both direct and indirect.

In the present perfect construction, you place **no** and other negative words either before the conjugated form of **haber** or, in certain cases, after the past participle. Either way, you never separate the verb **haber** and the past participle. See Chapter 17 for full details on using negative words.

In questions, the subject comes after the verb **haber** and the past participle; it can either follow directly after the verb structure or come at the end of the sentence. If you don't need the subject for clarity, you can omit it entirely. Here are a couple of examples:

> **¿Han hablado ellos al profesor?** (*Have they spoken to the professor?*)
>
> **¿Has visto esta película antes?** (*Have you seen this movie before?*)

Complete the following sentences by conjugating the verbs in parentheses into their present perfect form. Here's an example:

O. Tú _____ (comer) algo.

A. has comido

11. Usted _____ (hablar) con un/a amigo/a.

12. Ellos _____ (leer) un buen libro.

13. Pedro _____ (visitar) un museo.

14. Yo _____ (lavar) la ropa.

15. Alicia _____ (escribir) una carta.

16. Claudia y Felipe _____ (limpiar) la casa.

17. Vosotros _____ (comer) una pizza.

18. Tú _____ (servir) una comida.

19. Nosotros _____ (ver) una película buena.

20. Roberto _____ (sonreír) recientemente.

Knowing when to use the present perfect

You use the present perfect to talk about actions that *have happened* and *have been completed* before the present moment. You may remember that this use is almost exactly the same as the way you use the present perfect in English. Here are a few examples:

> **Tomás no ha hecho su tarea.** (*Tomás hasn't done his homework.*)
>
> **Hemos visto la película tres veces.** (*We have seen the movie three times.*)
>
> **Han pintado su cuarto antes.** (*They have painted their room before.*)

Note: When using the present perfect, you don't need to know or express the exact time of the occurrence. What's important is that the action was begun and completed in the past.

 Don't use the present perfect to describe action in progress. To describe an action that began in the past and is ongoing in the present, use the present tense, as shown in this example:

> **Hace cinco años que él trabaja aquí.** (*He has worked here for five years.*)

 Don't use the present perfect to express the sense of having just done something. Spanish usually uses the present tense form of the regular **-ar** verb **acabar de** (*to have just*) + an infinitive to describe an action that was recently completed, as in the following example:

> **Ella acaba de llegar de Arizona.** (*She just arrived from Arizona.*)

Constructing and Using the Pluperfect

When talking about a past action that was completed prior to another past action, use the *past perfect* or *pluperfect* tense. Expressions such as **ya** (*already*), **antes** (*before*), **nunca** (*never*), **todavía** (*yet*), and **después** (*later*) often hint that you need to use the pluperfect tense. In the following sections, I show you how to conjugate **haber** in the imperfect tense and then combine it with the action verb's past participle to form the pluperfect.

Conjugating the verb haber in the imperfect tense

To form the pluperfect tense, you use the imperfect form of the helping verb **haber** (*to have*) plus the past participle of the action verb. (The imperfect is a version of the past tense; see Chapter 19 for details.) The following table shows the imperfect forms of **haber:**

haber (*to have*)	
yo **había**	nosotros/nosotras **habíamos**
tú **habías**	vosotros/vosotras **habíais**
él/ella/usted **había**	ellos/ellas/ustedes **habían**

Forming the pluperfect

After you know how to form past participles and how to conjugate **haber** in the imperfect tense, you're ready to form the pluperfect. Simply combine the conjugated imperfect form of **haber** with the past participle of the action verb. For example: **nosotros habíamos hablado** (*we had spoken*).

Here are some examples of the pluperfect in action:

El portero había abierto la puerta para nosotros. (*The doorman had opened the door for us.*)

Cuando llegamos él ya había salido. (*When we arrived he had already left.*)

Todavía no habían cerrado la tienda. (*They hadn't closed the store yet.*)

Like with the present perfect, you never separate the form of **haber** and the past participle of the action verb, as shown in this example:

Ramón había leído el periódico. (*Ramón had read the newspaper.*)

When you replace the direct object in the preceding example with a direct object pronoun, the sentence looks like this:

Ramón lo había leído. (*Ramón had read it.*)

When you make a question with the perfect tense, you put the subject (if needed) after the past participle, as shown in this example:

¿Habían terminado ellos? (*Had they finished?*)

With the help of an English-Spanish dictionary (if needed), translate the following sentences into Spanish by using the imperfect conjugations of **haber.** Here's an example:

Q. *I had eaten.*

A. **Yo había comido.**

21. *They had gone out.*

_____

22. *You (singular, informal) had traveled all over Europe.*

_____

23. *They had built the house the previous year.*

_____

24. *The children had slept for eight hours.*

_____

25. *The newspaper had published a very controversial article.*

_____

26. *You (plural, informal) had greeted me on the street.*

_____

27. *We had waited an hour.*

_____

28. *The girls had danced all night.*

_____

29. *My brother had received lots of gifts.*

_____

30. *Alicia had driven my car to town.*

_____

Employing the pluperfect

Use the pluperfect when one past action was performed and completed before another past action. In some cases, the fact that one action preceded another action isn't always clearly stated. Instead, it may be implied. Here are a few examples to show you what I mean:

Stated: **José había llamado antes de llegar.** (*José had called before arriving.*)

Implied: **José había llamado.** (*José had called.*)

Stated: **El tren había salido antes de que ellos llegaron.** (*The train had left before they arrived.*)

Implied: **El tren había salido.** (*The train had left.*)

Constructing and Using the Future Perfect

It's time to move onto the future, the future perfect that is. In English, the *future perfect* describes an action or event that will be completed in the future before some other action or event occurs. In sentences such as *I will have been at the station for an hour by the time the train arrives*, the action of *being at the station* will take place before the action of the train arriving. (Note that in English, *the train arrives* is expressed in the present tense, not in the future.)

Fortunately, to use the Spanish future perfect tense, you only have to conjugate one verb in the future, the verb **haber,** and then attach it to any one of thousands of verb past participles. The following sections give you the info you need to start using the future perfect.

Conjugating the verb haber in the future tense

The following table shows the future tense forms of **haber:**

haber (*to have*)	
yo **habré**	nosotros/nosotras **habremos**
tú **habrás**	vosotros/vosotras **habréis**
él/ella/usted **habrá**	ellos/ellas/ustedes **habrán**

Forming the future perfect

After you know the conjugated forms of **haber** in the future and you know how to form the past participles of both regular and irregular verbs (see the earlier section "Forming Past Participles" for details), you're ready to combine them and put them to good use in the future perfect. For example: **nosotros habremos llamado** (*we will have called*).

Here is what the future of **haber** looks like with a past participle:

> **Yo habré comido una hamburguesa para el almuerzo.** (*I will have eaten a hamburger for lunch.*)

> **Nosotros habremos salido antes de las dos.** (*We will have left before two o'clock.*)

> **Ellos habrán llegado mañana por la mañana.** (*They will have arrived by tomorrow morning.*)

To help you figure out when to use the future perfect, take a look at the following list of time words that you're likely to see with the future perfect. (This is by no means a complete list, but it should help you get started.)

Spanish Time Word	English Translation
pronto	*soon*
mañana por la mañana	*(by) tomorrow morning*
mañana por la tarde	*(by) tomorrow afternoon*
mañana por la noche	*(by) tomorrow evening/night*
el próximo viernes	*(by) next Friday [fill in any day of the week]*
pasado mañana	*(by) the day after tomorrow*
la semana que viene	*(by) next week*

Remember that you never separate the form of **haber** and the past participle of the action verb, so if you want to use an object with the future perfect, you have to put it after the perfect tense structure, as shown in these examples:

> **Ella se habrá cepillado los dientes antes de acostarse.** (*She will have brushed her teeth before going to bed.*)

> **Nosotros habremos terminado el trabajo la semana que viene.** (*We will have finished the work by next week.*)

When you replace the direct object in the preceding example with a direct object pronoun, the sentence looks like this:

> **Nosotros lo habremos terminado la semana que viene.** (*We will have finished it by next week.*)

When you make a question with the future perfect tense, you put the subject (if needed) after the past participle, as shown in this example:

> **¿Habrían estudiado los estudiantes antes del examen?** (*Will the students have studied before the exam?*)

Conjugate the verbs given in parentheses into the future perfect tense to say that the subjects will have done the stated activities before going to bed tomorrow night, as shown in the example:

Q. Tú _____ (escribir) en tu diario.

A. habrás escrito

31. Lara _____ (mirar) la televisión.

32. Yo _____ (hacer) la tarea.

33. Vosotros _____ (hablar) con un amigo por teléfono.

34. Mi amigo _____ (jugar) un juego electrónico.

35. Los estudiantes _____ (estudiar).

36. Nosotros _____ (ducharse).

37. Norma _____ (cepillarse) los dientes.

38. Mi madre _____ (lavar) los platos.

39. Tú _____ (limpiar) la casa.

40. Mis padres y yo _____ (comer) una merienda.

Knowing when to use the future perfect

In Spanish, you use the future perfect to express an action that will occur in the future before another future action or event, to express conjecture or probability about the past, to express reservations, and to question the validity of a past action. Here are a few examples of the future perfect in action:

> **Ellos habrán terminado sus proyectos antes de las vacaciones.** (*They will have finished their projects before the vacation.*)

> **¿Quién habrá llamado?** (*Who could have called?*)

> **Ella no contestó. Se habrá acostado.** (*She didn't answer. Maybe she's gone to bed.*)

> **Los estudiantes habrán estudiado, pero todavía no hicieron bien en el examen.** (*The students might have studied, but they still didn't do well on the exam.*)

Answer Key

1 **servido** = *served*

2 **poseído** = *possessed*

3 **señalado** = *signaled*

4 **cortado** = *cut*

5 **oído** = *heard*

6 **encendido** = *lit*

7 **dicho** = *said, told*

8 **insistido** = *insisted*

9 **resuelto** = *resolved*

10 **puesto** = *put*

11 **ha hablado**

12 **han leído**

13 **ha visitado**

14 **he lavado**

15 **ha escrito**

16 **han limpiado**

17 **habéis comido**

18 **has servido**

19 **hemos visto**

20 **ha sonreído**

21 **Ellos habían salido.**

22 **Tú habías viajado por toda Europa.**

23 **Ellos habían construido la casa el año pasado.**

24 **Los niños habían dormido por ocho horas.**

25 **El periódico había publicado un artículo muy controvertido.**

26 **Vosotros me habíais saludado en la calle.**

27 Nosotros habíamos esperado una hora.

28 Las chicas habían bailado toda la noche.

29 Mi hermano había recibido muchos regalos.

30 Alicia había conducido mi coche al centro.

31 habrá mirado

32 habré hecho

33 habréis hablado

34 habrá jugado

35 habrán estudiado

36 nos habremos duchado

37 se habrá cepillado

38 habrá lavado

39 habrás limpiado

40 habremos comido

Part V

Expressing Conditions and Giving Commands

The 5th Wave   By Rich Tennant

SPANISH "GRAMMAR"

Olé!

In this part . . .

When you need to express a condition, such as "*If* you do this, *then* I'll do that," or order someone to do something, basic sentences won't help. You need to use the conditional or imperative mood.

The conditional mood enables you to describe cause-and-effect scenarios, in which one event must occur before another event can occur. You use the imperative mood to tell or ask someone to do something, as in this example: **Por favor, pase el guacamole** (*Please pass the guacamole*).

In this part, I explain how to form these often-used constructions and provide plenty of practice to help them become second nature to you.

Chapter 22

Wondering "What If" with the Conditional Mood

....

In This Chapter

▶ Conjugating regular and irregular verbs in the conditional mood

▶ Identifying expressions that require the conditional

....

English and Spanish speakers use the *conditional mood* to express actions that might or would happen *if . . . .* You can also use the conditional to wonder, express possibility or probability, or conjecture about possible future events.

In this chapter, I introduce you to the regular present tense conjugations of the conditional mood, show you how to form the conditional and use it in a sentence, and provide plenty of examples and exercises to get you accustomed to using it.

Forming the Conditional of Regular Verbs

In English, you add words like *would*, *could*, *must*, and *probably* to verbs to form the conditional, as in the following expressions:

> *She would have said so if that's what she believed.*
>
> *How much could it have cost?*
>
> *He was probably out of the office when you called.*
>
> *If I say so, you must come.*

In Spanish, you don't have to add words to form the conditional; it's built right into the verb. Nice, right? To conjugate regular Spanish verbs in the conditional mood, keep the following points in mind:

✔ The regular conditional mood is a combination of the future and imperfect tenses. You use the same verb stem that you use with the future tense (usually the infinitive) and add the same endings you use to form the imperfect. (See Chapter 19 for details about the imperfect and Chapter 20 for details about the future tense.)

✔ The regular conditional mood requires no spelling or stem changes, but several common verbs do have irregular stems in the conditional mood (see the next section for details).

✔ To conjugate regular **-ar**, **-er**, and **-ir** verbs in the conditional mood, take the entire verb infinitive (meaning don't drop anything) and add the imperfect verb endings you use for **-er** and **-ir** verbs (see the following table for a list of these endings).

Here are the imperfect endings for **-er** and **-ir** verbs:

-ía	**-íamos**
-ías	**-íais**
-ía	**-ían**

The following verb tables show a few regular **-ar**, **-er**, and **-ir** verbs conjugated in the conditional mood:

preparar (*to prepare*)	
yo **prepararía**	nosotros/nosotras **prepararíamos**
tú **prepararías**	vosotros/vosotras **prepararíais**
él/ella/usted **prepararía**	ellos/ellas/ustedes **prepararían**

vender (*to sell*)	
yo **vendería**	nosotros/nosotras **venderíamos**
tú **venderías**	vosotros/vosotras **venderíais**
él/ella/usted **vendería**	ellos/ellas/ustedes **venderían**

escribir (*to write*)	
yo **escribiría**	nosotros/nosotras **escribiríamos**
tú **escribirías**	vosotros/vosotras **escribiríais**
él/ella/usted **escribiría**	ellos/ellas/ustedes **escribirían**

Check out the following examples to see how the conditional mood looks in the context of a sentence and how it translates into English:

Jugarían con nosotros si tuviéramos mejores juguetes. (*They would play with us if we had better toys.*)

¿Pagarías $50.000 por un carro? (*Would you pay $50,000 for a car?*)

Ayer, dijo que discutiríamos el tema hoy. (*Yesterday, you said we would discuss the issue today.*)

¿Volaríamos a Buenos Aires? (*Could we fly to Buenos Aires?*)

Consideraríamos una oferta de $150.000. (*We would consider an offer of $150,000.*)

Planearíamos para la fiesta dos semanas de antelación. (*We could plan for the party two weeks in advance.*)

In each of the following sentences, supply the correct conditional form for the regular **-ar**, **-er**, or **-ir** verb provided in parentheses after the sentence. Here's an example:

0. Paco _____ la montaña si tuviera el equipo. (subir)

A. subiría

1. ¿Cuánto _____ tú por esa casa? (pagar)

2. Yo _____ en una isla. (vivir)

3. Me _____ volar un avión. (gustar)

4. ¿Cuándo _____ usted a los invitados? (llamar)

5. El equipo _____ en el gimnasio. (jugar)

6. Las plantas _____ sin agua. (morir)

7. Usted y yo _____ una gran cantidad de vino para 300 personas. (necesitar)

8. Probablemente ella _____ el regalo por correo. (recibir)

9. ¿_____ su hermano mi casa por $1.000? (pintar)

10. Vosotros _____ salir temprano. (preferir)

Dealing with Irregular Conditional Verbs

Spanish always has a few verbs that don't play by the rules. Fortunately, the verbs that are irregular in the conditional are the same verbs that require a stem change when conjugated in the future tense (see Chapter 20 for details). Like their future counterparts, the irregular conditional verbs fall into the following three groups:

Verbs That Drop the Final -e

Infinitive	Meaning	Conditional Stem
caber	*to fit*	cabr-
haber	*to have (helping verb)*	habr-
poder	*to be able*	podr-
querer	*to want*	querr-
saber	*to know*	sabr-

Verbs That Replace the Final -e or -i with -d

Infinitive	Meaning	Conditional Stem
poner	*to put*	pondr-
salir	*to leave*	saldr-
tener	*to have*	tendr-
valer	*to be worth*	valdr-
venir	*to come*	vendr-

Verbs You Just Have to Memorize

Infinitive	Meaning	Conditional Stem
decir	*to say*	dir-
hacer	*to make, to do*	har-

Other verbs have these same conditional stem changes, but many of them are related to the verbs in the preceding tables. For example, **detener** (*to stop, to hold back, to detain*) is comprised of **de** (*back*) and **tener** (*to hold*), so it has a conditional stem that's similar to that of **tener: detendr-**. Likewise, **oponer** (*to oppose*) has a conditional stem that's similar to that of **poner** (*to put*), so its stem is **opondr-**.

The only thing irregular about the conditional conjugation of these verbs is the stem. They use the same endings that all regular conditional verbs use (see the preceding section). Here are a few sentences that use irregular verbs in the conditional mood:

> **El plomero dijo que vendría esta tarde.** (*The plumber said he would come this afternoon.*)

> **¿Qué día lo harías?** (*What day would you do it?*)

> **La recepcionista habría llamado durante el almuerzo.** (*The receptionist must have called during lunch.*)

In each of the following sentences, supply the correct conditional form for the irregular **-ar**, **-er**, or **-ir** verb provided in parentheses after the sentence. Here's an example:

0. Nosotros _____ a la fiesta. (venir)

A. vendríamos

11. ¿Dónde _____ ella sus libros? (poner)

12. Ella no _____ que el producto era defectuoso. (saber)

13. El jarrón antiguo _____ más si estuviera en mejor condición. (valer)

14. ¿Cuándo _____ ellos salido? (haber)

15. _____ si el semáforo fuera roja. (detenerse)

16. Los gatos _____ más leche. (querer)

17. El ministro no _____ nada acerca de las acusaciones. (decir)

18. Vosotros _____ vuestros ensayos en la clase. (componer)

19. Las cajas _____ plátanos. (contener)

20. ¿ _____ los ciudadanos a la petición del alcalde para más dinero? (oponer)

Knowing When to Use the Conditional

Knowing *when* to use the conditional is just as important as knowing *how* to use it. Just as in English, the conditional in Spanish is very versatile, enabling you to describe a hypothetical event in the present or future, to conjecture about a past event, or to express future time within a past tense expression. In the following sections, I explain the variations in usage and provide examples so that you can see the conditional in action.

Describing hypothetical actions or events in the present or future

A *hypothetical* action or event would occur if a certain condition existed or will exist. In some cases, the implication is that the hypothetical action or event can't possibly occur because it relies on an unrealistic condition. Here are some examples:

Me compraría un Jaguar si tuviera el dinero. (*I would buy a Jaguar if I had the money.*)

¿Pasarías tres semanas en Portugal si tuvieras el tiempo de vacaciones? (*Would you spend three weeks in Portugal if you had the vacation time?*)

Irían si pudieran encontrar un medio de transporte. (*They would go if they could find transportation.*)

Communicating the probability of a past action or event

Use the conditional to describe an action or event that you're pretty sure (but not 100 percent certain) occurred in the past. For example, if someone asks you a question like **¿Sabes dónde se realizó la obra la semana pasada?** (*Do you know where they performed the play last week?*), you may answer by saying something like **Se realizaría la obra en el teatro** (*They probably performed the play at the theater*). Here are some additional examples:

Nosotros llamaríamos antes de aquel entonces. (*We would have called by then.*)

Eso ocurriría hace más de veinte años. (*That probably happened more than 20 years ago.*)

Saldríamos del país para aquel entonces. (*We probably left the country by then.*)

Instead of using the conditional, you can use **probablemente** (*probably*) plus the imperfect to conjecture about an action or event from the past. For example, instead of saying **Se realizaría la obra en el teatro** (*They probably performed the play at the theater*), you could say **Probablemente se realizaba la obra en el teatro.** Flip to Chapter 19 for the full scoop on the imperfect.

Indicating the future within a past tense expression

Sometimes you need to talk about the future within past tense expressions. Children master this use of the conditional early on when they tell their parents things like **Pero ayer, dijiste que iríamos al zoológico hoy** (*But yesterday, you said we were [would be] going to the zoo today*). Here are a few additional examples:

¡Yo te dije que arreglaría tu carro antes del viernes! (*I told you that I would have your car repaired before Friday!*)

El pronóstico del tiempo predijo que el fin de semana sería bonito. (*The weather forecast predicted that the weekend would be beautiful.*)

Tan pronto como nos conocimos, supe que nos casaríamos. (*As soon as we met, I knew we were going to get married.*)

Answer Key

1 pagarías

2 viviría

3 gustaría

4 llamaría

5 jugaría

6 morirían

7 necesitaríamos

8 recibiría

9 Pintaría

10 preferiríais

11 pondría

12 sabría

13 valdría

14 habrían

15 Nos detendríamos

16 querrían

17 diría

18 compondríais

19 contendrían

20 Opondrían

Chapter 23

Taking Command with the Imperative Mood

In This Chapter

▶ Commanding individuals or groups of people

▶ Adding subject pronouns to catch the listener's attention

▶ Making commands less authoritative with "Let's"

The *imperative mood* is a verb form that enables you to give commands and make requests. It's *imperative* because the action is urgent. It's a *mood* rather than a tense because it reflects the manner in which the action is expressed, not the time at which the action is performed. The time is always *right now*.

As in English, when you bark out a command, the subject of the sentence (in other words, the person you're addressing) is *you*, regardless of whether the subject is stated. For example, to command someone's attention, you'd say something like *Listen!*, which actually means *You listen!*

This process certainly seems easy enough, but in Spanish, forming commands is a more complex operation because Spanish has four different forms of *you* — **tú** (singular, informal), **vosotros** (plural, informal), **usted** (singular, formal), and **ustedes** (plural, formal) — which means it has four different command forms, as well. To further complicate matters, in certain cases, the verb form changes depending on whether the command is affirmative (*do something*) or negative (*don't do* something).

Confused? Never fear. This chapter shows you how to give commands no matter which *you* you're speaking to and regardless of whether you're dealing with regular or irregular verbs, verbs with stem or spelling changes, or affirmative or negative commands. I also show you how to use subject pronouns with the imperative and how to form "Let's" or "Let us" commands when you want to be a little less assertive.

To show emphasis, add an inverted exclamation point at the beginning of any command and a regular exclamation point at the end.

Giving Commands to Individuals

When you're telling or requesting an individual to perform an action, you use *you* singular commands. In the following sections, I explain how to form *you* singular commands, both informal and formal, and provide exercises so you can practice. I also describe a number of stem-changing, spelling-changing, and irregular verbs in the imperative.

You use the informal *you* when addressing friends and family. You use the formal *you* when addressing new acquaintances and people to whom you want to show respect or from whom you want to keep a formal distance. Flip to Chapter 9 for more details about different versions of *you*.

Constructing informal singular commands with regular verbs

To form **tú** (*you* informal, singular) commands using regular verbs, drop the **-s** ending from the verb's present tense **tú** form. That's it. You don't need to add anything. Easy, right? Here are a few examples:

Infinitive	Present Tense Tú Form	Positive Command
hablar	hablas (*you speak*)	habla (*speak*)
comer	comes (*you eat*)	come (*eat*)
decidir	decides (*you decide*)	decide (*decide*)

To form negative **tú** commands, you can't just add **no** to the beginning of the command. Sorry! To form a negative **tú** command, start with **no** and then take the **-o** off of the present tense **yo** form of the verb and add **-es** for regular **-ar** verbs and **-as** for regular **-er** and **-ir** verbs. Here are some examples:

Infinitive	Present Tense Yo Form	Negative Command
hablar	hablo (*I speak*)	no hables (*don't speak*)
comer	como (*I eat*)	no comas (*don't eat*)
decidir	decido (*I decide*)	no decidas (*don't decide*)

Creating formal singular commands with regular verbs

To form **usted** or **Ud.** (*you* formal, singular) commands using regular verbs, drop the **-o** ending from the verb's present tense **yo** form and then add **-e** for **-ar** verbs or **-a** for **-er** and **-ir** verbs.

Suppose a monster is approaching your teacher and you want to command her to run. You'd start with the verb **correr** (*to run*), take its present tense **yo** form (**corro**), drop the **-o**, and add **-a** to get **corra**. Then you'd yell to your teacher, ¡**Corra!** Here are some additional examples:

Infinitive	Present Tense Yo Form	Positive Command
firmar (*to sign*)	firmo (*I sign*)	firme (*sign*)
responder (*to respond*)	respondo (*I respond*)	responda (*respond*)
aplaudir (*to applaud*)	aplaudo (*I applaud*)	aplauda (*applaud*)

The good news is that forming negative *you* singular formal commands is pretty simple. All you have to do is add **No** (*No*) to the beginning of the command, as in **¡No corra!** (*Don't run!*)

Translate the following commands from English to Spanish by using the specified singular *you* form of the verb. All the verbs are regular; you can use an English-Spanish dictionary for any verbs you don't know or can't remember. Here's an example:

0. Read. (informal) _____

A. **Lee.**

1. Don't drink. (formal) _____

2. Eat. (formal) _____

3. Don't call. (informal) _____

4. Wear. (formal) _____

5. Pass. (informal) _____

6. Don't buy. (formal) _____

7. Live. (informal) _____

8. Listen. (formal) _____

9. Don't answer. (formal) _____

10. Don't receive. (informal) _____

Checking out verbs with stem changes in the singular imperative

Some verbs experience serious stem changes in the singular imperative, as shown in Table 23-1. (Check out Chapter 6 for an introduction to different types of stem changes.)

Table 23-1	Verbs with Stem Changes in Singular Commands				
Infinitive	*Stem Change*	*Informal*	*Negative*	*Formal*	*Negative*
-ar verbs					
cerrar (*to close*)	e to ie	cierra	no cierres	cierre	no cierre
mostrar (*to show*)	o to ue	muestra	no muestres	muestre	no muestre
-er and **-ir** verbs					
dormir (*to sleep*)	o to ue	duerme	no duermas	duerma	no duerma

(continued)

Table 23-1 *(continued)*

Infinitive	Stem Change	Informal	Negative	Formal	Negative
-er and -ir verbs					
mentir (*to lie*)	e to ie	miente	no mientas	mienta	no mienta
pedir (*to ask for*)	e to i	pide	no pidas	pida	no pida
perder (*to lose*)	e to ie	pierde	no pierdas	pierda	no pierda
volver (*to return*)	o to ue	vuelve	no vuelvas	vuelva	no vuelva

Here are a couple of these stem-changing verbs in the imperative mood (the first is informal and the second is formal):

> **No mientas sobre tu edad.** (*Don't lie about your age.*)
>
> **Pida cortésmente.** (*Ask politely.*)

Introducing verbs with spelling changes in the singular imperative

Some verbs undergo a change of spelling in certain singular forms of the imperative, as shown in Table 23-2.

Table 23-2 Verbs with Spelling Changes in Singular Commands

Infinitive	Informal	Negative	Formal	Negative
-ar verbs				
continuar (*to continue*)	continúa	no continúes	continúe	no continúe
enviar (*to send*)	envía	no envíes	envíe	no envíe
organizar (*to organize*)	organiza	no organices	organice	no organice
pagar (*to pay for*)	paga	no pagues	pague	no pague
sacar (*to take out, to get*)	saca	no saques	saque	no saque
-er and -ir verbs				
conducir (*to lead, to drive*)	conduce	no conduzcas	conduzca	no conduzca
destruir (*to destroy*)	destruye	no destruyas	destruya	no destruya
distinguir (*to distinguish*)	distingue	no distingas	distinga	no distinga
escoger (*to choose*)	escoge	no escojas	escoja	no escoja
exigir (*to demand*)	exige	no exijas	exija	no exija
obedecer (*to obey*)	obedece	no obedezcas	obedezca	no obedezca

Here are a couple of examples of commands using verbs that change spelling in the imperative (the first is formal and the second is informal):

Escoja el pescado. (*Choose the fish.*)

No pagues demasiado. (*Don't pay too much.*)

Handling verbs with stem and spelling changes in the singular imperative

When used in the imperative, some verbs undergo both stem and spelling changes. Table 23-3 lists the most common verbs of this type and shows what they look like in their singular informal and formal imperative.

Table 23-3	Verbs with Stem and Spelling Changes in Singular Commands				
Infinitive	*Stem and Spelling Change*	*Informal*	*Negative*	*Formal*	*Negative*
almorzar (*to eat lunch*)	o to **ue** and z to **c**	**almuerza**	**no almuerces**	**almuerce**	**no almuerce**
colgar (*to hang*)	o to **ue** and g to **gu**	**cuelga**	**no cuelgues**	**cuelgue**	**no cuelgue**
comenzar (*to begin*)	e to **ie** and z to **c**	**comienza**	**no comiences**	**comience**	**no comience**
corregir (*to correct*)	e to **i** and g to **j**	**corrige**	**no corrijas**	**corrija**	**no corrija**
empezar (*to begin*)	e to **ie** and z to **c**	**empieza**	**no empieces**	**empiece**	**no empiece**
jugar (*to play*)	u to **ue** and g to **gu**	**juega**	**no juegues**	**juegue**	**no juegue**
seguir (*to follow*)	e to **i** and gu to **g**	**sigue**	**no sigas**	**siga**	**no siga**

Dealing with irregular verbs in the singular imperative

Some verbs are just plain irregular, so you simply have to memorize their command forms. Table 23-4 lists some common verbs that have irregular **tú** (*you* singular, informal) command forms.

Table 23-4	Irregular Tú (Informal) Command Forms	
Infinitive	*Positive Command*	*Negative Command*
decir (*to say, to tell*)	di	**no digas**
hacer (*to do, to make*)	haz	**no hagas**
ir (*to go*)	ve	**no vayas**
poner (*to put*)	pon	**no pongas**
salir (*to leave*)	sal	**no salgas**
ser (*to be*)	sé	**no seas**
tener (*to have*)	ten	**no tengas**
valer (*to be worth*)	**val** or **vale**	**no valgas**
venir (*to come*)	ven	**no vengas**

Fortunately, Spanish has only three irregular **usted** (*you* singular, formal) commands:

Infinitive	*Positive Command*	*Negative Command*
ir (*to go*)	**vaya** (*go*)	**no vaya** (*don't go*)
saber (*to know*)	**sepa** (*know*)	**no sepa** (*don't know*)
ser (*to be*)	**sea** (*be*)	**no sea** (*don't be*)

Translate the following commands from English to Spanish by using the specified singular *you* form of the verb. These verbs may have spelling and/or stem changes. Here's an example:

0. *Don't extinguish.* (formal) _____

A. **No extinga.**

11. *Eat lunch.* (informal) _____

12. *Begin.* (formal) _____

13. *Don't sleep.* (formal) _____

14. *Go.* (formal) _____

15. *Pay.* (formal) _____

16. *Don't have.* (informal) _____

17. *Choose.* (informal) _____

18. *Do.* (informal) _____

19. *Don't play.* (formal) _____

20. *Don't correct.* (formal) _____

Issuing Commands to Two or More People

Whether you're telling a few close friends to meet you at the movie theater or instructing a group of students to sit down and be quiet, you need to know how to form and use the imperative in its two *you* plural forms — informal and formal. In the following sections, I explain how to form plural informal and formal commands with regular verbs and then how to deal with verbs that have spelling and/or stem changes and verbs that are irregular in the imperative mood.

Constructing informal plural commands with regular verbs

In most Spanish-speaking countries, you don't have to worry about forming informal *you* plural commands because **vosotros** (second person *you* plural, informal) is used primarily in Spain. In Spanish American countries, people generally use the third person plural **ustedes** form for *you* plural formal and informal commands (see the next section for details). If you happen to find yourself in Spain, however, you need to know how to form informal *you* plural commands with **vosotros.** So don't skip this section just yet!

Forming regular affirmative informal **(vosotros)** plural commands is a snap. Just replace the final **-r** in the infinitive with **-d.** This works whether the verb is regular, has an irregular **yo** form, or has a spelling and/or stem change. Here are a few examples:

Infinitive	Positive Command
firmar (*to sign*)	**firmad** (*sign*)
responder (*to respond*)	**responded** (*respond*)
aplaudir (*to applaud*)	**aplaudid** (*applaud*)

Unfortunately, replacing **-r** with **-d** doesn't work for negative commands. To form regular negative **vosotros** commands, follow these three steps:

1. **Drop the final -o from the verb's present tense yo form.**

2. **Add the imperative ending:**

   • For infinitives ending in **-ar**, add **-éis.**

   • For infinitives ending in **-er** or **-ir**, add **-áis.**

3. **Add no before the verb.**

Following are a few examples of negative **vosotros** commands with regular verbs:

Infinitive	Present Tense Yo Form	Negative Command
firmar (*to sign*)	**firmo** (*I sign*)	**no firméis** (*don't sign*)
responder (*to respond*)	**respondo** (*I respond*)	**no respondáis** (*don't respond*)
aplaudir (*to applaud*)	**aplaudo** (*I applaud*)	**no aplaudáis** (*don't applaud*)

Creating formal plural commands with regular verbs

When issuing commands or making requests in a formal setting to a group of people, use the formal plural **(ustedes)** imperative. For example, if you're addressing colleagues at an annual convention, you probably want to politely say, "Please be seated," rather than, "Sit!"

To form formal plural commands with regular verbs, follow these steps:

1. **Start with the present tense yo form of the verb.**

2. **Drop the -o from the end.**

3. **Add the formal imperative ending:**

    • For infinitives ending in **-ar**, add **-en.**

    • For infinitives ending in **-er** or **-ir**, add **-an.**

4. **To form the negative, add no before the verb.**

Imagine that you're having lunch with your boss and a few of her associates. You want to ask her and them to look at the wine list. Here's what you do:

1. **Start with the present tense yo form of the verb mirar, which is miro.**

2. **Drop the -o from the end to get mir.**

3. **Add -en to the end (because it's an -ar verb) to get miren.**

4. **Add please and the wine list to get this: Por favor, miren la lista de vinos.**

Here are some additional examples:

Infinitive	Present Tense Yo Form	Positive Command	Negative Command
firmar (*to sign*)	**firmo** (*I sign*)	**firmen** (*sign*)	**no firmen** (*don't sign*)
responder (*to respond*)	**respondo** (*I respond*)	**respondan** (*respond*)	**no respondan** (*don't respond*)
aplaudir (*to applaud*)	**aplaudo** (*I applaud*)	**aplaudan** (*applaud*)	**no aplaudan** (*don't applaud*)

As long as you know how to form regular formal singular commands (as I describe earlier in this chapter), forming formal plural commands is a cinch. Just add **-n** to the formal singular imperative. This works for all verbs — regular, irregular, and those with stem and/or spelling changes.

Translate the following commands from English to Spanish by using the specified plural form of the verb. All the verbs are regular; you can use an English-Spanish dictionary for any verbs you don't know or can't remember. Here's an example:

0. *Eat.* (informal) _____

A. **Comed.**

21. *Don't talk.* (formal) _____

22. *Attend.* (informal) _____

23. *Don't shake.* (formal) _____

24. *Finish.* (informal) _____

25. *Decide.* (formal) _____

26. *Don't prepare.* (informal) _____

27. *Sell.* (formal) _____

28. *Adore.* (informal) _____

29. *Don't insist.* (formal) _____

30. *Don't break.* (informal) _____

Checking out verbs with stem changes in the plural imperative

Some verbs experience serious stem changes in the plural imperative, as shown in Table 23-5.

Table 23-5	Verbs with Stem Changes in Plural Commands				
Infinitive	*Stem Change*	*Informal*	*Negative*	*Formal*	*Negative*
-ar verbs					
cerrar (*to close*)	e to ie	cerrad	no cerréis	cierren	no cierren
mostrar (*to show*)	o to ue	mostrad	no mostréis	muestren	no muestren
-er and **-ir** verbs					
dormir (*to sleep*)	o to ue	dormid	no durmáis	duerman	no duerman
mentir (*to lie*)	e to ie	mentid	no mintáis	mientan	no mientan
pedir (*to ask for*)	e to i	pedid	no pidáis	pidan	no pidan
perder (*to lose*)	e to ie	perded	no perdáis	pierdan	no pierdan
volver (*to return*)	o to ue	volved	no volváis	vuelvan	no vuelvan

Here are a couple of these stem-changing verbs in the imperative mood (the first is informal and the second is formal):

> **No durmáis todavía.** (*Don't sleep yet.*)
>
> **Por favor, vuelvan.** (*Please return.*)

Introducing verbs with spelling changes in the plural imperative

Some verbs change spelling in certain forms of the plural imperative, as shown in Table 23-6.

Table 23-6	Verbs with Spelling Changes in Plural Commands			
Infinitive	*Informal*	*Negative*	*Formal*	*Negative*
-ar verbs				
continuar (*to continue*)	**continuad**	**no continuéis**	**continúen**	**no continúen**
enviar (*to send*)	**enviad**	**no enviéis**	**envíen**	**no envíen**
organizar (*to organize*)	**organizad**	**no organicéis**	**organicen**	**no organicen**
pagar (*to pay for*)	**pagad**	**no paguéis**	**paguen**	**no paguen**
sacar (*to take out, to get*)	**sacad**	**no saquéis**	**saquen**	**no saquen**
-er and **-ir** verbs				
conducir (*to lead, to drive*)	**conducid**	**no conduzcáis**	**conduzcan**	**no conduzcan**
destruir (*to destroy*)	**destruid**	**no destruyáis**	**destruyan**	**no destruyan**
distinguir (*to distinguish*)	**distinguid**	**no distingáis**	**distingan**	**no distingan**
escoger (*to choose*)	**escoged**	**no escojáis**	**escojan**	**no escojan**
exigir (*to demand*)	**exigid**	**no exijáis**	**exijan**	**no exijan**
obedecer (*to obey*)	**obedeced**	**no obedezcáis**	**obedezcan**	**no obedezcan**

Here are a couple of examples of commands with verbs that change spelling in the imperative (the first is formal and the second is informal):

> **No exijan demasiado.** (*Don't demand too much.*)
>
> **Conduzcáis mi vehículo.** (*Drive my car.*)

Handling verbs with stem and spelling changes in the plural imperative

When used in the imperative, some verbs undergo both stem and spelling changes. Table 23-7 lists some of the most common verbs of this type and shows what they look like in their plural formal and informal imperative forms.

Table 23-7	Verbs with Stem and Spelling Changes in Plural Commands				
Infinitive	Stem and Spelling Change	Informal	Negative	Formal	Negative
almorzar (*to eat lunch*)	o to **ue** and z to **c**	almorzad	no almorcéis	almuercen	no almuercen
colgar (*to hang*)	o to **ue** and g to **gu**	colgad	no colguéis	cuelguen	no cuelguen
comenzar (*to begin*)	e to **ie** and z to **c**	comenzad	no comencéis	comiencen	no comiencen
corregir (*to correct*)	e to **i** and g to **j**	corregid	no corrijáis	corrijan	no corrijan
empezar (*to begin*)	e to **ie** and z to **c**	empezad	no empecéis	empiecen	no empiecen
jugar (*to play*)	u to **ue** and g to **gu**	jugad	no juguéis	jueguen	no jueguen
seguir (*to follow*)	e to **i** and gu to **g**	seguid	no sigáis	sigan	no sigan

Dealing with irregular verbs in the plural imperative

Some verbs are just plain irregular, so you have to memorize their command forms. Several verbs have irregular informal (**vosotros**) command forms, as shown in Table 23-8.

Table 23-8	Irregular Informal Command Forms	
Infinitive	Positive Command	Negative Command
decir (*to say, to tell*)	decid	no digáis
hacer (*to do, to make*)	haced	no hagáis
ir (*to go*)	id	no vayáis
poner (*to put*)	poned	no pongáis
salir (*to leave*)	salid	no salgáis
ser (*to be*)	sed	no seáis
tener (*to have*)	tened	no tengáis
valer (*to be worth*)	valed	no valgáis
venir (*to come*)	venid	no vengáis

Spanish has three irregular formal **(ustedes)** commands:

Infinitive	Positive Command	Negative Command
ir	**vayan** (*go*)	**no vayan** (*don't go*)
saber	**sepan** (*know*)	**no sepan** (*don't know*)
ser	**sean** (*be*)	**no sean** (*don't be*)

Translate the following commands from English to Spanish by using the specified plural form of the verb. These verbs may have spelling and/or stem changes. Here's an example:

Q. *Don't tell.* (informal) _____

A. **No digáis.**

31. *Don't leave.* (informal) _____

32. *Do.* (informal) _____

33. *Don't go.* (informal) _____

34. *Play.* (formal) _____

35. *Organize.* (formal) _____

36. *Don't put.* (formal) _____

37. *Begin.* (informal) _____

38. *Don't take.* (formal) _____

39. *Don't sleep.* (informal) _____

40. *Pay.* (informal) _____

Using Subject Pronouns with Commands

Like English, Spanish usually omits subject pronouns in the imperative form. However, unlike in English, when you want to use a subject pronoun with the imperative in Spanish, you normally place the subject pronoun after the command verb.

Why would you use the subject pronoun? In formal commands, the subject pronoun shows extra consideration. In informal commands, it emphasizes or clarifies the subject. Here are a couple of examples (the first is formal and the second is informal):

¡Vengan ustedes! (*You guys, please come!*)

Siéntate tú, y yo te traigo tu comida. (*You sit down, and I'll bring you your food.*)

Forming "Let's" Commands

If you ever flip through verb conjugation charts in a Spanish grammar or verb book, you may notice that the imperative includes a **nosotros** (*we*) form. How can you possibly command *we* to do something? Well, the **nosotros** form of the imperative enables you to make suggestions to your friends or a group of people, including yourself, about what to do; for example, **¡Vamos al cine!** (*Let's go to the movies!*)

To form a *let's* command, drop the **-o** from the present tense **yo** form of the verb and add **-emos** for **-ar** verbs and **-amos** for **-er** or **-ir** verbs. To make the command negative, simply add **no** before the verb. Here are a few examples of regular verbs that you can transform into *let's* commands:

Infinitive	Present Tense Yo Form	Positive Command	Negative Command
saltar (*to jump*)	**salto** (*I jump*)	**saltemos** (*let's jump*)	**no saltemos** (*let's not jump*)
aceder (*to agree*)	**acedo** (*I agree*)	**acedamos** (*let's agree*)	**no acedamos** (*let's not agree*)
urdir (*to scheme*)	**urdo** (*I scheme*)	**urdamos** (*let's scheme*)	**no urdamos** (*let's not scheme*)

The following three troublemakers are irregular in the **nosotros** command form:

Infinitive	Positive Command	Negative Command
ir	**vamos** (*let's go*)	**no vayamos** (*let's not go*)
saber	**sepamos** (*let's know*)	**no sepamos** (*let's not know*)
ser	**seamos** (*let's be*)	**no seamos** (*let's not be*)

Note that **ir** (*to go*) is different in both its positive and negative forms. You don't just add **no** before the affirmative to create the negative command.

Translate the following *let's* commands from English to Spanish by using the specified verb, as in the following example (consult an English-Spanish dictionary if necessary):

0. Let's eat! _____

A. ¡Comamos!

41. Let's read! _____

42. Let's jump! _____

43. Let's not forget! _____

44. Let's repeat! _____

45. *Let's write!* _____

46. *Let's not shout!* _____

47. *Let's not spend.* _____

48. *Let's stop!* _____

49. *Let's repair.* _____

50. *Let's not talk.* _____

Answer Key

1 No beba.

2 Coma.

3 No llames.

4 Lleve.

5 Pasa.

6 No compre.

7 Vive.

8 Escuche.

9 No conteste.

10 No recibas.

11 Almuerza.

12 Empiece. or Comience.

13 No duerma.

14 Vaya.

15 Pague.

16 No tengas.

17 Escoge.

18 Haz.

19 No juegue.

20 No corrija.

21 No hablen.

22 Asistid.

23 No sacudan.

24 Terminad.

25 Decidan.

26 No preparéis.

27 Vendan.

28 Adorad.

29 No insistan.

30 No rompáis.

31 No salgáis.

32 Haced.

33 No vayáis.

34 Jueguen.

35 Organicen.

36 No pongan.

37 Empezad. or Comenzad.

38 No saquen.

39 No durmáis.

40 Pagad.

41 ¡Leamos!

42 ¡Saltemos!

43 ¡No olvidemos!

44 ¡Repitamos!

45 ¡Escribamos!

46 ¡No gritemos!

47 No gastemos.

48 ¡Paremos!

49 Reparemos.

50 No hablemos.

Part VI
The Part of Tens

In this part . . .

The Part of Tens is a standard fixture in all *For Dummies* titles, and I'm not one to break with tradition. This particular Part of Tens is part work and part play. The work consists of a list of ten common Spanish grammar mistakes with advice on how to avoid making them. The fun part is a list of ten Spanish idioms that'll make you sound like a native Spanish speaker — enjoy!

Chapter 24

Ten Common Spanish Grammar Mistakes (And How to Avoid Them)

In This Chapter

▶ Sounding more like a native speaker by avoiding common beginner errors

▶ Avoiding the pitfalls of false cognates and idiomatic expressions

▶ Recognizing the subtle differences between similar words

*W*hen learning any language, including your own, you're bound to make a few usage mistakes along the way. You learn by taking chances with the language and being corrected when you guess wrong. As a general rule, the more chances you take and the more mistakes you make, the better you get at the language. Otherwise, you'd be communicating in simple sentences your entire life: *Jane walks. Dick cooks dinner. Mary walks the dog.*

You usually make mistakes when words or expressions are irregular or don't follow the normal usage patterns. For example, you may hear a young child say, "I goed to my friend's house yesterday," instead of, "I went to my friend's house yesterday." These errors occur often when you're learning a new language, so don't feel incompetent or somehow deficient when you fall prey to a few common Spanish usage errors. You're taking chances and making mistakes so you can learn from them. That's a good thing.

This chapter points out ten of the more common grammar mistakes that people make when learning Spanish. Hopefully, by being forewarned, you can learn from other people's mistakes instead of making these particular mistakes yourself.

Forgetting to Change the Gender of "cientos" When Describing Feminine Nouns

When using the word **cientos** (*hundred*) to describe feminine nouns, don't forget to change the **o** to **a** in **cientos** to make it agree with the noun. You may have **doscientos libros** (*two hundred books*), for example, but if you have *two hundred calculators,* you have to say **doscientas calculadoras**. (Flip to Chapter 3 for an introduction to feminine and masculine nouns; Chapter 5 deals with numbers.)

Adding "un" or "una" to "otro" or "otra"

The word **otro** or **otra** means *other* or *another,* so you don't need to say **un otro** or **una otra** to say *another.* Just say **otro** or **otra,** as in these examples:

Correct: **Necesito otro libro para leer.** (*I need another book to read.*)

Incorrect: **Necesito un otro libro para leer.** (*I need a another book to read.*)

Correct: **Ellos tienen otra hija.** (*They have another daughter.*)

Incorrect: **Ellos tienen una otra hija.** (*They have a another daughter.*)

Chapter 4 introduces adjectives in more detail.

Overusing Subject Pronouns

In English, every sentence must have a subject — either a noun or a subject pronoun — to perform the action. You can't just say *ran* or *cook* and expect people to figure out who or what you're talking about.

Spanish is different because the verb ending usually clearly indicates who the subject of the sentence is. **Yo corrí** and **Corrí** have the same meaning: *I ran.* Adding the subject pronoun **yo** is redundant. Use the subject pronoun only if you need to clarify or emphasize the subject of the sentence. (Check out Chapter 9 for more information about subject pronouns.)

Repeating the Preposition in Verbs That Already Include a Preposition

Some Spanish verbs, such as **buscar** (*to look for*), include a preposition in their definitions, so adding another preposition, such as **para** (*for*), when using these verbs is redundant. If you say **Busco para mi bolsa,** you're essentially saying *I'm looking for for my purse.* Instead, say **Busco mi bolsa** (*I'm looking for my purse*). Following are some other Spanish verbs that come complete with a preposition:

Spanish Verb	*English Translation*
apagar	to turn off
aprobar	to approve of
bajar	to go down
caerse	to fall down
conocer	to be acquainted with
encender	to turn on
envolver	to wrap up
escuchar	to listen to
esperar	to hope for, to wait for
lograr	to succeed in
mirar	to look at
pagar	to pay for
pedir	to ask for
sacar	to take out
subir	to go up

See Chapter 13 for more details on prepositions.

Using Possessive Adjectives to Refer to Body Parts or Clothing with Reflexive Verbs

When you use reflexive verbs in Spanish, you don't need to use possessive adjectives when referring to body parts or articles of clothing because the reflexive verb already indicates that the body parts or the articles of clothing belong to the subject of the sentence. For example, you'd say **Me lavo el pelo** (_I wash my hair_) rather than **Me lavo mi pelo.** Here's another example: You'd say **Ella se viste el vestido** (_She puts on her dress_) rather than **Ella se viste su vestido.** (Chapter 14 has full details on reflexive verbs.)

Assuming Spanish Words That Look Like English Words Mean the Same Thing

Spanish and English have a large number of *cognates* — similar words that have similar meanings — like *abandon* and **abandonar**, *function* and **función**, and *music* and **música**. Cognates generally make learning Spanish easier for English speakers, but you need to be careful. Sometimes a Spanish word doesn't mean the same thing as the English word that it resembles.

When a word looks and sounds similar in English and Spanish but has a different meaning, it's known as a *false cognate*. Here are just a few of the false cognates that can get you into trouble:

- ✔ **Embarazada** doesn't mean embarrassed; it means *pregnant*. The word for *embarrassed* is **avergonzado**.

- ✔ **Vaso** isn't a vase; it's a *drinking glass*. If you want a *vase*, ask for a **jarrón**.

- ✔ **Éxito** doesn't show up over the doors at the movie theater because it means *success*. If you're looking for the exits, look for a sign that says **salida** (*exit*).

- ✔ **Carpeta** isn't carpet; it's a *folder*. So if you order **carpeta** for the floors of your new **casa** (*house*), whatever company you're ordering from is likely to know that you're just starting to learn Spanish. Order **alfombra** (*carpet*) instead.

Translating Idioms Word for Word

Idioms are phrases that mean something other than what the words themselves convey. For example, if I say *It's raining cats and dogs,* you know I don't mean that cats and dogs are literally falling from the sky. Instead, I mean a lot of rain is coming down.

Spanish also has plenty of idiomatic expressions, and to keep things interesting, they vary from one locale to another. In Mexico, for example, if someone says **Tú estás como un queso hoy** (*You're like cheese today*), they mean *You're looking good today.* To understand idiomatic expressions, you simply have to memorize their meanings and forget their literal translations.

If you encounter an expression that doesn't make logical sense in its context, you're probably dealing with an idiomatic expression. Ask the speaker what she means or ask a native speaker what the phrase means. You may also want to look up the expression online with your favorite search engine, but don't try to use an online translator because it'll give you the literal translation!

See Chapter 25 for some common Spanish idiomatic expressions.

Confusing Definite and Indefinite Articles

Spanish students often confuse the definite articles **el, la, los,** and **las** (*the*) and the indefinite articles **un** and **una** (*a, an*) and **unos** and **unas** (*some*). For example, instead of saying **Fui al concierto de Enrique Iglesias ayer por la noche** (*I went to the Enrique Iglesias concert last night*), a novice might say **Fui a un concierto de Enrique Iglesias ayer por la noche** (*I went to an Enrique Iglesias concert last night*), as if Enrique had more than one concert last night.

Discover the difference between definite and indefinite articles, as explained in Chapter 3, and use them accordingly. Doing so can go a long way toward making your Spanish sound more polished.

Mixing Up "pedir" and "preguntar" and "conocer" and "saber"

Spanish has two words that mean *ask:* **pedir** (*to ask for*) and **preguntar** (*to ask [a question]*). When you're ordering something in a restaurant or requesting an item in a store, use **pedir.** When you're asking for information, use **preguntar.** Here are a few examples to illustrate the difference:

> **En el restaurante, pedimos más tortillas y salsa.** (*At the restaurant, we asked for more tortilla chips and salsa.*)

> **Rosario preguntó qué hora es.** (*Rosario asked what time it is.*)

> **El conductor se había perdido, y por eso se detuvo y preguntó por el camino.** (*The driver was lost, so he stopped and asked for directions.*)

Spanish also has two verbs that mean *to know:* **conocer** (*to be acquainted with*) and **saber** (*to know [certain facts or information]*). Use **conocer** when discussing familiarity or lack thereof with a certain person, place, or object. Use **saber** to describe knowledge or ignorance of facts or information.

Confusing Different Types of Movement

In Spanish, you can *move* in several different ways, but the two movement verbs most often confused are **mudarse** (*to move [to a different place or residence]*) and **moverse** (*to change position*). If you're describing a move from one house to another, use **mudarse.** Use **moverse** to describe body movement. Here are two examples:

> **Nosotros nos mudamos a Austin el próximo verano.** (*We are moving to Austin next summer.*)

> **Ella se mueve muy elegantemente.** (*She moves very gracefully.*)

Chapter 25

Ten Useful Spanish Idioms

In This Chapter

▶ Getting to the point

▶ Describing a person in terms of cheese and goats

▶ Pulling your hair rather than your leg

▶ Using food-related terms to describe people, events, and more

*E*very language has *idioms* — words or phrases whose common-usage meanings are far different from their literal meanings. In English, for example, you may describe someone as being "cool as a cucumber," meaning the person remains calm under pressure. Everyone knows that you're not describing the person as physically being as cool as a cucumber.

Because they're based on usage, idioms have their roots not only in language but also in culture and locale. For this reason, they can be fun and interesting to look at, and they can help you communicate more like a native speaker. This chapter introduces you to ten common Spanish idioms that you can start using as soon as you figure out what they really mean.

Ir al grano

Literally, **ir al grano** means *to go to the grain*, but when Spanish speakers use this phrase, they mean let's get down to brass tacks or let's get to the point. Here are a couple of examples:

> **Ya bastante de bromas, vamos al grano.** (*Enough [already] of joking around, let's get to the point.*)

> **No tengo todo el día, por favor vaya al grano.** (*I don't have all day, please just get to the point.*)

Estar para comerte

Describing someone as **estar para comerte** (literally: *ready to be eaten*) doesn't make you a cannibal. In Spanish, you can use the expression **Estás para comerte** to tell someone that she's so adorable you could just "eat her up." Similarly, in English, people sometimes say, "You're so cute I could just eat you up," often in a baby voice.

Estar como un flan

Literally, **estar como un flan** means *to be like flan*. Because *flan* is a deliciously sweet dessert made of custard and caramelized sugar, you may think that *being like flan* means being sweet, but that's not the case. *Being like flan* means that you're nervous. To tell someone that you're nervous, you can say, **Estoy como un flan** (*I am so nervous*). Perhaps this idiomatic meaning comes from the fact that flan shakes even when subjected to the slightest movement.

Estar chupado

Literally, **estar chupado** means *to be sucked* or *to be licked*. For simplicity's sake, focus on the *to be licked* part because the expression **está chupado** means *it is super easy*. Contrary to what you may have originally thought, **está chupado** isn't the equivalent of the English expression *this sucks*.

Estar como un queso

If someone says to you, **"Tú estás como un queso hoy"** (literally: *"You are like cheese today"*), he probably isn't comparing you to a block of cheddar or saying that you smell like Limburger. You're actually on the receiving end of a very nice compliment. After all, used idiomatically, **Tú estás como un queso hoy** means *You are so beautiful/sexy today*.

The verb **estar** (*to be*) is one of the most basic verbs in Spanish; flip to Chapter 7 for details.

Estar como una cabra

As a native English speaker, you may not think about comparing someone to a goat, but making this comparison is fairly common in Spanish-speaking countries. **Estás como una cabra** (*You are crazy*) literally means *You are like a goat*. I suppose if you wanted to tell someone that she's beautiful and crazy, you could say something like this: **Estás como queso de cabra.** (Literally: *You are like goat cheese.*)

Faltar un tornillo

This particular idiom is nearly identical in English and Spanish. In Spanish, **faltar un tornillo** literally means *to lack a screw*. In English, the phrase is *to have a screw loose*. In both instances, you use the phrase to describe someone who's "crazy," as in this example:

> **Te falta un tornillo.** (*You are crazy.*)

Note: The indirect object pronoun **te** (*you*) in the preceding example indicates who is missing the screw. For more on verbs that conjugate like **faltar** (*to need, to be lacking*), see Chapter 10.

Tomar el pelo

In English, when you want to fool someone, you pull his leg. In Spanish, you pull his hair. **Tomar el pelo** literally means *to pull someone's hair,* but figuratively, it means *to joke around with someone.* For example, if you think someone is kidding you, you might say something like this:

> **¿Me tomas el pelo?** (*Are you kidding me?*)

Importarse un pimiento

When something is **importarse un pimiento** (*important as a small pepper*), it's trivial. So when someone tells you **me importa un pimiento,** that person is saying, *I couldn't care less* or *I don't care.*

Es de toma pan y moja

Es de toma pan y moja (literally: *it takes bread and dip*) is one of the more interesting idiomatic expressions in Spanish. It comes from the idea that when a meal is really good, you wipe the plate clean with bread. Hence, you use the phrase to describe anything that's really good, as in the following example:

> **¡Este trabajo es de toma pan y moja!** (*This essay is amazing!*)

Index

Business/Accounting & Bookkeeping
Bookkeeping For Dummies
978-0-7645-9848-7

eBay Business
All-in-One For Dummies,
2nd Edition
978-0-470-38536-4

Job Interviews
For Dummies,
3rd Edition
978-0-470-17748-8

Resumes For Dummies,
5th Edition
978-0-470-08037-5

Stock Investing
For Dummies,
3rd Edition
978-0-470-40114-9

Successful Time
Management
For Dummies
978-0-470-29034-7

Computer Hardware
BlackBerry For Dummies,
3rd Edition
978-0-470-45762-7

Computers For Seniors
For Dummies
978-0-470-24055-7

iPhone For Dummies,
2nd Edition
978-0-470-42342-4

Laptops For Dummies,
3rd Edition
978-0-470-27759-1

Macs For Dummies,
10th Edition
978-0-470-27817-8

Cooking & Entertaining
Cooking Basics
For Dummies,
3rd Edition
978-0-7645-7206-7

Wine For Dummies,
4th Edition
978-0-470-04579-4

Diet & Nutrition
Dieting For Dummies,
2nd Edition
978-0-7645-4149-0

Nutrition For Dummies,
4th Edition
978-0-471-79868-2

Weight Training
For Dummies,
3rd Edition
978-0-471-76845-6

Digital Photography
Digital Photography
For Dummies,
6th Edition
978-0-470-25074-7

Photoshop Elements 7
For Dummies
978-0-470-39700-8

Gardening
Gardening Basics
For Dummies
978-0-470-03749-2

Organic Gardening
For Dummies,
2nd Edition
978-0-470-43067-5

Green/Sustainable
Green Building
& Remodeling
For Dummies
978-0-470-17559-0

Green Cleaning
For Dummies
978-0-470-39106-8

Green IT For Dummies
978-0-470-38688-0

Health
Diabetes For Dummies,
3rd Edition
978-0-470-27086-8

Food Allergies
For Dummies
978-0-470-09584-3

Living Gluten-Free
For Dummies
978-0-471-77383-2

Hobbies/General
Chess For Dummies,
2nd Edition
978-0-7645-8404-6

Drawing For Dummies
978-0-7645-5476-6

Knitting For Dummies,
2nd Edition
978-0-470-28747-7

Organizing For Dummies
978-0-7645-5300-4

SuDoku For Dummies
978-0-470-01892-7

Home Improvement
Energy Efficient Homes
For Dummies
978-0-470-37602-7

Home Theater
For Dummies,
3rd Edition
978-0-470-41189-6

Living the Country Lifestyle
All-in-One For Dummies
978-0-470-43061-3

Solar Power Your Home
For Dummies
978-0-470-17569-9

Internet

Blogging For Dummies,
2nd Edition
978-0-470-23017-6

eBay For Dummies,
6th Edition
978-0-470-49741-8

Facebook For Dummies
978-0-470-26273-3

Google Blogger
For Dummies
978-0-470-40742-4

Web Marketing
For Dummies,
2nd Edition
978-0-470-37181-7

WordPress For Dummies,
2nd Edition
978-0-470-40296-2

Language & Foreign Language

French For Dummies
978-0-7645-5193-2

Italian Phrases
For Dummies
978-0-7645-7203-6

Spanish For Dummies
978-0-7645-5194-9

Spanish For Dummies,
Audio Set
978-0-470-09585-0

Macintosh

Mac OS X Snow Leopard
For Dummies
978-0-470-43543-4

Math & Science

Algebra I For Dummies
978-0-7645-5325-7

Biology For Dummies
978-0-7645-5326-4

Calculus For Dummies
978-0-7645-2498-1

Chemistry For Dummies
978-0-7645-5430-8

Microsoft Office

Excel 2007 For Dummies
978-0-470-03737-9

Office 2007 All-in-One
Desk Reference
For Dummies
978-0-471-78279-7

Music

Guitar For Dummies,
2nd Edition
978-0-7645-9904-0

iPod & iTunes
For Dummies,
6th Edition
978-0-470-39062-7

Piano Exercises

For Dummies
978-0-470-38765-8

Parenting & Education

Parenting For Dummies,
2nd Edition
978-0-7645-5418-6

Type 1 Diabetes
For Dummies
978-0-470-17811-9

Pets

Cats For Dummies,
2nd Edition
978-0-7645-5275-5

Dog Training For Dummies,
2nd Edition
978-0-7645-8418-3

Puppies For Dummies,
2nd Edition
978-0-470-03717-1

Religion & Inspiration

The Bible For Dummies
978-0-7645-5296-0

Catholicism For Dummies
978-0-7645-5391-2

Women in the Bible
For Dummies
978-0-7645-8475-6

Self-Help & Relationship

Anger Management
For Dummies
978-0-470-03715-7

Overcoming Anxiety
For Dummies
978-0-7645-5447-6

Sports

Baseball For Dummies,
3rd Edition
978-0-7645-7537-2

Basketball For Dummies,
2nd Edition
978-0-7645-5248-9

Golf For Dummies,
3rd Edition
978-0-471-76871-5

Web Development

Web Design All-in-One
For Dummies
978-0-470-41796-6

Windows Vista

Windows Vista
For Dummies
978-0-471-75421-3